T0305116

Entrepreneurship and Innovation in
Evolving Economies

ELGAR LAW AND ENTREPRENEURSHIP

Series Editors: Shubha Ghosh, *Vilas Research Fellow and Professor of Law, Honorary Fellow and Associate Director, INSITE, University of Wisconsin School of Law* and Robin Paul Malloy, *E.I. White Chair and Distinguished Professor of Law and Director of the Center on Property, Citizenship and Social Entrepreneurism at Syracuse University, US.*

The primary goals of this series are two-fold. The first is to develop the theoretical foundation for law and entrepreneurship. As to this goal, central research questions involve but are not limited to developing an understanding of the various meanings of entrepreneurship. Although superficially associated with the creation of a profit-making business enterprise, the concept of entrepreneurship extends to any motivation and effort to create something new. What does it mean to create? In what sense is an enterprise or project new? Is creation a process or an instantaneous, unpredictable event? What are the channels of creativity and in what venues does it occur? Is creativity in art, science, and business a coherent whole or completely different exercises? These questions serve to define the contours of entrepreneurship and its relationship to law and legal institutions.

The second goal is to translate the theoretical understanding of law and entrepreneurship into concrete policy. At one level, this goal entails identifying key legal policy levers (taxation, property rights, competition policy, financial regulation, contract law) that structure and direct entrepreneurship. At a deeper level, the second goal mandates a detailed institutional analysis of successful and unsuccessful entrepreneurship activity. This deeper goal invites an inquiry into the definitions of success and its measures. These definitions and measures, in turn, provide a benchmark for accessing and defining implementable policies.

At its core, the Law and Entrepreneurship series examines the role of law and legal institutions in promoting and sustaining entrepreneurial activity.

Titles in the series include:

Creativity, Law and Entrepreneurship
Edited by Shubha Ghosh and Robin Paul Malloy

Entrepreneurship and Innovation in Evolving Economies
The Role of Law
Edited by Megan M. Carpenter

Entrepreneurship and Innovation in Evolving Economies

The Role of Law

Edited by

Megan M. Carpenter

Texas Wesleyan School of Law, USA

ELGAR LAW AND ENTREPRENEURSHIP

Edward Elgar

Cheltenham, UK • Northampton, MA, USA

Published by
Edward Elgar Publishing Limited
The Lypiatts
15 Lansdown Road
Cheltenham
Glos GL50 2JA
UK

Edward Elgar Publishing, Inc.
William Pratt House
9 Dewey Court
Northampton
Massachusetts 01060
USA

A catalogue record for this book
is available from the British Library

Library of Congress Control Number: 2012935295

ISBN 978 0 85793 469 7 (cased)

Typeset by Servis Filmsetting Ltd, Stockport, Cheshire
Printed and bound by MPG Books Group, UK

For my dad.

And for people who fight for what can be in places where others are
focused on what has always been.

MMC

Contents

Contributors

Megan M. Carpenter, Associate Professor of Law and Director of the Center for Law and Intellectual Property at Texas Wesleyan School of Law.

Shubha Ghosh, Vilas Research Fellow and Professor of Law, Honorary Fellow and Associate Director, INSITE, University of Wisconsin School of Law.

Eric J. Gouvin, Professor of Law and Director, Law and Business Center for Advancing Entrepreneurship, Western New England University School of Law, B.A., Cornell University, J.D., LL.M., Boston University, M.P.A. Harvard University.

Steven D. Jamar, Professor of Law, Howard University School of Law, and Associate Director, Institute for Intellectual Property and Social Justice.

Andrea L. Johnson is Professor of Law and Director of the Center for Intellectual Property, Technology and Telecommunications at California Western School of Law.

Brian Krumm is Associate Professor at the University of Tennessee School of Law, where he teaches Business Associations, Secured Transactions, Representing Enterprises, and Business Clinic. He was formerly policy advisor to the Governor of Tennessee.

Patricia H. Lee, Visiting Associate Professor and Director, West Virginia University College of Law, Entrepreneurship, Innovation and Law Program; B.A., Northwestern University; J.D., Northwestern University School of Law. She was the founding Director of The University of Chicago Law School's IJ Clinic on Entrepreneurship program and formerly, Corporate Counsel and Staff Director for McDonald's Corporation.

Michael J. Madison, Professor of Law and Faculty Director, Innovation Practice Institute, University of Pittsburgh School of Law.

Lateef Mtima, Professor of Law, Howard University School of Law, and Director, Institute for Intellectual Property and Social Justice.

Sean M. O'Connor, Professor of Law and Faculty Director; Law, Business, and Entrepreneurship Program, University of Washington School of Law.

Michael Risch, Associate Professor of Law, Villanova University School of Law.

Franklin G. Snyder, Professor of Law, Texas Wesleyan School of Law.

Elizabeth Townsend Gard is Associate Professor, Director, Durationator® Experiment, Co-Director, Tulane Center for Intellectual Property Law and Culture, Tulane University Law School.

Foreword

Franklin G. Snyder

Exactly one hundred years ago the British Distributivist Hilaire Belloc
wrote that "[t]he control of the production of wealth is the control of
human life itself."[1] In the ensuing century, this control has increasingly
been exercised by governments, which today pervasively regulate every
aspect of wealth production. In the 21st-century United States there is not
a single significant economic decision made by a producer or consumer
that is not affected directly or indirectly by government controls.

Because the American government generally exercises such controls
via laws applied through its legal system, and because in America lawyers
enjoy monopoly power over the legal system, lawyers inevitably play
an enormously important role in the process. Lawyers are the group in
society who as judges and advocates manipulate[2] the legal system on
behalf of their clients, whether government or private entity. What the law
should be may perhaps be a legislative question (in which non-lawyers are
allowed to have a say), but once the legislative text is settled, nearly all the
rest of its implementation will be in the hands of lawyers. Legislators may
pass statutes, but, as Chief Justice Marshall said, "[i]t is emphatically the
province and duty of the judicial department to say what the law *is*."[3] As
the American judicial department is totally under the control of lawyers,[4]

---

[1] Hilaire Belloc, The Servile State (1912).

[2] "Manipulate" has something of a bad connotation, but I am using it in its
broader sense, that is, to move, arrange, and operate things by hand, to achieve a
desired (often therapeutic) result. It is in this sense that a chiropractor manipulates
one's spine. Unfortunately, I have not found another word that carries this broad
meaning but does not carry the negative connotations. While some lawyers do in
fact "manipulate" facts and laws in the most pejorative sense—lawyers are no more
honest than most other groups in society—even such therapeutic things as qualify-
ing a family for Social Security benefits involve "manipulation" in the sense I use
it here.

[3] *Marbury v. Madison*, 5 U.S. (1 Cranch) 137, 177 (1803) (emphasis added).

[4] Any citizen, regardless of background, can become a Member of Congress, a
Cabinet official, or a lobbyist, and exercise substantial influence over the legislative
and executive branches. But with some trivial exceptions, only lawyers can become

virtually every decision about who will be punished or rewarded by the government will ultimately be made by lawyers.

It is thus not surprising that the question of what law and lawyers can do to stimulate desirable economic activity has received a good deal of attention from legal scholars. This new volume of original essays is a significant contribution to that discussion. The individual essays are of high quality, but one of the volume's chief virtues is its breadth—the essays range from how to improve the training of lawyers, to how lawyers can better serve clients, to specific policy prescriptions about how laws can encourage certain kinds of desirable economic effects. Several of the contributions reflect the personal experiences of the authors in their own efforts to achieve these things, and their remarkably open and honest assessments of what did and did not work. While each of the contributions can and does stand on its own, reading them together in this volume allows a non-specialist reader to make interesting and valuable connections between such apparently disparate issues as how to conceive of the rule of law in international trade, how to transform a Rust Belt urban economy, and how to start a small technology business.

The editors who assembled these contributions have done an admirable job in encouraging a wide range of views. This diversity means that both proponents and opponents of greater government intervention (or of particular types of intervention) are likely to find substantial food for thought. There are certainly success stories here, such as the revitalization of Pittsburgh[5] and a successful law school entrepreneurship clinic,[6] but there are also honestly acknowledged failures, such as the past history of state-sponsored venture capital funds[7] and the attempt to create an intellectual property community from scratch through development of a

---

judges. Judges, in return, set the requirements for and control the admission of new lawyers. Judges and lawyers together set the accreditation policies for law schools, the graduates of whom are (with similarly trivial exceptions) the only persons eligible to become lawyers. And only lawyers can appear on behalf of others in judicial proceedings.

[5] Michael J. Madison, 'Contrasts in Innovation: Pittsburgh Then and Now', in Entrepreneurship and Innovation in Evolving Economies: The Role of Law (*infra*, Chapter 7).

[6] Patricia H. Lee, 'The Role and Impact of Clinical Programs on Entrepreneurship and Economic Growth', in Entrepreneurship and Innovation in Evolving Economies: The Role of Law (*infra*, Chapter 9).

[7] Brian Krumm, 'State Legislative Efforts to Improve Access to Venture Capital', in Entrepreneurship and Innovation in Evolving Economies: The Role of Law (*infra*, Chapter 2).

law school IP clinic.[8] Yet on closer inspection things are not so clear—there are (as the authors are careful to point out) valuable lessons to be drawn from the failures and reasons for at least some doubts about the successes.

Different readers are also likely to take different lessons from the other contributions, many of whose policy prescriptions have not yet been tried. Reading these essays together allows us to evaluate them on a deeper level. For example, the thoughtful discourse on the "strategic" role of lawyers[9] can inform our understanding of what their role should be (and how it can be encouraged) in "regional innovation ecosystems"[10] while simultaneously drawing attention to the contrast between what law schools generally teach and what lawyers do in practice. The fascinating story of one law professor's near-Herculean quest to become an entrepreneur[11] not only shows up the gaps in legal education—this trained lawyer who teaches in the business law field candidly admits she was unable to understand virtually any of the advice given to her by a successful entrepreneur she consulted—but illuminates on a micro level the struggles that the law on a larger scale has had to face in trying to create an innovation-friendly, background legal regime,[12] support the rule of law in economic affairs around the world,[13] and foster economic justice.[14] An economy, after all, is nothing more than the aggregate of all of the individual decisions made

---

[8] Michael Risch, 'IP and Entrepreneurship in an Evolving Economy: A Case Study', in Entrepreneurship and Innovation in Evolving Economies: The Role of Law (*infra*, Chapter 8). The clinic Professor Risch describes was most certainly not a failure, but its aims, as he explains, have changed over time.

[9] Shubha Ghosh, 'The Strategic Lawyer', in Entrepreneurship and Innovation in Evolving Economies: The Role of Law (*infra*, Chapter 5).

[10] Sean M. O'Connor, 'Transforming Professional Services to Build Regional Innovation Ecosystems', in Entrepreneurship and Innovation in Evolving Economies: The Role of Law (*infra*, Chapter 4).

[11] Elizabeth Townsend Gard, 'The Making of the Durationator®: An Unexpected Journey into Entrepreneurship', in Entrepreneurship and Innovation in Evolving Economies: The Role of Law (*infra*, Chapter 11). Like Professor Townsend Gard, I have been a business entrepreneur and can testify to the extraordinary complexity of the choices she has to face.

[12] Eric J. Gouvin, 'Of Small Businesses and Entrepreneurs: Toward a Public Policy that Supports New Venture Formation', in Entrepreneurship and Innovation in Evolving Economies: The Role of Law (*infra*, Chapter 3).

[13] Andrea L. Johnson, 'The Rule of Law, Privatization, and the Promise of Transborder Licensing', in Entrepreneurship and Innovation in Evolving Economies: The Role of Law (*infra*, Chapter 10).

[14] Steven D. Jamar and Lateef Mtima, 'A Social Justice Perspective on Intellectual Property, Innovation, and Entrepreneurship', in Entrepreneurship and Innovation in Evolving Economies: The Role of Law (*infra*, Chapter 6).

by its participants, and these contributions remind us that the smallest and largest decisions are inevitably bound together.

Another strength of this volume is, perhaps paradoxically, the way it vividly illustrates the potential conflict between desirable economic goals. Entrepreneurship is not the same thing as innovation, and neither entrepreneurship nor innovation has any necessary connection with creating or preserving "jobs." Policies designed to spur entrepreneurship may actually reduce innovation;[15] policies designed to encourage innovation may destroy jobs in existing industries;[16] policies whose goal is to preserve jobs may discourage both innovation and entrepreneurship.[17] Laws aimed at any one of these things may actually reduce overall wealth production and may well conflict with social justice goals. Given that resources are finite, every government decision allocating resources to *A* means that they must be taken from *B*, *C*, and *D*. A cautionary lesson from these contributions is that it is very important to understand the goal that one is trying to achieve. In the words of the old proverb, "The man who tries to chase two rabbits at the same time will catch neither."

Given that most of these contributions are from scholars at American law schools, it is not surprising that these essays would resonate strongly with legal educators. Each of them illustrates lawyers at work, and they throw a strong light on the connection—or, as some might say, the disconnection—between what law students are taught and what they will be doing when they go to work for clients. They illustrate both the strengths and the weaknesses of how law schools go about exercising their responsibility to train the people who will control an entire third of the tripartite United States government.

For those outside the academy, however, the lessons are perhaps even more valuable. The choices that governments make about intervention in the economy, and the way lawyers and judges go about enforcing them, affect the lives of every citizen. And in an increasingly interconnected world, decisions made in the United States (or any major developed country) have consequences for people in every other country. Many of the contributors to this volume offer their own proposals for how these decisions can or should be made. But even those who disagree with the

---

[15] As in those countries where there are thriving industries built on piracy of intellectual property rights.

[16] Clayton M. Christensen, *The Innovator's Dilemma* (1997). This has become very nearly a cliché, but is still the seminal work on "disruptive technology."

[17] As can be seen from the very mixed success of governments in trying to prop up uncompetitive domestic industries that face competition from more innovative and entrepreneurial foreign firms.

particular policy suggestions need to understand that the answers we give to the questions raised are going to be crucial to achieving our own ultimate goals, whether those goals are increasing innovation, fostering entrepreneurship, improving international competitiveness, ensuring adequate living standards, creating or preserving "good jobs," or promoting social justice.

Bosque County, Texas
October 2011

Acknowledgments

I would like to acknowledge the support of those who helped to make this project a reality.

First, I would like to thank Shubha Ghosh and Robin Paul Malloy, Series Editors of the Law and Entrepreneurship Series for Edward Elgar Publishing, for supporting this project. I would also like to thank Dean Frederic White and Texas Wesleyan School of Law for the financial support for the conference that brought these authors together, and Deborah Barnett for her hard work in making the conference a success. In addition, I would like to thank Dean White and the Texas Wesleyan School of Law for the ongoing support of the Center for Law and Intellectual Property (CLIP) at Texas Wesleyan.

For administrative support in publishing the book, I thank Elizabeth Wilhelm Hayes (JD 2012) for her time and for her dedication to the project.

I also appreciate the support of the book's editors at Edward Elgar Publishing, Alan Sturmer and Jane Bayliss.

ACKNOWLEDGEMENTS

1. Introduction

Megan M. Carpenter

In the book *Creativity, Law, And Entrepreneurship*,[1] I discussed growing up with the comforting undertones of the mine reports on radio stations in Appalachia in the 1970s. *"Loveridge, will work. Blacksville, will work. Sentinel, will work."* For a mining community, the mine reports provided announcements for the workers as to which coal mines (and therefore, which coal miners) would and would not work on any given day. More indirectly, those reports served as an indicator of economic vitality. There was a comfort in hearing those reports in the mornings. There was stability in the mines. Men would set their career path at the age of 18 or 19, and they were thereafter part of a much larger economic engine. Eventually, however, the economic climate shifted. Mechanization of mining activity created less demand for workers. The mine reports did not report "will work" as often. Eventually, the reports stopped altogether.

The small town where I grew up is like thousands of other communities in the United States. This small town had in its boom been dependent upon primary and secondary sector industries—specifically, mining and manufacturing. Because of a decrease in traditional industry, the economy of the town at large began to suffer; this problem was exacerbated in the downtown area when a shopping mall was built outside city limits. By the time I was growing up, the town seemed much closer to bust than boom. The tales recounted to me by my grandmother, tales of a thriving and vibrant community, had long passed. In those days, when her father was the Sheriff and the family lived downtown in the Sheriff's residence, people would gather and greet each other outside, shop and eat, walk and busy themselves on the downtown streets. As my generation entered high school in the mid-1980s, we walked past shuttered shops to get to the movie theatre. As my generation graduated from college, we knew we had

---

[1] Megan Carpenter, "'Will Work': The Role of Intellectual Property in Transitional Economies," in Shubha Ghosh & Robin Paul Malloy, (eds), *Creativity, Law, and Entrepreneurship*, Cheltenham, UK, Northampton, MA, U.S.A.: Edward Elgar Publishing (2011).

to seek professional opportunities elsewhere. I watched my peers leave, one by one, and they left nearly always with some measure of wistfulness and a longing to return. I did the same.

Across the United States, primary and secondary sector industries are no longer as viable as they once were—because the particular businesses are no longer profitable, because the underlying resources are no longer as plentiful or desirable, or because human activity is not essential to various aspects of an industry's operations. In character, the foundation of our very economy is changing. As early as 2004, Alan Greenspan noted that the U.S. economy is no longer based on traditional industries, but rather on content and information.[2] As economies evolve from traditional industrial resources, such as mining and manufacturing, to "new" resources, such as information and content, innovation and entrepreneurship become key.

Cities such as Detroit are exemplars of this kind of transition, where the automotive manufacturing industry suffered a substantial collapse, and more auto industry-related jobs were lost than were left in the region as a whole.[3] While there ultimately may be some resurgence in these sectors, thus far it has not reversed the overall trend.[4] Rather, cities like Detroit are seeking necessarily to diversify their economies, looking for ways to embrace new sectors of the economy. This is an issue that communities of all sizes face across the country and around the world as one of the key issues of modern entrepreneurship. In part, these economic transitions involve a move away from the old and into the new. But also in part, the new must at some level utilize traditional resources in new economy ways.

While the seeds of this project germinated in my childhood, they began to sprout when I returned home to teach law as a Visiting Associate Professor. I organized a conference in 2006 called "From Coal to Content: The Role of Intellectual Property and Technology in a New Economy." This project sought to begin a dialogue about the role that intellectual property can play as communities evolve from primary and secondary sector industrial resources to new economy resources, such as intellectual property and high technology. The conference speakers included policy-

---

[2]   *See, e.g.*, Alan Greenspan, *Intellectual Property Rights*, Remarks at the Stanford Institute for Economic Policy Research Economic Summit, *available at* http://www.federalreserve.gov/boarddocs/speeches/2004/200402272/default.htm (Feb. 27, 2004) (accessed Oct. 2, 2011).

[3]   John Austin, *The New Republic: Pinning the Problem in Detroit*, *available at* http://www.npr.org/templates/story/story.php?storyId=113959508 (Oct. 20, 2009) (accessed Oct. 2, 2011).

[4]   One such resurgence is discussed, in part, in Chapter 8.

makers, thought leaders, foundations and non-profit organizations, attorneys, entrepreneurs, and prominent members of the arts community. The dialogue focused on the ways that technology and intellectual property resources can foster a dynamic and profitable environment for entrepreneurship, including how to best protect and make effective use of human capital and natural resources.

However, it is clear that the legal structure that has developed to incentivize innovation and creativity is not enough. Intellectual property law seeks in part to incentivize creativity by creating legal mechanisms for the protection of inventions and creative works, but it does little to facilitate entrepreneurship or the business side of innovation. This book operates within that space: it examines the role of law in supporting innovation and entrepreneurship in communities whose economies are in transition. It contains a collection of works from different perspectives looking at questions of policy and practice, including how support for entrepreneurship can be translated into policy, as well as more concrete questions of practical efficacy, including measures of how successful or unsuccessful legal efforts to incentivize entrepreneurship may be, through intellectual property law and otherwise (and what might define success to begin with). We ask: What role does the law play in this transition? Does it play any role at all? And by what measurement do we determine success?

This book is unique in a couple of ways. First, its direct focus on economies in transition is something that distinguishes it from other books on entrepreneurship or law. Second, the book pulls together a set of works that in their compilation create a unique mix—pieces that focus on the role of individuals, including both lawyers and non-lawyers, in supporting entrepreneurship; pieces that present specific examples or proposals for creative thinking that address the realities of modern innovation; practical pieces on legal education and experiential learning; and a discussion about the social justice implications of the rule of law. Within this collection is a rich diversity of experience, thought, and scholarship. As such, it is relevant not just to scholars, but to practitioners, policy-makers, and others interested in entrepreneurship and innovation from many angles.

In the first section, authors examine the role that various societal actors play in supporting entrepreneurship and innovation in transitional economies; in the second section, the focus will transition from policy to application, including specific pragmatic perspectives related to a variety of particular endeavors. In Chapter 2, Professor Brian Krumm examines efforts by state legislatures toward venture capital funds formed with the intent to support fledgling entrepreneurs. Krumm notes that because the initial stages of venture capital are the most risky, it is a particularly open area for state involvement. In that vein, he evaluates the pros and cons of differing state programs, and provides a thorough explication of one program as a model for future legislative efforts. In Chapter 3, Professor Eric Gouvin discusses how the infrastructure of a particular area can either clear the path for business start-ups or threaten to obscure it. In that vein, he notes the importance of details such as municipal licensing requirements, land use ordinances, employment law issues, and regulatory schemes. Professor Sean O'Connor extends this discussion in Chapter 4 to examine the role that professional service providers play in supporting new technology sectors, including not just lawyers, but accountants, architects, designers, management consultants, and fellow entrepreneurs. Professor O'Connor discusses the important characteristics of these professional service providers and advocates for building this part of the innovation ecosystem. In Chapter 5, Professor Shubha Ghosh focuses on lawyers as entrepreneurs. Professor Ghosh argues that lawyers can aid the entrepreneurship process through changing the culture, and that change in attitudes towards law and business can affect the shaping of rules that are the most suitable for a particular local business climate. Chapter 6 wraps up the first section of the book, and lays the groundwork for the second, by considering the social justice implications of fostering entrepreneurship through policies and law. By using copyright as an example, Professors Steven Jamar and Lateef Mtima discuss how intellectual property law can empower individuals as well as advance societal development collectively.

The second part of the book focuses on specific pragmatic perspectives on the topic related to a variety of particular endeavors. In Chapter 7, Professor Michael Madison takes a snapshot of one recovering post-industrial economy, Pittsburgh, Pennsylvania. After the collapse of the steel industry, the city has spent the last 30 years building a new economy, one that has been frequently hailed as a success story. Professor Madison dives deeper into that story, describing the characteristics of Pittsburgh today and measuring the state of its rebirth. He considers the extent, if any, to which law and the legal system have contributed to Pittsburgh's modern success, and identifies lessons that this case study might offer for other transitioning regions. In Chapter 8, Professor Michael Risch provides a narrative discussion of his experience creating an entrepreneurship clinic at a law school in the context of an evolving economy. Risch generalizes from his experience to note that an entrepreneurship clinic's best clients may be the least expected—that is, other university and law school students—because of the symbiotic relationship they can bring to an IP-based business culture. Professor Patricia Lee follows this groundwork by providing a synopsis of the history and current state of clinical entrepreneurial programs in law schools across the United States. In Chapter 9, Professor Lee assesses the relationship of these programs to economic growth, and presents a conceptual model to examine the importance of clinical programs. Professor Andrea Johnson looks at another specific application of policy to practice in Chapter 10, through her examination of the insufficiency of legal and regulatory infrastructure and the possibilities for trans-border licensing to fit within those gaps. Like other authors in the book, Professor Johnson emphasizes the importance of non-legal factors in providing a stimulus for sustainable economic development in a transitional economic structure. Finally, Professor Elizabeth Townsend Gard wraps up the book in Chapter 11 with a first-hand account of her experience at the intersection of law, entrepreneurship, and innovation from the ground level. Professor Townsend Gard recounts her experience as a tenure-track law professor who found herself playing the part of unexpected entrepreneur, needing to come up with a "pitch", a business plan, and an appropriate choice of corporate entity for a university spin-out. She discusses some of the challenges she has encountered along the way at the intersection of law, business, and personal entrepreneurship.

This project departs from the notion that intellectual property law is itself an instrument of innovation and entrepreneurship. It moves into a larger space, one that considers the role of law both generally and particularly in the context of evolving economic realities. One challenge is to consider ways that this evolution demands a different role for the law, with different responsibilities and opportunities, than that demanded by primary and secondary sector economies. Another challenge is to consider the role of law in what are, in part, extra-legal endeavours. In this book, we seek to do this by exploring both policy and practice (and the interplay between them). Several authors consider the role that various societal actors play in facilitating entrepreneurship and supporting the business side of innovation, from funding to infrastructure, from innovation ecosystems to creative lawyering. Several others contribute pragmatic, empirical perspectives on the issue, whether in the context of case studies, law clinics, or personal entrepreneurship. All of them offer insights relevant to quintessential questions of entrepreneurship and innovation for communities transitioning from traditional, industrial economies to economies largely based in information and content—the communities we live in today. The daily mine reports no longer exist as a barometer of vitality in our current economic climate. And the decline of vertically integrated, primary sector industries has often left communities struggling. As communities seek to find a foothold in a new economy through entrepreneurship and innovation, it is my hope that this book can help scholars, policy-makers, and innovators navigate space – to "will work" in new economic times.

2. State legislative efforts to improve access to venture capital

Brian Krumm[1]

The 1983 cover article in *TIME* magazine entitled "The New Economy" was one of the first to discuss the transition from heavy industry to a new, technology-based economy in the United States. That article described a massive complex of aged, red-brick buildings, the former home of a wool mill which was reborn as the new corporate headquarters of Digital Equipment Corporation, the second largest computer manufacturer in the world at the time. The development and growth of Digital Equipment was made possible through financing obtained through venture capital. Venture capital has played an integral part in the evolution from the old to the new economy, yet not all areas of the country have fully participated in this renaissance. This chapter will discuss the role that law, in the form of legislation that creates state-sponsored venture capital programs, can play in providing the capital necessary for states to create an environment that supports entrepreneurs in commercializing their intellectual property.

Access to capital is critical for business startups and expansions and, more importantly, to the health of state and local economies. Despite the need for startup capital, many small businesses find that obtaining such funding is a difficult, or sometimes an even impossible, challenge. The difficulty of small businesses to raise capital is primarily because banks are reluctant to provide conventional debt financing to companies with little to no track record. In the recent economic downturn, this practice has only intensified, with reports suggesting that small business lending has declined as much as 57% in some sectors.[2] Accordingly, traditional debt financing is not an option for many small and emerging businesses.

---

[1] This chapter is based on research conducted for *Understanding the New Tennessee Small Business Investment Company Credit Act: Stimulating Economic Growth at the Intersection of Free Market Capitalism and Government Intervention,* Transactions: the Tennessee Journal of Business Law, 11 TRANSACTIONS: TENN. J. BUS. 93 (2009).

[2] Emily Maltby, *Small business lending drops 57%,* CNNMONEY.COM, Apr. 3,

As an alternative to conventional financing, venture capital is another resource small businesses turn to when seeking to raise funds. However, like traditional bank financing, access to venture capital by small businesses is also limited. In addition, the supply of venture capital has been traditionally concentrated geographically, focused in a relatively small number of regions and industries. Due to the same risks that prevent banks from lending to startup and emerging businesses, venture capital firms also have an incentive to refrain from investing in companies without a track record of success. In the absence of venture capital funds or traditional bank lending, many small businesses are left with few resources from which they can effectively grow their businesses while maintaining a sufficient cash flow to stay solvent.

THE VENTURE CAPITAL LANDSCAPE

Traditional venture capital financing, in its most basic form, involves three parties: an investor, a venture capitalist, and a target company. Generally, venture capitalists can be viewed as financial intermediaries, meaning they first must convince wealthy individuals, pension funds, corporations, and foundations to trust the venture capitalists with their money, which the venture capitalists will use to make equity investments in privately held companies. Obtaining investments is a difficult task, requiring venture capitalists to prove that they have the experience and track record of making equity investments in companies, monitoring and assisting in their growth, and exiting those investments in such a way as to make substantial profits for themselves and the investors.

Venture capital investment also creates a unique investment dynamic; it typically involves an investment in a company whose stock is essentially illiquid and worthless. Venture capitalists, like many equity investors, bet on the future success of the target company. This success will, in turn, benefit the entrepreneur due to the increased price of their stock and stock options. Typically, even the rank-and-file employees benefit from the stock and option appreciation. Increases in stock prices, however, does not mean much until the asset is sold and the increase in value is realized. Unless the target company is later acquired or goes public after its stock value has appreciated, there is little actual value in the venture capital firm's initial investment. Venture capitalists understand this dynamic and

2009, http://money.cnn.com/2009/04/02/smallbusiness/smallbiz_loans_drop.smb/index.htm.

invest in companies based on the hope that success will materialize and the venture capitalist and its investors split the profits from the future sale of the company based upon a predetermined formula.[3]

The benefits of venture capital investment in small businesses go far beyond those realized by the direct participants and investors, and are also felt by the overall economy as well. Those companies financed by venture capital investments have historically created jobs at a faster pace than their non-ventured counterparts.[4] Venture-capital-backed companies also demonstrate greater sales growth and comprised 16.6% of the nation's gross domestic product in 2005.[5] All together, the nation's venture-capital-backed companies were directly responsible for 10 million jobs and $2.1 trillion in sales during this same time period.[6] The jobs and revenue generated are largely in innovative, cutting-edge technology and products. Such industries typically benefit the entire economy because they create jobs in high-wage occupations and benefit governmental bodies through their ability to tax such growth.

While investments in risky new ventures are as old as commerce itself, the current venture capital landscape only dates back to 1946 with the

---

[3] Venture capitalists are compensated through a combination of management fees and carried interest (often referred to as a "two and 20" arrangement). Management fees are annual payments made by the investors in the fund to the fund's manager to pay for the private equity firm's investment operations. The typical venture capital fund is created as a limited partnership. The general partners receive an annual management fee equal to up to 2% of the committed capital. Carried interest is a share of the profits of the fund (typically 20%), paid to the private equity fund's management company as a performance incentive. The remaining 80% of the profits are paid to the fund's investors. Strong limited partner interest in top-tier venture firms has led to a general trend toward terms more favorable to the venture partnership, and certain groups are able to command carried interest of 25–30% on their funds. Metrick, *infra* note 7, at 11.

[4] Stephane Dupont, *Venture Impact The Economic Importance of Venture Capital Backed Companies To The U.S. Economy*, in ADVANCED VENTURE CAPITAL 2007, 68, 74 (2007). Statistics show that venture capital-backed companies generated an annual jobs growth rate of 4.1% compared to a 1.3% total annual private sector growth rate between 2003 and 2005. *Id.*

[5] Dupont, *supra note* 4 at 65. Venture capital-backed businesses demonstrated an 11.3% annual growth rate in total sales compared to an overall, annual private-sector sales growth rate of 8.5%. Venture capital investments totaled $23 million in 2005, which represented just 0.02% of gross domestic product. The corresponding revenue generated was $2.1 trillion.

[6] *Id.* Venture capital-financed companies are not limited to one segment of the economy. Computers and peripherals, media/entertainment/retail, industrial and energy, software, and telecommunications were the five leading industries by revenue. *Id.* at 77.

formation of the American Research and Development Corporation as the first true venture capital firm.[7] However, this innovation did not significantly change the supply of equity for small and startup businesses. Recognizing this fact, coupled with the desire to take advantage of the benefits conferred on the government by venture capital investment, the federal government sought to encourage venture capital investment as part of the Small Business Investment Act of 1958. This legislation created the Small Business Administration, which led to the creation of Small Business Investment Companies (SBICs). While this legislation did little to immediately increase the available venture capital funding, the SBIC program proved to be an effective vehicle for training future professional venture capitalists. SBICs still exist today and share many of the same characteristics of private venture capital firms; however, they have been prevented from becoming a dominant institutional form because of regulatory restrictions.

One of the most significant changes in venture capital investment occurred in 1979, when U.S. pension fund rules were relaxed to allow pension funds to invest in this asset class. With vast amounts of money to invest compared to the individual investor, pension funds soon began to dominate the venture capital market. In fact, pension funds presently supply nearly half of the money for all venture capital in the United States.[8] Following a surge in venture capital investment after the relaxation of

---

[7] ANDREW METRICK, VENTURE CAPITAL AND THE FINANCE OF INNOVATION 3, 10 (Hoboken, NJ: John Wiley & Sons Inc.,2007), *available at* http://ssrn.com/abstract=929145. American Research and Development Corporation was established in 1946 as the first institutional private equity firm. It was a publicly traded corporation and during its 25-year existence it earned an annualized return on its investment of 15.8%. The company is also credited with the first venture capital success story when in 1957 it invested $70,000 in Digital Equipment Corporation, an investment that would be valued at $355 million after the company's initial public offering in 1968. Without this investment, 25-year annualized investment drops to 7.4%. *Id.*

[8] METRICK, *supra* note 7 at 11. The U.S. Labor Department relaxed certain of the Employee Retirement and Security Act (ERISA) restrictions, under the "prudent man rule," thus allowing corporate pension funds to invest in more risky investments and providing a major source of capital available to venture capitalists. The "prudent man rule" is a fiduciary responsibility of investment managers under ERISA. Under the original application, each investment was expected to adhere to risk standards on its own merits, limiting the ability of investment managers to make any investments deemed potentially risky. Under the revised 1978 interpretation, the concept of portfolio diversification of risk, measuring risk at the aggregate portfolio level rather than the investment level to satisfy fiduciary standards, would also be accepted.

ERISA laws, growth in the venture capital industry remained relatively stable throughout the 1980s. This growth continued throughout the first half of the 1990s, increasing from $3 billion in 1983 to just over $4 billion in 1994.

Then, in the late 1990s, the United States market experienced extraordinary growth in internet and computer technology investments, and venture capitalists were there to share in the profit. Venture capital investments in such companies were yielding spectacular returns, and institutional investors rushed in to participate. Venture capital investments grew from a previous high of around $4 billion in the early 1990s, to an unprecedented level of $105.9 billion in 2000. (See Figure 2.1.) This boom in venture capital investments, however, was short lived. The stock market crash and technology slump that started in March of 2001 shook the entire venture capital market as valuations for technology companies collapsed. Venture capital investments fell by nearly half from the fourth quarter of 2000 to the first quarter of 2001. Nevertheless, current venture capital levels have settled at a considerable increase over those that existed prior to 1995.

Despite the increased prevalence of venture capital funding in the 1980s and 1990s, its availability is isolated in a select few regions of the United States. (See Figure 2.2.) Economic research suggests that there are a number of variables that influence the regional allocation of venture capital. Factors that affect when and where venture capital investments are made include macroeconomic conditions, supply and demand conditions concerning markets for innovations and technological opportunities, and willingness to take risks. Since the regions are not homogeneous with regard to technological areas of expertise, some regions also have a comparative advantage over others as it pertains to regional allocation of venture capital investments.

Currently, the Silicon Valley and New England regions attract the greatest proportions of venture capital, mainly due to the fact that they were centers for information technology innovation during the late 1990s. While Silicon Valley has consistently led the regional allocation of venture capital, the New England region's success is relatively new, as it recently moved to second place among American venture capital hubs, up from fourth out of eighteen regions analyzed in 1995. In 2008, these two regions attracted more than 50% of the total venture capital financing, with the top seven regions attracting 78%.[9] The importance of such agglomeration cannot

---

[9]   George Erber, *Regional Patterns of Venture Capital Financing in the US* 10-11 (DIW Berlin, Working Paper No. 2008/WP03-04, Nov. 2008), 12, 14 *avail-*

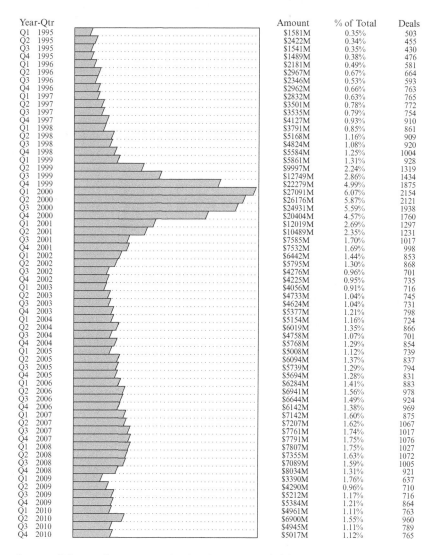

Year-Qtr		Amount	% of Total	Deals
Q1	1995	$1581M	0.35%	503
Q2	1995	$2422M	0.34%	455
Q3	1995	$1541M	0.35%	430
Q4	1995	$1489M	0.38%	476
Q1	1996	$2181M	0.49%	581
Q2	1996	$2967M	0.67%	664
Q3	1996	$2346M	0.53%	593
Q4	1996	$2962M	0.66%	763
Q1	1997	$2832M	0.63%	765
Q2	1997	$3501M	0.78%	772
Q3	1997	$3535M	0.79%	754
Q4	1997	$4127M	0.93%	910
Q1	1998	$3791M	0.85%	861
Q2	1998	$5168M	1.16%	909
Q3	1998	$4824M	1.08%	920
Q4	1998	$5584M	1.25%	1004
Q1	1999	$5861M	1.31%	928
Q2	1999	$9997M	2.24%	1319
Q3	1999	$12749M	2.86%	1434
Q4	1999	$22279M	4.99%	1875
Q1	2000	$27091M	6.07%	2154
Q2	2000	$26176M	5.87%	2121
Q3	2000	$24931M	5.59%	1938
Q4	2000	$20404M	4.57%	1760
Q1	2001	$12019M	2.69%	1297
Q2	2001	$10489M	2.35%	1231
Q3	2001	$7585M	1.70%	1017
Q4	2001	$7532M	1.69%	998
Q1	2002	$6442M	1.44%	853
Q2	2002	$5795M	1.30%	868
Q3	2002	$4276M	0.96%	701
Q4	2002	$4225M	0.95%	735
Q1	2003	$4056M	0.91%	716
Q2	2003	$4733M	1.04%	745
Q3	2003	$4624M	1.04%	731
Q4	2003	$5377M	1.21%	798
Q1	2004	$5154M	1.16%	724
Q2	2004	$6019M	1.35%	866
Q3	2004	$4758M	1.07%	701
Q4	2004	$5768M	1.29%	854
Q1	2005	$5008M	1.12%	739
Q2	2005	$6094M	1.37%	837
Q3	2005	$5739M	1.29%	794
Q4	2005	$5694M	1.28%	831
Q1	2006	$6284M	1.41%	883
Q2	2006	$6941M	1.56%	978
Q3	2006	$6644M	1.49%	924
Q4	2006	$6142M	1.38%	969
Q1	2007	$7142M	1.60%	875
Q2	2007	$7207M	1.62%	1067
Q3	2007	$7761M	1.74%	1017
Q4	2007	$7791M	1.75%	1076
Q1	2008	$7807M	1.75%	1027
Q2	2008	$7355M	1.63%	1072
Q3	2008	$7089M	1.59%	1005
Q4	2008	$8034M	1.31%	921
Q1	2009	$3390M	1.76%	637
Q2	2009	$4290M	0.96%	710
Q3	2009	$5212M	1.17%	716
Q4	2009	$5384M	1.21%	864
Q1	2010	$4961M	1.11%	763
Q2	2010	$6900M	1.55%	960
Q3	2010	$4945M	1.11%	789
Q4	2010	$5017M	1.12%	765

Source: PricewaterhouseCoopers/National Venture Capital Association Money Tree Report, based on data from Thomson Reuters.

Figure 2.1 *Venture capital investments by year*

able at http://ssrn.com/abstract=1338633. The top 7 regions in 2008 were: Silicon Valley 39.3%; New England 11.1%; LA/Orange County 7.5%; NY Metro 6.8%; Northwest 4.6%; Midwest 4.4%; and San Diego 4.4%. *Id.* at 25.

Investments by Region/Q4 2010

Regions Defined	Total $ Invested	Average $ Per Deal	Deals
All	$5,017,002,700	$6,558,173	765

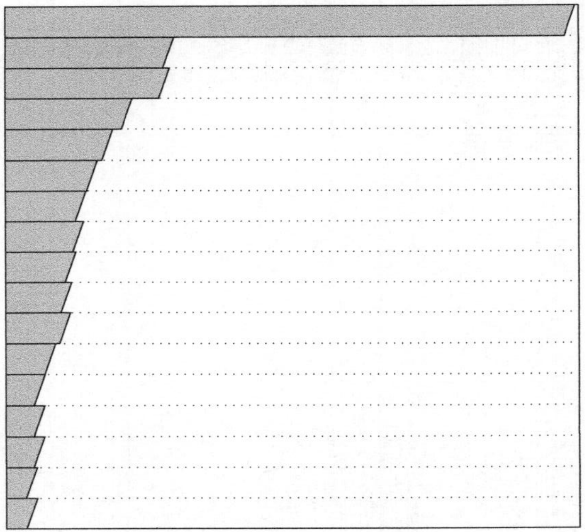

	Amount	% of Total	Deals
Silicon Valley	$2001M	39.88%	231
New England	$536M	10.68%	88
NY Metro	$513M	10.22%	83
Midwest	$378M	7.54%	62
LA/Orange County	$305M	6.07%	48
Colorado	$254M	5.06%	24
San Diego	$193M	3.85%	26
Southeast	$191M	3.81%	33
Northwest	$160M	3.20%	33
DC/Metroplex	$143M	2.84%	23
Texas	$138M	2.74%	34
Philadelphia Metro	$85M	1.69%	30
North Central	$46M	0.92%	14
South Central	$34M	0.69%	18
Southwest	$31M	0.61%	8
Unknown	$8M	0.16%	6
Upstate NY	$2M	0.04%	4

Source: PricewaterhouseCoopers/National Venture Capital Association Money Tree Report, based on data from Thomson Reuters.

Figure 2.2 Venture capital investments by region

be overstated, as innovators and startup entrepreneurs all over the world relocate their activities to regional centers in order to have better access to venture capital markets than they have in their own counties and states.

States seeking to take advantage of the benefits of venture capital funding must recognize the driving forces behind the geographic isolation of venture capitalists. Specifically, if states wish to increase their ability to attract an increased share of venture capital, states need to establish a threshold level of venture capital investors. In addition, it is critical that states facilitate a concentration of technological innovation expertise, which promises to contribute to the development of products and services that are in demand in the marketplace.

STATE-SPONSORED VENTURE CAPITAL PROGRAMS

In the late 1970s, a number of states began establishing state-sponsored venture capital programs in order to overcome the market constraints associated with regional concentration of venture capital investment. Several states recognized that they were underserved by the private venture capital market and established state-sponsored venture capital programs attempting to emulate the success of their private sector counterparts. These programs can be categorized in three primary types of venture capital funding: (1) publicly funded and publicly managed funds; (2) public funding provided for privately managed funds; and (3) tax credits or incentives for businesses and individuals making venture capital investments. In addition, some states have undertaken a purely facilitative role by supporting networks of individual investors and venture capital fairs. Under this scheme, the state avoids the obligation of managing the investments of the fund, leaving these responsibilities up to experienced fund managers. In that respect, the state is able to limit both its financial liability and risk.

From a political standpoint, venture capital investments are extremely risky and the total returns on these investments, with a few exceptions, are not as high as popularly believed, given the amount of risk involved.[10]

---

[10] *See generally,* YOCHANAN SHACHMUROVE, ECONOMIC GEOGRAPHY, VENTURE CAPITAL AND FOCAL POINTS OF ENTREPRENEURIAL ACTIVITY (PIER Working Paper 09-032, 2009), *available at* http://ssrn.com/abstract=1460823 (This study utilizes thirty years of data concerning companies that initially were backed by venture capital. These firms are located in Entrepreneurial Focal Points in the United States, namely California, Massachusetts, New York, Pennsylvania, and Texas. The study evaluates the returns of both successful and unsuccessful venture capital

State government officials who seek reelection are not typically willing to take on the political risk from lackluster returns or losses, nor are they willing to provide the necessary leadership to make such programs successful. There is a marked difference between an individual making a personal decision to invest their risk capital in a venture capital fund and an elected politician making a decision to invest the public's funds in a risk-laden venture. Thus, the organizational structure of the state-assisted venture capital program selected may be evaluated on a risk/reward continuum.

At one extreme, publicly funded and managed programs allow for greater governmental control by the targeting of investment decisions, allowing the state to focus their investments on specific economic development objectives. These state-sponsored venture capital programs have been met with mixed results. The programs are most often managed by employees of state agencies or quasi-public organizations. The individuals responsible for making investment decisions and providing oversight are typically appointed by the governor. These funds are most often capitalized by public funds generated from state appropriations or bond sales. Because of the substantial reliance on state funding, such funds typically come with restrictions that all or part of the investments must be made within the state and that the investments comply with the state's economic development agenda.

The primary advantage of publicly funded, publicly managed funds is their ability to direct funding toward particular policy objectives or industries. This allows for economic and social impacts to be considered during the investment decision-making process. However, these funds can also face substantial political pressure to make investments in specific areas of the state or in specific businesses that otherwise might not be considered good investments. In addition, publicly managed firms may not be able to attract the most qualified or competent fund managers. States are often at a disadvantage when they seek to take on the management of venture capital investments because their compensation restrictions typically prevent state-managed venture capital programs from attracting top talent from better compensated private firms. Moreover, under this management structure the state also assumes greater direct responsibility for funding the program and for all financial gains and losses that might occur. Such programs have also been criticized for inadequate financing for capitalization and management, government regulations that impeded fund operations, and poor financial returns on fund investments.

---

investments. The results show that despite popular beliefs, returns on investment are only adequate given their substantial risk.).

Furthermore, private venture capital firms may not be willing to co-invest with the state-managed funds because of the perception that such funds are overly susceptible to political influence and less responsive to private sector investors. This may limit the fund's ability to invest in a broader range of opportunities and leverage private-sector venture capital.

The Iowa Product Development Corporation (IPDC) was formed in 1983 in response to the downturn in the state's farm economy. The IPDC was housed in the Department of Economic Development, designed to promote economic development by providing seed capital to small businesses with innovative products, services, or ideas. While initially state appropriations and staffing was limited, starting in 1987 annual appropriations increased to approximately $1.5 million a year through the dedication of state lottery receipts for economic development programs. However, state payroll guidelines precluded the hiring of an experienced professional venture capitalist and there was political pressure to make investments outside its investment criteria.

In 1994, the IPDC was restructured as a private, non-profit corporation in response to the State Auditor's questions that IPDC's equity investments were in violation of the Iowa Constitution. Although the financial performance of the fund improved under this new management structure and investment decisions were more insulated from political influence, the fund still suffered from an inability to attract and retain qualified staff due to state pay restrictions. In addition, the program lost its supporters in the state legislative and executive branches due to retirements and election turnover, and the annual appropriations ended in the fiscal year 1997. The fund was forced to operate out of its limited reserves and investment returns and as a result, the fund was terminated in 1998.

While other publicly funded, publicly managed programs such as the Minnesota Technology Corporation Investment Fund created in 1991 and the Small Enterprise Growth Fund created by Maine in 1997 are still in existence in some form today, they have evolved refining their focus from that of their original strategy and objectives, in response to some of the program limitations described above.

Like publicly funded, publicly managed funds, publicly funded but *privately* managed funds generally receive the bulk of their capitalization from public sources. However, unlike their publicly managed counterparts, privately managed funds are organized with a somewhat different purpose. The purpose of these funds is typically to increase the supply of professionally managed venture capital in a region, or to enhance the infrastructure and management capacity of venture capital already existing in the region. These funds tend to focus more on maximizing profits and less on social or economic development objectives. Although the state sacrifices direct management control over investment management decisions, it gains more limited financial risk and may receive better economic returns.

The structure of capitalization of this type of fund has varied among state programs. Some have obtained state funding with a requirement for a private match or provided additional inducements to encourage private investment. For instance, some funds guarantee a minimum return on investment before the state receives its return; other states forgo a return in order to provide private investors with a premium on their investments. Although publicly funded, privately managed funds have many advantages over their publicly managed counterparts but they are not without disadvantages. These funds are less subject to political pressure, are better positioned to attract experienced managers, and have greater leverage to obtain private capital investments. However, the state's economic development objectives may be overlooked because management's primary focus is on maximizing returns.

The state of Oklahoma has developed perhaps one of the most promising publicly funded, privately managed programs for enhancing and targeting venture capital investments. The state obtains capital for venture investments by borrowing it from institutional lenders and investors. Principal and interest are guaranteed by $50 million in tax credits that are only used if necessary, through prearranged contracts currently with a consortium of public utility companies that have contractually agreed to purchase tax credits through 2015. The Oklahoma Capital Investment Board (OCIB), whose five trustees are appointed by the governor, choose venture capital firms based upon the fund's track record, industry emphasis, interest in the state, and plans for generating deal flow and conducting business in the state. The OCIB seeks to invest $1–5 million in a venture fund as a limited partner representing 10–20% share of the fund with the understanding that the fund will actively seek Oklahoma deals, and that the other private-sector, limited-partner investors and the general partners will conduct the appropriate due diligence on the fund investments and insure that politicians do not influence the fund's investment decisions. If the limited partnerships are successful, the state will realize economic benefits at no cost, and can potentially become self-financing through income from prior investments. Finally, the selection of the portfolio companies for investments is made by professional venture capitalists whose compensation is tied to the success of those investments.

The state of Mississippi, which passed the Venture Capital Act of 1994, provides a classic example of the problems that publicly sponsored venture capital programs can have if appropriate government oversight is not exercised and where the incentive systems do not reward making sound investment decisions. During the fund's two-and-one-half year history, the $18 million fund incurred expenses of over $4.5 million while approving only one venture capital investment of $650,000. Management misappropriation caused the fund's private investor to withdraw most of its contribution, and the program was placed under the protection of Chapter 11 reorganization.

Regardless of whether publicly funded venture capital funds are privately or publicly managed, there are several public-funding issues that policy makers and venture capitalists trying to create new funds should consider. Public funding should be provided in one lump sum rather than as an annual appropriation over a period of time in order to ensure effective program buy-in and continuity. While it may be more difficult to convince state legislators to make large, lump-sum investments, the uncertainties of the economy and the political process make program dependency on annual appropriations unappealing to private-sector venture capital funds. In addition, funds receiving annual appropriations may be prone to make suboptimal investment decisions because of pressure to use the appropriation before year end for fear that additional appropriations will not be authorized. Furthermore, capital venture investments may experience failures before successes occur. Such failures can have a cooling effect on the legislative support for future appropriations, jeopardizing both current and future investment decisions.

A third type of state-sponsored venture capital program provides incentives, often in the form of tax credits, to encourage private venture capital investments. In this form of venture capital legislation, the state's control is limited to the restrictions outlined in the enabling legislation and the state does not always share in the direct financial gains that these investments may achieve. These programs have been referred to as Certified Capital Corporation programs (CAPCOs). The first CAPCO legislation was passed in Louisiana in 1983. Since this time a number of other states have adopted similar legislation.[11] Under the typical CAPCO-enabling legislation, the state offers tax credits to insurance companies in return for "certified investments" in CAPCOs.[12] The tax credits are available to

---

[11] Other states that have adopted the CAPCO model are Missouri, New York, Wisconsin, Florida, Kansas, Texas, Vermont, Colorado, Alabama, and the District of Columbia.

[12] David L. Barkley et al., *Certified Capital Companies (CAPCOs): Strengths and Shortcomings of the Latest Wave in State-Assisted Venture Capital Programs*, 15 ECON. DEV. Q. 290, 352 (2001), *available at* http://edq.sagepub. com/cgi/content/ abstract/15/4/350. For various legal and practical reasons, the benefits of investing in CAPCO programs have generally been restricted to

offset future tax obligations that insurance companies pay on premiums collected in the state.[13] Thus they are basically investing in a guaranteed security rather than a risky investment. In addition, these tax credits are usually salable or transferable by the insurance companies.

In order to build upon and enhance the existing venture capital infrastructure in the state, CAPCOs are generally selected from well-established, private-sector venture capital funds that become certified with the state. Certification requirements established by the state include, among other things, minimum capitalization requirements, investment experience requirements, and the establishment of an in-state office. Once the funds are selected and certified as CAPCOs, they must meet certain

---

insurance companies. Insurance companies are a significant source of investment funds and, in every state, are subject to a premium tax (a levy imposed on the premiums insurers receive). Because the insurance companies typically pay premium taxes in lieu of income taxes, they generally do not benefit from income tax credits. Thus, to encourage insurance companies to invest their considerable cash reserves in state-restricted venture capital funds, states include the premium tax credits as a key component of their CAPCO programs. Velislava Groudkova et.al., *CAPCO Programs Offer Tax Credits to Attract Venture Capital for Small Businesses*, THE JOURNAL FOR MULTISTATE TAXATION AND INCENTIVES, June 2002 *available at* http://capcoprogram.com/2009/09/capco-programs-offer-tax-credits-to-attract-venture-capital-for-small-business.

[13]   Insurance company regulations prohibit insurance companies from investing in venture capital funds as a limited partner, as is typically the case with traditional venture capital funds. The CAPCO model is a mechanism that is approved by the National Association of Insurance Commissioners, which provides a relatively secure rate of return on the insurance company's investment. A premium tax credit is unique because of the consistent nature of premium taxes, which are less prone to year-to-year fluctuation than income tax credits. While predicting taxable income in future years can be difficult, insurance companies may easily estimate the future receipts on which their premium tax will be based. As a result, states can predict with increased accuracy the fiscal impact of a credit against premium tax. Because of the greater certainty of the premium tax credit, an insurance company is more likely to factor the value of the credit into its investment calculations. Because insurance companies generally are sophisticated, long-term investors in fixed-income instruments, the premium tax credit enhances the expected return and encourages participation in the CAPCO program. For these reasons, states may derive more predictable economic development benefits from a premium tax credit for investments in CAPCOs than from a credit claimed against income taxes. The premium tax credit for CAPCO investments attracts funding that otherwise would not have been invested in the newly formed venture funds. Velislava Groudkova et.al., *CAPCO Programs Offer Tax Credits to Attract Venture Capital for Small Businesses*, THE JOURNAL FOR MULTISTATE TAXATION AND INCENTIVES, (June 2002), *available at* http://capcoprogram.com/2009/09/capco-programs-offer-tax-credits-to-attract-venture-capital-for-small-business.

established investment criteria, and invest 100% of the certified capital, before any of the investment gains can be distributed to the partners. Traditionally, CAPCO fund managers have been allowed to receive an annual management fee, usually no more than 2.5% of capital available for investment for expenses necessary to operate the fund.

The state-enabling legislation also commonly creates a means for CAPCOs to become decertified, either voluntarily or as a result of non-compliance with the rules established for their operation. Generally, involuntary decertification occurs when it fails to meet the requirements for raising certified capital, or when it has not met the investment requirement under the legislation. Voluntary decertification typically occurs when the CAPCO has met its investment objectives, and the small business is ready to go public, be acquired, or otherwise repay the investment. The CAPCO may then choose to decertify, and consequently make distributions of its profits.

CAPCOs must make investments in "qualified businesses" as defined in the enabling legislation. In defining "qualified businesses," the state is essentially targeting the types of businesses it wants to support in order to meet its economic development objectives. Generally, qualified businesses must be small, located and operated within the state, with most of the employees residing in the state.[14] Once again, depending on the state's particular economic development objectives, certain sectors of the economy are specifically excluded from participating as qualified businesses. CAPCO investments must be made in qualified businesses in order to ensure the availability of tax credits for insurance company investors.

In return for the sacrificed tax revenues from the insurance companies that receive the tax credits, the state anticipates receiving sufficient new tax revenues from the businesses that start, expand, and remain within the state as a result of the CAPCO investments. There are also ancillary tax revenues in the form of increased sales tax and income tax from the employees who work in these businesses, not to mention indirect and induced benefits from the increased economic activity.[15] Some states have

---

[14] The Small Business Administration definition of a small business varies by major industry group but generally includes businesses of fewer than 500 employees for manufacturing and less than $5 million in annual sales for retail trade and services.

[15] Tucker Adams, GROWTH CAPITAL ALLIANCE, THE COLORADO CAPCO PROGRAM: AN ANALYSIS 22 (2003), *available at* http://www.coloradoeconomy.com/downloads/ CAPCOstudy.pdf. Indirect benefits are "generated by the purchase of goods and services by the businesses that are the original recipients of CAPCO dollars. For example, the purchase of computers, office supplies and cleaning services by" the

also incorporated provisions in their legislation that would allow them to participate directly in the investment returns of the CAPCO investments, in addition to the anticipated increase in future tax revenues.

State governments provide oversight of CAPCOs by requiring that they report on an annual basis to designated regulatory authorities. Typically, CAPCOs are required to report the identity of each investor, the amount of each investment, and the amount of the investment tax credit allocated on the basis of such investment. Information is also collected on the identity, type, size, location, and the amount invested in each of the target companies invested in by the fund manager. Some states require the CAPCO to also report the number of jobs created by the investment in the qualified business, along with their audited financial statements.

As mentioned above, state-managed venture capital programs are heavily criticized for inadequate financing for capitalization and management, lack of expertise in fund management, perception of political influence in investment decisions, government regulations that impeded fund operations, and poor financial returns on fund investments. CAPCO programs, however, are not nearly as susceptible to such criticisms. First, because CAPCOs are capitalized through the use of tax credits, they do not require current state budget expenditures or bond sales.[16] The actual cost of the tax credits to the state is reduced by the allocation of tax credits over time. Funding CAPCOs with tax credits and spreading tax credits over ten years make CAPCOs an attractive alternative when compared to programs that require current expenditures of debt. Furthermore, CAPCOs have another advantage over other publicly funded venture capital programs in that they can usually raise significant funding from insurance companies in a relatively short period of time.

Second, traditional publicly funded and managed venture capital programs are also commonly constrained by state pay regulations and are

---

companies being funded by the venture capital. *Id.* Induced benefits are those that are generated by the economic activity produced from "the purchase of goods and services by the individuals whose incomes are derived directly or indirectly from [the venture capital-funded] companies. The purchase of groceries, a car, or a home is an example of induced economic activity." *Id.*

[16]   CAPCOs do not require current expenditure of funds or bond sales as do publicly funded and publicly managed and publicly funded and privately managed venture capital funds. The cost to the state for CAPCOs is the present value of future tax revenues lost due to tax credits over a ten-year period. For public investments in public or private venture capital funds, the cost to the state is typically the current lump-sum value of state funds invested. If returns from program investments were poor, the state treasury would lose less with a program financed with ten years of tax credits than with a program funded with one lump-sum payment.

limited to how much they can compensate public fund managers. This creates problems because experienced venture capital fund managers are highly compensated and, thus, not attracted to manage public funds due to relatively low compensation structures. CAPCOs, on the other hand, are more able to attract experienced fund managers because of higher salary, profit sharing allowances, and other benefits.

Third, with respect to publicly managed venture capital funds, there is a perception of, if not the potential for, political interference with investment decisions. Similarly, with publicly funded and privately managed funds, there is the potential for political interference in the selection of the private firms. The CAPCO management structure, which limits the state's role to certifying the capital companies, reduces the political pressure to place state monies with specific private venture firms. The participating insurance companies select the certified CAPCOs in which to place their funds, which diminishes any political pressure to make an investment in a specific business. Because the CAPCO is insulated from political influence, private venture funds are more inclined to co-invest with the privately managed CAPCO, thus increasing the fund's ability to participate in syndicated deals and leverage their certified capital.

While the CAPCO model appears to offer advantages over other types of state-sponsored venture capital programs, policy makers who are considering implementing a venture capital program need to evaluate the CAPCO model in conjunction with an understanding of their state economy, the availability of venture capital resources, and the political environment, in order to develop a model which is appropriate for their state.

ECONOMIC AND PROGRAM EVALUATION

It has been over twenty-five years since the first CAPCO legislation was passed. During this time similar legislation has been implemented in nine additional states and the District of Columbia. As is the case with many government programs, disparities often exist between the vision and intent of legislation and the reality of its programmatic implementation. Only after the passage of time can one evaluate whether a program is meeting its intended objectives and whether it is being managed in an efficient and cost-effective manner. Once an evaluation is conducted, policy makers can then determine whether the legislation should be repealed, amended, or improved upon through the implementation of additional management and oversight controls.

Evaluations of CAPCO programs conducted to date tend to emphasize the economic development benefits of growing high-wage professional, scientific, and technical service industries within the state as opposed to focusing primarily on the recruitment of large-scale manufacturing projects. The highly competitive bidding process that takes place between states for high-profile manufacturing projects, where each state attempts to out bid the other using subsidies and tax abatements, is an expensive zero-sum game. It is important to remember that the overriding objective of CAPCO programs is economic development. By instituting a CAPCO program, states seek benefits much broader than direct venture capital profit. As those who are familiar with economic development know, these broader benefits are more meaningful for the state's long-term economic well being, but extremely difficult to quantify or attribute to one specific program. The very nature of venture capital for seed or early-stage financing does not immediately translate into quantitative measures such as "number of jobs created" or "average salary of jobs created" that are standard measures when measuring the impact of economic development programs. While the effects of venture capital investment in terms of these quantitative measures are often not immediately realized, each state can point to success stories where the outcomes far exceed the investment. However, despite the promising economic development impact of CAPCO programs, there exist opportunities for improvement in program implementation.

The expansion of CAPCO programs since the late 1990s was due in large part to the lobbying efforts of relatively concentrated CAPCO fund management groups. Four CAPCO fund management groups control the bulk of the industry across the United States.[17] One criticism of CAPCO programs is that they have enriched fund management groups while doing little to support early-stage entrepreneurship within the state. In fact, CAPCO programs have been accused of actually hurting the state venture capital industry. This criticism originates from the fact that CAPCO management groups have existing relationships with insurance companies through CAPCO programs in other states. Accordingly, these management groups have traditionally been able to use these preexisting relationships to quickly obtain insurance company investment commitments, locking up all of the tax credits among themselves and precluding local venture capital funds from participation in the program. Additionally,

---

[17]   *Id.* The four major CAPCO fund management groups are: Advantage Capital, Enhanced Capital, Stonehenge Capital, and Newtek. These four fund-management groups accounted for approximately 80% of the $1.65 billion of the total state tax credits granted between 1986 and 2001 in all CAPCO programs across the United States. *See* Daniel Sandler, *State-Sponsored Venture Capital: Are CAPCOs a Solution or a Problem?*, (2004) *available at* http://prowlingowl.com/Scams/CAPCO/CAPCOsAProblem2.cfm.

because CAPCOs have cost advantages in raising capital, they often offer more favorable investment terms to their portfolio companies. This may result in existing out-of-state, fund-management groups crowding out other in-state venture capital providers and discouraging new venture capital formation in the state.

Evaluations of other CAPCO programs also reveal that they tend to make few seed or startup investments. This is because their primary focus is on maximizing profitability within the parameters outlined in the state-enabling legislation. As such, to the greatest extent possible, they try to make later-stage investments that carry lower risk and present the best potential for a quick return on investment. In addition, in contrast to their private sector counterparts that profit from exiting carefully chosen investments in high-growth companies, CAPCO profits come from decertifying from the CAPCO program once they have invested 100% of their tax credit allocation. Once decertified, the CAPCO is able to retain all of the taxpayer money that is not lost through the investment process. As a result, there is an incentive for the CAPCOs to invest the taxpayers' dollars in a manner that insures the fastest and safest return, and a disincentive to making long-term equity investments in high-growth companies that maximizes economic growth and job creation.

While all state-sponsored venture programs result in new costs as well as potential new revenues, CAPCOs can be a more costly way of increasing equity capital in the state compared to other state venture capital programs. Under the CAPCO model, the net cost to the state depends on the performance of the fund, as represented by the present value of future tax revenues exercised ratably over a ten-year period. In contrast, the cost to the state for alternative investments in private or public venture capital funds is typically the current value of the lump-sum investment. All things being equal, if investment returns are poor or if there is a loss, the state will lose less with a program financed by ten years of tax credits compared to a program that is funded in one lump sum. On the other hand, in situations where CAPCOs and other publicly funded venture capital programs break even or are profitable, CAPCOs will have a higher net cost to the state. Unlike the other forms of publicly funded programs, the proceeds from CAPCO investments are distributed to the insurance companies, other equity investors, and fund managers, and the state does not usually receive a share of the returns from the CAPCO investments to defray program costs.

The state of Tennessee is the most recent state to enact a state-sponsored venture capital program. The Tennessee legislation, while initially promoted by the CAPCO industry, has diverted significantly from the traditional CAPCO model, with an eye toward overcoming many of the CAPCO shortcomings. While the Tennessee Program is designed to vest fund management in private fund managers, it also has established clear parameters and metrics for the investment of funds that help place greater emphasis on the state's economic development objectives. In addition, it allows for the state to participate as a limited partner in any profits that are generated through the program.

THE TNINVESTCO PROGRAM

The Tennessee Small Business Investment Company Credit Act[18] (the "Act") is similar in many respects to the legislation that created CAPCO programs that have been established in a number of other states. The Act and its 2010 amendment creates ten certified venture capital funds, each referred to as a "TNInvestco,"[19] which have been authorized to receive a total of $200 million in investment tax credits to be offered to insurance companies ("Participating Investors") in exchange for capital commitments in the TNInvestco. These tax credits can be used incrementally, beginning in 2012, by Participating Investors to offset certain tax liabilities imposed by the state on the collection of insurance premiums. While the Act's passage has produced some skeptics, the Tennessee business community has lauded this initiative as a mechanism for the state to diversify its economy into higher wage industries at a time when Tennessee is experiencing declining nominal personal income growth, declining wage growth, and a state revenue shortfall.[20]

---

[18]   §§ 4-28-101 to 112 (Supp. 2009) (approved by the Tennessee General Assembly as H.B. 2085, 106th Gen. Assy. (Tenn. 2009)). The legislation had a total of 82 formal co-sponsors in the Tennessee House and Senate. Tenn. Gen. Assy., Bill Summary, *available at* http://wapp.capitol.tn.gov/ apps/billinfo/BillSummaryArchive.aspx? BillNumber=HB2085&ga=106. The TNInvestco program passed in the Senate 30-0 and in the House 94-0, with one abstention. Tenn. Gen. Assy., Floor and Committee Votes, *available at* http://wapp.capitol.tn.gov/apps/BillInfo/BillVotesArchive. aspx?chambervoting =s&BillNumber=SB1203&ga=106; Tenn. Gen. Assy., Floor and Committee Votes, *available at* http://wapp.capitol.tn.gov/apps/BillInfo/ BillVotesArchive.aspx?chambervoting=H&BillNumber=HB2085&ga=106.

[19]   TENN. CODE ANN. §§ 4-28-101 to 112 (Supp. 2009) at § 4-28-102(16). TNInvestco is the name given in Tennessee's legislation to the venture capital firms that are certified by the Tennessee Department of Economic and Community Development to receive an investment tax credit allocation. *Id.* In essence, TNInvestco is merely the term adopted by the state legislature to describe Tennessee's version of a CAPCO.

[20]   THE UNIVERSITY OF TENNESSEE CENTER FOR BUSINESS AND ECONOMIC RESEARCH, AN ECONOMIC REPORT TO THE GOVERNOR OF TENNESSEE 22, 24-26 (2009), *available at* http://cber.bus.utk.edu/tefs/erg2009.pdf.

The TNInvestco program was designed to overcome some of the shortcomings of the CAPCO programs. For example, the TNInvestco program has avoided the undue influence of the out-of-state CAPCO management groups by giving a preference to venture capital funds with a well-established history of investing in Tennessee small businesses. Notably, the Act requires that each TNInvestco applicant be based, and have its principal office, in the state of Tennessee for at least five years or, alternatively, have at least five years' experience in investing primarily in Tennessee-domiciled companies. For those applicants that did not meet these criteria, an opportunity was afforded to enter into a joint venture with applicants meeting these standards. This provision is designed to ensure that the state develops and expands its own venture capital base and prevents the preexisting relationships that exist between the insurance industry and CAPCO management groups from limiting the TNInvestco's access to capital from insurance companies.

The Act also incorporates parameters that require all TNInvestco applicants to present a strategy for focusing investment of capital in seed or early-stage companies with high growth potential. In addition, it reinforces this policy through the application of investment performance measures, which places strict requirements on TNInvestcos to provide seed and early-stage financing. Qualified investments that are seed or early-stage investments receive a 300% credit toward the yearly investment performance measurement thresholds that the TNInvestcos have to meet beginning two years after the tax credit allocation. This encourages TNInvestco fund managers to seek out small business investments, especially during the initial few years of the TNIvestco program, in order for them to more easily meet their performance objectives. This also serves to temper the venture fund manager's tendency to make investments in businesses that insure the fastest and safest return, and an incentive to make long-term equity investments in high-growth companies that maximizes economic growth and job creation.

From a fiscal standpoint, perhaps the most significant improvement in the CAPCO model is the requirement that the state receive a portion of any non-qualified distributions made by the TNInvestcos. The Act's imposition of a "Profit Share Percentage," which imposes a fee of 50% of all non-qualified distributions made by the TNInvestco, allows the state to equitably participate in the fund's upside potential. In the event that TNInvestco is profitable, not only can the state enjoy potential future tax revenues, but it will also repay the treasury for the amount of revenue foregone pursuant to the tax credits allocated to the insurance industry. In addition, the Act prevents TNIvestcos from making any investment distributions that include the base investment amount until after the seventh year of the fund's operation. This provision should help to provide an equitable balance between the TNInvestco's desire to rapidly maximize its return on investment, and the economic development objectives of making longer-term investments in high-growth companies.In sum, the enhancements made to the fundamental CAPCO model through the TNInvestco-enabling legislation certainly have the potential to make the program a more cost-effective mechanism to stimulate small business development in Tennessee. The drafters of the legislation have obviously benefited from the lessons learned in other states that have adopted the CAPCO model.

CONCLUSION

State-sponsored venture capital programs, if established correctly and managed properly, can prove to be an effective economic development tool that enables a state to encourage private sector investment activity in target industries and geographic areas. Those states that have implemented venture capital programs based upon the fundamental CAPCO model have made numerous changes over time. For example, the Louisiana program has subsequently instituted a state profit-sharing component to their program. The state of Florida, in addition to incorporating a profit-sharing provision, has required any business receiving venture funds to keep their headquarters and any manufacturing facilities in the state for ten years. New York's legislation targets investment in early-stage businesses by requiring that at least 50% of the fund be invested in such businesses within four years. These changes to the fundamental CAPCO model have evolved over time, based upon the lessons learned from both internal operations and the sharing of experiences between state programs.

The TNInvestco-enabling legislation incorporates a number of unique improvements that are designed to avoid many of the problems encountered by other state-sponsored venture capital programs. Despite these improvements, one should anticipate new issues arising. On-going program monitoring is essential to address such unanticipated issues and correct them proactively. Those states that anticipate embarking upon a state-sponsored venture capital program should continue to refine and build upon the lessons learned to date.

3. Of small businesses and entrepreneurs: toward a public policy that supports new venture formation

Eric J. Gouvin*

INTRODUCTION

The United States likes to think of itself as a nation of entrepreneurs. We idolize people whose rags-to-riches life stories seem to track the storyline of the fictional hero Horatio Alger.[1] Our popular culture tends to mythologize the entrepreneurial experience. In the popular mind, entrepreneurs get to be their own boss, set their own hours, follow their passion, and, of course, make a lot of money. The romantic notion of entrepreneurship is so attractive the idea of the "entrepreneur" has mutated from being a way to refer to someone who identifies and exploits an economic prospect to being someone who develops any kind of idea or opportunity.[2]

Indeed, we are so fond of entrepreneurship that a recent survey found a majority of Americans have either started a business or thought about starting one.[3] Of course, thinking about starting a business is a lot easier

* ©2011 The author thanks the participants at the Evolving Economies Conference at Texas Wesleyan Law School and his research assistant, Michael Stein.

[1] Bernard Sarachek, *American Entrepreneurs and the Horatio Alger Myth*, 38 J. ECON. HIST., issue 2, 439–56 (1978) (analyzing the actual life experiences of 20th century entrepreneurs and finding that although many successful entrepreneurs were drawn from the elite classes and were not true "rags to riches" stories, they did often overcome some kind of adversity on their way to the top).

[2] *See,* David E. Pozen, *We Are All Entrepreneurs Now*, 43 WAKE FOREST L. REV. 283 (2008) (analyzing the evolution of entrepreneurship's "linguistic migration" and evaluating the significance of the terms used in new contexts).

[3] *Findlaw Survey Indicates a Nation of Entrepreneurs: Most Americans Are Interested in Owning a Business*, 26 No. 14 LAWYER'S PC, April 15, 2009 at 9 (reporting on a survey by FindLaw.com showing that 61% of Americans have

than actually starting one. Many people fail to grasp how much work it takes to be one's own boss and many more fail to appreciate that owning a business is not a guarantee of a regular income.[4] Still fewer stop to think about the legal barriers that stand in the way of creating a new business. Nevertheless, Americans love small businesses and entrepreneurs; regardless of party affiliation, polling shows Americans have an overwhelmingly favorable view of both.[5]

Not surprisingly, given the universal popularity of small businesses and entrepreneurs, political leaders on both sides of the aisle also hold small business owners in the highest regard. It has become an article of political faith that small business owners create jobs and therefore are the engine of recovery needed to bring the economy out of a slump.[6] Given

---

either started a small business or thought about starting one: 30% say they have started at least one small business, and another 31% have thought about starting their own business at some point).

   [4]   Sara Carter, *The Rewards of Entrepreneurship: Exploring the Incomes, Wealth, and Economic Well-Being of Entrepreneurial Households*, 35 ENTREPRENEURSHIP THEORY AND PRACTICE 39–55 (2011) *available at* http://onlinelibrary.wiley.com/doi/10.1111/j.1540-6520.2010.00422.x/full (noting paradox of earlier research showing entrepreneurs make less money than would be anticipated compared to other employed people and exploring whether the lower income is compensated for through non-pecuniary factors such as autonomy and satisfaction, while ultimately concluding that the analysis of overall economic well-being of entrepreneurs is determined in significant part by household needs that evolve over time). The mismatch between the myths of entrepreneurship and the reality of business ownership has spawned a host of self-help products and services to address that disconnect, *see, e.g.,* MICHAEL E. GERBER, THE E-MYTH REVISITED (New York, NY, U.S.A.: HarperCollins, 1995) (one of long series of books addressing common problems of small business owners who have been caught up in the myths of entrepreneurship).

   [5]   An opinion poll conducted by the Gallup Organization in 2010 showed that 97% of Republicans and 95% of Democrats held a positive opinion of small business and 88% of Republicans and 82% of Democrats held a positive view of entrepreneurs. Frank Newport, *Socialism Viewed Positively by 36% of Americans*, Gallup.com, Feb. 4, 2010, *available at* http://www.gallup.com/poll/125645/socialism-viewed-positively-americans.aspx (last visited June 3, 2011).

   [6]   Such references are so ubiquitous that perhaps no citation is necessary, but examples from the State of the Union addresses of both President Obama and President George W. Bush lionizing small businesses and entrepreneurs illustrate the point. President Obama in his 2010 State of the Union offered a short paean to entrepreneurs by saying "Now, the true engine of job creation in this country will always be America's businesses. But government can create the conditions necessary for businesses to expand and hire more workers. . . . We should start where most new jobs do – in small businesses, companies that begin when an entrepreneur takes a chance on a dream, or a worker decides it's time she became her own boss. Through sheer grit and determination, these companies have weathered the

the heroic role politicians and pundits have assigned to small businesses, it is safe to say that the shop-owner on Main Street is now in the special pantheon of unassailable American icons along with mom, apple pie, and baseball.

Because small businesses and entrepreneurs enjoy such popular and political support, it seems natural that our law should be geared toward promoting the development of new businesses. But the law frequently falls short on that score and erects obstacles to new business formation. Those obstacles sometimes occur as disincentives or barriers that are part of the overall environment in which would-be entrepreneurs operate. Ironically, part of the reason for the creation of barriers to entrepreneurship is a failure among policymakers to appreciate that the interests of "entrepreneurs" are distinct from, and sometimes in opposition to, the interests of "small businesses." Although those terms are often used interchangeably in public discourse, they are by no means synonymous.

Law and policy discussions ostensibly about designing legal regimes to promote entrepreneurship frequently focus on broad legal and regulatory issues that are more important to existing small businesses than they are to potential entrepreneurs. The issues most relevant to entrepreneurs are those affecting the decision to start a new business—which often means the decision to leave an incumbent position. A legal regime designed to promote entrepreneurship should strive to develop a policy environment that is conducive to new venture creation by identifying and removing impediments to new venture creation.

Creating an appropriate environment requires an appreciation of the factors influencing the entrepreneur's decision to leave an incumbent position to start a new business. Issues surrounding the would-be entrepreneur's concern about specific details such as continuing medical insurance coverage, or the potential liability for misuse of intellectual property claimed by a former employer, or for running afoul of a non-competition agreement, are the kinds of environmental issues that weigh on an entrepreneur's mind and make the decision to leave an incumbent position difficult.

This chapter will start with a discussion about the differences between "small businesses" and "entrepreneurs." It will then proceed to examine some salient issues that affect the creation of a legal environment that is

---

recession and they're ready to grow." Barack Obama, State of the Union Address (Jan. 27, 2010), *available at* http://www.whitehouse.gov/the-press-office/remarks-president-state-union-address (last visited June 3, 2011) (redundancies and applause pauses removed). For a quote from President Bush noting small businesses job creation role, *see infra* note 57 and accompanying text.

hospitable for entrepreneurial activity. Finally, it will conclude with the suggestion that policymakers analyze regulatory schemes with an eye toward creating an entrepreneur-friendly environment by imagining the impact of policy choices on the typical entrepreneur.

I.   DIFFERENTIATING BETWEEN "SMALL BUSINESSES" AND "ENTREPRENEURS"

The widespread popular and political regard for "small business," is a little odd because people have strong positive feelings about something that eludes precise definition. "Small business" as a term of art has various meanings in various contexts and often keys off of the number of people the firm employs—sometimes fewer than 500, or 100, or 20. Alternatively, it is sometimes useful to talk about small business by reference to the size of the firm's capitalization, asset value, or revenues.[7]

Economists have long recognized significant overlap between the notions of "small businesses" and "entrepreneurial ventures," but they have noted the important differences between the two ideas as well.[8] In political discourse, and even in policy debate, however, we often find people discussing small business, self-employment, and entrepreneurship as if they were synonyms. In some discussions, any individual with income as a sole proprietor listed on Schedule C, or Schedule E income from partnerships, S corporations, or rents and royalties is considered to be an "entrepreneur."[9] In fact, many of those people are just self-employed and are not true entrepreneurs.

Unfortunately, the idea of "entrepreneurship" is not easy to define. Since the term "entrepreneur" first gained currency in economics discourse in the 1750s, it has gone through several articulations in the literature,

---

[7]   *See* Anthony Luppino, *A Little Of This, A Little Of That: Potential Effects On Entrepreneurship Of The McCain And Obama Tax Proposals*, 31 W. NEW ENG. L. REV. 717, 719–20 (2009) (providing a tidy summary of the multiple definitions of "small business").

[8]   *See, e.g.,* James W. Carland, Frank Hoy, William R. Boulton, and JoAnn Carland, *Differentiating Entrepreneurs from Small Business Owners: A Conceptualization*, 9 ACAD. OF MGMT. REV. no. 2, 354 (1984) (discussing the differences between small business and entrepreneurial ventures and offering the suggestion that entrepreneurial ventures are those which engage in at least one of Schumpeter's four categories of behavior, i.e., introduction of new products, introduction of new methods of production, opening of new markets, or reorganization of industry).

[9]   *See* Luppino, *supra* note 7 at fn. 10.

not all of which are consistent with one another.[10] One major school of thought centers on the work of Joseph Schumpeter, a highly influential 20th century economist. Schumpeter's entrepreneurs are innovators whose activities disrupted the status quo. His view of the role of entrepreneurs in the capitalist system can be summarized as follows:

> "[T]he function of the entrepreneur," Schumpeter maintained, "is to reform or revolutionize the pattern of production" by exploiting a new technology, developing a new source of supply, reorganizing an industry, or the like.[11]

Another important 20th century economic thinker, Frank Knight, had a different perspective on the entrepreneur's role. He saw the entrepreneur as a species of risk arbitrageur—taking on the uncertainty inherent in creating a business enterprise in exchange for the potential of economic gain.[12] In either case, whether the "true" entrepreneur is a Schumpeterian innovator or a Knightian risk bearer, that person differs from both the self-employed person, who is basically "entrepreneuring" their way into a job, and the small business owner who may be happy to operate a staid business in a steady state without introducing new products, techniques, markets or innovations. Sometimes the self-employed, and even some small business owners, are called "lifestyle entrepreneurs": businesspersons whose goal is to support themselves in a particular lifestyle.[13]

Although the terms mean different things, in public discourse "entrepreneur" is often used as a synonym for "small business." While many entrepreneurial enterprises are small businesses, not all small businesses are entrepreneurial. It may be useful to define the term "small business." The Small Business Administration (SBA) has a definition for that term, but it is not a simple one.[14] For most industry sectors, however, the SBA considers a business to be "small" if it employs fewer than 500 employees.

---

[10] *See*, Pozen, *supra* note 2 at 284–94 (providing an overview of the development of the idea of the entrepreneur in economic thinking).
[11] *Id.* at 291.
[12] *Id.* at 291–92.
[13] *See* Amar Bhide, *The Questions Every Entrepreneur Must Answer*, HARV. BUS. REV., (Nov.–Dec. 1996) 120, 122–23 (discussing the differences between lifestyle entrepreneurs and other entrepreneurs).
[14] The definition is found in 13 C.F.R. §121. The regulation goes on at great length about the procedural details for determining eligibility for various programs. At 13 C.F.R. §121.201 the regulation provides size standards for SBA programs to be effective November 5, 2011, by reference to annual receipts in dollars and/or number of employees for businesses engaged in activities defined by various North American Industry Classification System (NAICS) codes. In rough summary, the

To see how the SBA definition works in practice, consider the business ecosystem in western Massachusetts, the area west of the city of Worcester defined by the four western counties of the Commonwealth, Hampden, Hampshire, Franklin and Berkshire. About 830,000 people live in western Massachusetts.[15] According to the website of the regional economic development agency, there are more than 30,500 businesses in the region, almost all of which have fewer than 100 employees, while about 500 have more than 100 employees.[16]

According to the website, western Massachusetts has twenty-eight employers whose workforces exceed 500 employees. When that list is reduced by removing the United States Postal Service and the non-profit organizations—primarily hospitals and colleges[17]—the list consists of only twelve (out of 30,500) employers that do not meet the SBA definition of "small business." In a nutshell, the way the SBA defines small business includes almost all of the businesses operating in western Massachusetts. While this is not a scientific survey and it is hard to tell if western Massachusetts is a typical geographic area, we might assume it is not too atypical. With that in mind, the significance of the SBA definition is clear: it is extremely inclusive—virtually all businesses are "small" businesses.

There may be good policy reasons for such a broad definition, but there are obviously compelling political reasons for it as well. Given such a broad

---

eligible businesses include: for most manufacturing and mining industries, those with 500 or fewer employees (but for a significant number of industries 750, 1,000, or 1,500 employees are permissible); for all wholesale trade industries, 100 or fewer employees; receipts for most retail and service industries (with some exceptions), $7 million per year in sales; for most general & heavy construction industries, $33.5 million per year in sales receipts; for all special trade contractors; $14 million per year in sales receipts; and $0.75 million per year in sales receipts for most agricultural, forestry, and fishing industries (with some exceptions). 13 C.F.R. § 121.201.

[15]   U.S Census Bureau, State & County QuickFacts, http://quickfacts.census. gov/qfd/states/25/25015.html (last visited June 3, 2011).

[16]   *See* Economic Development Council of Western Massachusetts, Companies *available at* http://www.westernmassedc.com/Data__Demographics/companies/ (last visited June 3, 2011).

[17]   Although the so-called "meds and eds" are being removed from the list of "businesses," they are important economic innovators that can catalyze economic growth in their communities. *See, e.g.,* Timothy J. Bartik and George Erickcek, *The Local Economic Impact of "Eds & Meds": How Policies to Expand Universities and Hospitals Affect Metropolitan Economies Education, Cities, Jobs and the Economy, Labor, Economic Development,* Brookings, Dec. 2008 (available online at: http://www.brookings.edu/~/media/Files/rc/reports/2008/1210_metropolitan_ economies_bartik_erickcek/metropolitan_economies_report.pdf)(discussing the positive impact of medical center and university expansion on host municipalities).

definition, proponents of any piece of pro-business legislation, even policies designed primarily to benefit big businesses, can claim the proposed
legislation has a big impact on "small" businesses. Polls show that across
the political spectrum people are much less favorably disposed toward "big
business" than they are toward "small business."[18] With the almost all-
inclusive definition of "small" business, however, proponents of just about
any provision favored by business generally, from loosening environmental
protections, to weakening worker safety standards, to defanging consumer
protection agencies, to eliminating the estate tax, can proceed under the
rallying cry that such changes are necessary to protect "small" businesses.
In our national mythology we care about the little guy. We want to nurture
small businesses because we believe they are the most important players in
our distinctly American entrepreneurial economy. Except that they are not.

Although small businesses clearly are important in our economy, big
businesses are still at least as important as small businesses and probably more so. About 45% of the U.S. working population is employed in
large, mature firms.[19] A report from the Center for Economic and Policy
Research shows that among western nations American businesses rank
near the bottom on several measures of "smallness."[20] Using Organization
for Economic Cooperation and Development (OECD) data, the report
shows that among the world's major economically developed democracies[21] the U.S. actually has a lower percentage of its workforce employed
in small business than just about any other country. For example, we have
a relatively low rate of self-employment[22] and in the manufacturing sector

---

[18]   *See* Gallup Poll *supra* note 5 (showing Republicans and Democrats having
a 97% and 95% favorable view of small business, respectively, and only a 54% and
46% favorable view of big business).

[19]   John C. Haltiwanger, Ron S. Jarmin, and Javier Miranda, *Who Creates
Jobs? Small Vs. Large Vs. Young*, National Bureau of Economic Research Working
Paper 16300 at 10 (2010) available at http://www.nber.org/papers/w16300 (noting
that "it is the mature and large firms that account for most employment (about
45%) and most job creation and destruction").

[20]   John Schmitt and Nathan Lane, *An International Comparison of Small
Business Employment*, Center for Economic and Policy Research (2009) *available at*
http://www.cepr.net/documents/publications/small-business-2009-08.pdf.

[21]   *Id.* at 3, fn. 3 (noting that the study examined data from the 21 major
democracies, specifically: Australia, Austria, Belgium, Canada, Denmark, Finland,
France, Germany, Greece, Ireland, Italy, Japan, Luxembourg, Netherlands, New
Zealand, Norway, Portugal, Spain, Sweden, Switzerland, the United Kingdom,
and the United States).

[22]   *Id.* at 4 (noting a self-employment rate in the United States of 7.2% and
showing that compared to the other 20 countries in the data set (data for Japan was
not available) only Luxembourg at 6.1% had a lower rate of self-employment).

only a modest percentage of our manufacturing workforce is employed by firms of fewer than twenty employees.[23] Among our industrialized peers, the United States has the lowest percentage of its manufacturing workforce employed in firms smaller than 500 employees.[24]

This empirical data does not fit well with the story we tell ourselves about small firms being the backbone of the U.S. economy. Our national discussion about business and job creation—on both sides of the aisle—clings to the popular (mis)perception that small businesses make all the new jobs. This piece of folklore, in turn, has been the basis of public policy that caters to small business ostensibly with the aim of creating new jobs. The problem is, when controlled for other factors, big firms and small firms create new jobs roughly in proportion to the overall percentage of the job market those firms control.[25]

A study from the National Bureau of Economics Research adds an important dimension to the job-creation discussion. It found that a subset of small firms—start-ups—do in fact produce more jobs than other firms, but the distinguishing characteristic of those job-creating companies is firm age, not firm size.[26] Relying on data from the Census Bureau, the study confirmed that smaller companies created more jobs than larger companies during the period 1992–2005. The study also confirmed that the real force for disproportionate job growth was not the size of the company, but the age of the company. The researchers concluded that the younger companies are, the more jobs they create, regardless of their size. It appears that start-up firms are responsible for generating the new jobs that policy makers usually attribute to small companies generally.

There is, however, another side of the start-up firm job creation story. New firms not only create more jobs than more mature firms, they destroy more jobs, too. Because start-ups operate in highly competitive and turbulent markets, the rigor of competition weeds out a significant number of start-up firms during the early years. Within five years of inception,

---

[23]   *Id.* at 7 (noting that 11.1% of the manufacturing workforce in the United States is employed in firms with fewer than 20 employees—third lowest in the 21-country data set—only Ireland at 9.6% and Luxembourg at 8.5% were lower).

[24]   *Id.* at 8 (showing the United States with only 51.2% of its manufacturing workforce employed in firms of fewer than 500 employees—the other countries ranged from 56.5% to 85.6%).

[25]   *See* Haltiwanger, et al., *supra* note 19 at 30–31 (noting that large, mature firms—those more than ten-years-old and with more than 500 workers—employed about 45% of all private-sector workers and accounted for almost 40% of job creation and destruction).

[26]   *Id.* at 31 (showing that although firm start-ups account for only 3% of employment, they were almost 20% of gross job creation).

many of the newly formed, job-creating businesses have failed and, in doing so, have destroyed, on a net basis, about 40% of the jobs created by all new companies. Those start-up firms that do not fail often continue to grow, adding jobs faster than more mature companies, and creating a disproportionate share of jobs relative to their size.[27]

These new firms are the businesses that are creating new jobs. The family-owned florist that has been a fixture on Main Street for fifty years and always had a staff of four is probably going to continue in stasis for quite a while; it will not be creating jobs just because it is a small business. The start-up firms, on the other hand, are making something out of nothing—the jobs they create did not exist before.

Given the difficulty in defining "self-employment," "small business," and "entrepreneurial activity" in ways that are easy to grasp and apply, it may make more sense to adopt a pragmatic working definition of "entrepreneurs" as the people who are starting new businesses, regardless of whether those firms are truly entrepreneurial under either a Schumpeterian or Knightian definition. Because most job creation comes from new firms,[28] not necessarily small firms, we ought to make sure we have a legal regime in place that is informed by a policy that fosters business formation and does not unnecessarily burden would-be entrepreneurs with obstacles that make the decision to leave an incumbent position difficult.

II. FOSTERING AN ENTREPRENEURSHIP-FRIENDLY ENVIRONMENT

To promote the formation of new businesses we must first develop an environment that is supportive of and, conducive to, that activity.[29] The

---

[27] *Id.* at 30.

[28] We should, however, keep the magnitude of the job creation aspect of start-ups in perspective: most start-ups do not employ anyone other than the founder and those that do have employees have relatively few. SCOTT A. SHANE, THE ILLUSIONS OF ENTREPRENEURSHIP: THE COSTLY MYTHS THAT ENTREPRENEURS, INVESTORS AND POLICY MAKERS LIVE BY, 65 (New Haven, CT, U.S.A.: Yale University Press, 2008) (citing statistics showing that only 24% of new businesses have any employees and of new businesses with employees, only 10% employed more than five people and only 4.5% of those start-ups with employees had more than 20 employees).

[29] *See, e.g.,* WESLEY D. SINE & ROBERT J. DAVID, INSTITUTIONS AND ENTREPRENEURSHIP (Bingley, UK: Emerald Group Publishing Limited, 2010) (examining how the institutional environment affects entrepreneurial organizations, and vice versa); and DOUGLASS C. NORTH, INSTITUTIONS, INSTITUTIONAL CHANGE AND ECONOMIC PERFORMANCE (Cambridge, UK: Cambridge University

entrepreneur's crucial decision is whether or not to start a business. Policy
that promotes entrepreneurship should focus on that decision and strive
to eliminate barriers that prevent people from taking the leap of faith
necessary to go out on their own. The literature recognizes that an environment supportive of entrepreneurship is a function of both appropriate
institutions and supportive cultural attitudes.[30]

By most accounts, the United States satisfies these environmental conditions quite well.[31] The United States embodies the cultural aspects of
a pro-entrepreneurship economy: our society changes constantly, failure
does not carry the heavy social stigma that it does in many other cultures,[32]
and, for better or worse, Americans seem relatively unconcerned about the
gap between the "haves" and the "have-nots."[33] In addition, our institutions are governed by the rule of law, and property rights are enforced.[34]
We do, however, continue to have a vigorous debate about whether we
unreasonably constrain economic activity.

Press, 1990) (articulating the importance of both governmental and other institutional structures and also cultural norms and incentives as part of the environment
for entrepreneurship).

[30] William J. Dennis, Jr., *Entrepreneurship, Small Business and Public Policy
Levers*, 49 J. SMALL BUS. MGMT. 92, 95 (2010) (spelling out the fundamental institutional issues as being: (1) whether there is the rule of law; (2) whether enforceable
property rights exist; and (3) whether private economic activity is unreasonably
constrained; while the basic cultural issues are: (1) whether society easily accepts
change; (2) whether failure is tolerated; and (3) whether economic inequity is
tolerated). For an account of how difficult it is to establish a business when these
institutional and cultural factors are missing, *see* Max Chafkin, *A Constant Feeling
of Crisis*, INC., June 2011 at 76 (describing the dire entrepreneurship environment
in Argentina).

[31] The World Bank annually conducts a survey of countries around the world
to assess the relative ease or difficulty of starting and running businesses. The
United States places consistently in the top ten. The data is available at http://www.
doingbusiness.org/rankings (last visited June 12, 2011).

[32] *See, e.g.,* Brendan Burchell and Alan Hughes, *The Stigma Of Failure: An
International Comparison Of Failure Tolerance And Second Chancing*, Centre
for Business Research, University of Cambridge, Working Paper No. 334 (2006)
(finding a high tolerance for failure in the United States, but not necessarily a
higher tolerance for giving failed entrepreneurs a second chance).

[33] LARRY M. BARTELS, UNEQUAL DEMOCRACY: THE POLITICAL ECONOMY OF THE
NEW GILDED AGE (New Jersey, U.S.A.: Princeton University Press, 2008) (exploring the complicated interplay among economic, political, and social factors that
allows historically high levels of income inequality in the U.S. to persist).

[34] *See* Zoltan J. Acs and Roger R. Stough, *Introduction to Public Policy in an
Entrepreneurial Society*, *in* Zoltan J. Acs and Roger R. Stough, eds., PUBLIC POLICY
IN AN ENTREPRENEURIAL ECONOMY (New York, NY, U.S.A.: Springer, 2008), 1, 13
(noting the fitness of American institutions for promoting entrepreneurship).

While having a tradition of respect for the rule of law appears to be a prerequisite for an entrepreneurship-friendly environment, the content of those rules matters, too.[35] The possibility exists that wise design of legal rules and institutions could contribute to the level of innovation and growth in the economy.[36] A complete discussion of this idea is well beyond the scope of this chapter, but a couple of examples where the substantive content of public policy or legal rules affect the environment for entrepreneurship will illustrate the importance of the idea that focusing on issues that matter to "small businesses" is not the same as developing rules that are good for "entrepreneurs."

Legal rules that are especially helpful to entrepreneurs are those that facilitate the decision to start a business. These rules are not always obvious, but many different aspects of our legal/regulatory scheme come to bear on the entrepreneur's decision to start up a new venture. Before exploring this territory, however, it may be helpful to place the would-be entrepreneur in context. The Kauffman Foundation has published a profile of the attributes of entrepreneurs and it suggests a good starting point for thinking through the legal issues that would-be entrepreneurs wrestle with before deciding to start a new business.

While the image of Bill Gates dropping out of Harvard to start Microsoft (or Steve Jobs dropping out of Reed College to start Apple or Michael Dell dropping out of the University of Texas to start his eponymous computer company or Mark Zuckerberg dropping out of Harvard to start Facebook) tends to dominate our view of the modern entrepreneur, in fact, the actual demographic profile of the typical entrepreneur does not look like a single, workaholic, childless twenty-something college dropout who has no experience in the "real world" of industry. According to the study, the majority of entrepreneurs had worked at other companies for more than six years before starting their own firms.[37] Almost 70% of the

---

[35] *See, e.g.,* KAUFFMAN TASK FORCE ON LAW, RULES FOR GROWTH: INNOVATION AND GROWTH, PROMOTING INNOVATION AND GROWTH THROUGH LEGAL REFORM (Kansas City, MO, U.S.A.: Ewing Marion Kauffman Foundation, 2011) *available at* http://www.kauffman.org/uploadedfiles/Rules-for-Growth.pdf (legal scholars offering suggestions for improving the legal system in a wide array of substantive areas with an eye toward removing barriers to innovation).

[36] *See* Viktor Mayer-Schönberger, *The Law as Stimulus: The Role of Law in Fostering Innovative Entrepreneurship,* 6 I/S: J. L. & POL'Y FOR INFO. SOC'Y 153 (2010) (arguing that the law has capacity to foster economic growth, though that potential is not realized).

[37] VIVEK WADHWA, RAJ AGGARWAL, KRISZTINA "Z" HOLLY, AND ALEX SALKEVER, THE ANATOMY OF AN ENTREPRENEUR: FAMILY BACKGROUND AND MOTIVATION, 16 (Kansas, MO, U.S.A.: the Ewing Marion Kauffman Foundation,

entrepreneurs were married when they launched their business and almost 60% had at least one child in their household at the time of launch.[38] Only about a quarter of them were "extremely interested" in starting a new business at the time they graduated from college; a fairly significant portion, 48%, either never thought about it or were not interested in starting a business when they left college.[39]

One writer provided a tidy summary of the literature profiling the demographic traits of American entrepreneurs this way:

> The typical entrepreneur looks a lot less like Bill Gates and a lot more like the guy who lives across the street from you or sits next to you at church:
>
> - He is a white man in his forties.
> - He is married with a working spouse.
> - He attended college but might not have graduated.
> - He was born in the United States and lived here his whole life.
> - He has spent much of his life in the town where he started his business.
> - He is just trying to make a living, not trying to build a high-growth business.
> - He worked previously in the industry in which he started his company, something like construction, insurance or retail.
> - He has no special psychological characteristics.[40]

The last point is worthy of additional examination. Despite the persistent myth that there are special people with a particular psychological makeup who naturally become entrepreneurs, research tends to show there are no entrepreneur-specific psychological traits. Although we still do not have a satisfactory articulation of what motivates entrepreneurs,[41] in light of current research we cannot uncritically adhere to the old notion that entrepreneurs have a "risk-taking propensity" that distinguishes them from other organizational managers or from the general population.[42] It

---

2009) *available at* http://ssrn.com/abstract=1431263)(showing that 75.4% of entrepreneurs surveyed had at least six years of experience with a previous employer before starting their own firm).

[38] *Id.* at 12 (showing 69.9% of entrepreneurs were married and 59.7% had at least one child at the time of new venture launch).

[39] *Id.* at 13 (showing 24.5% were "extremely interested," 27.5% were "somewhat interested," 34.7% "didn't think about it," 6.1% were "not very interested," and 7.2% were "not interested at all").

[40] *See* SHANE *supra* note 25 at 40–41 (summarizing the scholarship on the characteristics of entrepreneurs).

[41] *See* Alan Carsrud & Malin Brannback, *Entrepreneurial Motivations: What Do We Still Need to Know?*, 49 J. SMALL BUS. 9 (2011) (surveying literature and pointing the direction for more research on "entrepreneurial motivation").

[42] Wayne H. Stewart, Jr., Warren E. Watson, Joanne C. Carland, and James W.

may very well be that rather than embracing the risks inherent in a new business, entrepreneurs are actually overly optimistic about the profit potential when they identify opportunities.[43] In any event, it would be wrong to say that entrepreneurs seek out risk or gratuitously embrace it.

In his book, *Principles of Innovation*, Peter Drucker summarizes the entrepreneur's approach to risk by recounting an exchange he witnessed at a conference where an entrepreneur was responding to some academic discussion about the "entrepreneurial personality" being one that embraced risk taking. According to Drucker, the entrepreneur made this comment:

> I have never come across an 'entrepreneurial personality.' The successful ones I know all have, however, one thing—and only one thing—in common: they are *not* 'risk-takers.' They try to define the risks they have to take and to minimize them as much as possible. Otherwise none of us could have succeeded.[44]

Envisioning the characteristics of the typical entrepreneur allows us to imagine the kinds of issues that might weigh heavily on the decision to start a business. Appreciating that entrepreneurs do not gratuitously assume risks but rather consider risks carefully and prudently helps round out the picture. Imagining the issues that will worry a middle-aged, married, business person with children as he or she contemplates leaving an existing employer to strike out on a new venture is perhaps easier than trying to identify the possible issues that might, in the abstract, affect some theoretical entrepreneur who could be just out of college and independently wealthy, or could be someone in mid-career living paycheck-to-paycheck.

With that in mind, how is policy made that takes into account the concerns of entrepreneurs? Ordinarily in our system we expect interest groups to petition the government to hear their concerns and to lobby for policies that further the group's agenda. As a matter of interest group formation, however, potential entrepreneurs would seem to be a difficult group to organize. Many of them would not realize they belong in the group, since many people who become entrepreneurs do so only after a unique opportunity arises and they find themselves pursuing it. Then, after creating a

---

Carland, *A Proclivity for Entrepreneurship: A Comparison of Entrepreneurs, Small Business Owners, and Corporate Managers*, 14 J. OF BUS. VENTURING, no. 2, March 1999, 189 (1999) (reviewing the literature on entrepreneurs as risk-takers).

[43] *See* Gavin Cassar, *Are Individuals Entering Self-Employment Overly-Optimistic? An Empirical Test of Plans and Projections of Nascent Entrepreneur Expectations* (2008) (*available at* http://ssrn.com/abstract=945206 (finding substantial over-optimism in the expectations of nascent entrepreneurs).

[44] PETER F. DRUCKER, INNOVATION AND ENTREPRENEURSHIP: PRACTICE AND PRINCIPLES 139 (New York, NY, U.S.A.: HarperCollins,1985).

new business, some of them will go on to create other businesses, but many of them will no longer be personally affected by the problem of business formation again. Indeed, after establishing their businesses, many entrepreneurs may just as soon see barriers to entry for potential new competitors remain high—including the obstacles to starting a new firm, which, after all, was a cost their firm had to bear when it entered the market.

Because entrepreneurs *qua* entrepreneurs may be difficult to mobilize politically, it leaves the entrepreneurship policy portfolio on the table for other lobbying organizations to appropriate. Since many entrepreneurs start ventures that evolve into small businesses, there is a natural tendency for organizations purporting to represent the interests of small business to carry the banner for entrepreneurship as well.

Many lobbying groups claim to speak for small businesses, but chief among them is the U.S. Chamber of Commerce. In its Mission Statement the U.S. Chamber of Commerce purports to speak for "3 million American businesses,"[45] yet its actual paid membership is closer to 300,000 businesses and its operations are funded primarily by huge corporations like Chevron, Dow Chemical, Prudential Insurance, Aegon (a Dutch insurance company), and Goldman Sachs,[46] which might explain the Chamber's virulent opposition to financial reform, environmental policy, and the healthcare overhaul. The Chamber casts all of those issues as being extremely detrimental to small business. The lack of at least some ambivalence in the Chamber's stance on financial reform is odd, since the primary beneficiaries of a roll-back of the financial services law would be big bankers who have not exactly distinguished themselves as friends of small business. Similarly, its super-charged rhetoric in opposition to climate change legislation seems more concerned with the interests of big energy companies and utilities than with small businesses, since small businesses are most likely to be the innovative firms that will benefit from the opportunities that are arising in the emerging green economy. Finally, the much maligned healthcare law, although opposed for various reasons, might have been a net positive for entrepreneurs had it been crafted properly.

Although the U.S. Chamber of Commerce is not the only lobbying

---

[45]   *See* U.S. Chamber of Commerce, Mission Statement, http://www.uschambersmallbusinessnation.com/about-us/mission-statement (last visited June 13, 2011).

[46]   Eric Lipton, Mike Mcintire and Don Van Natta Jr, *Large Donations Aid U.S. Chamber In Election Drive*, N.Y. TIMES, Oct. 22, 2010 at A1 (noting that half of the U.S. Chamber of Commerce's $140 million operating budget came from just 45 donors).

group purporting to speak for small businesses, it is a very significant presence in the public debate. Because of that, we end up with a political debate about what is good for entrepreneurship being conducted by people who ostensibly represent the interests of small business, but who are in fact funded by big business.

The health-care-reform debate conducted during the first two years of the Obama administration illustrates some of the problems that arise when the "pro-business" side of the argument is focused on extant small businesses and not on would-be entrepreneurs. The debate to impose some order on the healthcare system with the goals of extending coverage to the uninsured and bringing costs down has been controversial, protracted, and divisive. Many voices were heard in the debate, but the impact of the various possible health-care models on entrepreneurial activity— specifically the question of how the reform might affect the decision to start a new business—did not receive much attention.

As background for the discussion, one should first appreciate that the American system of providing healthcare insurance is an historical accident.[47] For various path-dependent reasons, Americans came to expect that they would get health insurance from their employers, but employers were not required to provide that benefit. People who were not employed or whose employers did not provide coverage had to buy insurance in the open market, where it was very expensive.

Many decided to forgo the expense. Nevertheless, when uninsured people went to the hospital they received care. The hospitals billed the uninsured patients, but often could not collect the full amount due. In order to cover the costs incurred by uninsured patients, those patients with insurance were charged more, essentially cross-subsidizing the uninsured. Costs went ever-higher, making private insurance even more expensive, causing more people to go uninsured, which created the need for more cross-subsidization, which caused costs to go higher, and so on. The system was unsustainable primarily because not enough people were covered by insurance, especially healthy young people. As Milton Friedman was fond of saying, "There is no such thing as a free lunch."[48] Although Friedman

---

[47] During the New Deal FDR wanted to create a national healthcare system as part of the safety net, but it was a political bridge too far. Not many people had health insurance until the Second World War, when wages at home were frozen by law. Since employers couldn't raise wages, they started providing fringe benefits as a way to retain their best people. Health insurance turned out to be a very popular fringe benefit. When those benefits were also determined to be not subject to the income tax as compensation, we were off to the races.

[48] *See* Richard Lederer, *On Language; Haunted Words*, N.Y. Times, Sept. 3,

railed against government benefits as the classic "free lunch," the health care provided to the uninsured is a free lunch problem, too; somebody has to pay for it and that somebody is the patients with insurance.

These escalating costs affected business in at least two ways. First, in order to attract a quality workforce, businesses, both big and small, found they needed to offer a good health care plan. These plans were expensive and added significantly to personnel costs.

Second, these costs hampered U.S. businesses in the global market. Our competitors in Europe and Japan have health care systems, too. Although their systems vary a quite a bit from one to the other, the government tends to play a more central role—sometimes as the single payer, sometimes as the provider of service, sometimes as the coordinator of many providers and many payers.[49] Eschewing government involvement, the United States has relied on the market to control healthcare costs with the result that we Americans pay significantly more of our GDP for healthcare than do other developed nations[50] even though we do not enjoy better health outcomes.

1989 at sec. 6 (noting that the phrase is the title of one of Friedman's books and also relating the anecdote that Friedman once summarized his entire scholarly agenda by saying: "There is no such thing as a free lunch. That is the sum of my economic theory. The rest is elaboration.").

[49]   *See,* Valérie Paris, Marion Devaux, & Lihan Wei, *Health Systems Institutional Characteristics: A Survey of 29 OECD Countries,* OECD HEALTH WORKING PAPERS, No. 50 (2010) *available at* http://dx.doi.org/10.1787/5kmfxfq9qbnr-en (describing the variety of health care systems in the OECD countries, where some countries provide the medical service through government doctors while others use private practitioners; some countries have a single payer, while others have multiple payers; some countries have automatic coverage provided by the state, while others require the citizens to obtain insurance.). The quality of public discourse was extremely low, even by modern American standards. Opponents merely resorted to labeling any government involvement "socialism" without any hint of sophistication about how varied "socialized medicine" systems are or acknowledging that the United States already has "socialized" medicine such as the Indian Health Service and the Veterans Administration health system, which share characteristics with the UK healthcare system where the government pays for the service and provides the service through government doctors; on the more moderate part of the scale, our Medicare system is similar to the "socialized" Canadian system where private parties provide the services, but the government pays for them.

[50]   *Disparities In Health Expenditure Across OECD Countries: Why Does The United States Spend So Much More Than Other Countries?* Hearing Before the S. Special Committee on Aging, Sept. 30, 2009 (written Statement of Mark Pearson, Head, Health Division, OECD) (noting that the U.S. spent 16% of its GDP on health in 2007, the highest share in the OECD, and more than 7 percentage points higher than the average of 8.9% in OECD countries. Even France, which had the

The net result of the pre-reform health care system was to make it more expensive for American businesses to compete internationally, while at the same time making it more expensive to retain good workers at home. On the eve of the health reform debate, the status quo situation presented the following scenarios for existing small businesses, among others. First, some businesses wanted the flexibility not to offer health insurance to their workers and by doing so to receive the back-door wealth transfer from the insured patients, who provided a cross-subsidy for the uninsured. Second, some businesses that provided health care insurance had a competitive advantage in the labor market and had no desire to level the playing field by providing a new government program covering all workers, including those at competitor firms. Third, some businesses wanted the government to take over the health insurance benefit—which is a nuisance for small businesses to administer and takes energies away from the business of the firm—but their voices were lost in the noise.

Also lost in the histrionics was any serious discussion about how the existing healthcare system affected entrepreneurship, as opposed to how it affected small businesses. There were very few voices drawing the connection between healthcare and entrepreneurship, but one study made a salient observation:

> . . . entrepreneurial decision-making involves making non-optimizing decisions where the reward or loss suffered by the entrepreneur, the "entrepreneurial profit," and the decision to exploit an entrepreneurial opportunity rely on the perception that the expected value of the opportunity exceeds the opportunity costs. This occurs when an individual has lower opportunity costs, and one way to lower the opportunity cost is to affect health insurance costs either by directly reducing the insurance costs, reducing the cost of searching for re-insurance, or eliminating the need to search for insurance altogether. The poison pill, however, is that the specific mechanism for reducing the opportunity costs could have negative effects.[51]

Considering the demographics of the typical entrepreneur—middle-aged, married, with children, employed at another firm, and not a gratuitous risk taker—one would naturally assume that healthcare coverage

---

second greatest percent outlay, spent over 5 percentage points of GDP less than the U.S. However, almost all OECD countries, with the exception of the U.S., Mexico, and Turkey, have full insurance coverage of their population.).

[51] Scott Jackson, *Entrepreneurial Healthcare: A Study in State Policy Arbitrage*, *in* Zoltan J. Acs and Roger R. Stough, (eds), PUBLIC POLICY IN AN ENTREPRENEURIAL ECONOMY (New York, U.S.A.: Springer 2008), 117, 120 (citations and internal quotations omitted).

figures significantly into the cost/benefit calculation in the decision to start a new company. Prior to healthcare reform medical insurance coverage affected entrepreneurship in that it tended to keep talented people anchored in jobs for fear of losing their health-care coverage.[52] People with special health issues, or who were just starting a family, may have valued the incumbent employer's health insurance very highly and may have stayed put instead of going out on their own.[53]

Existing studies had already shown that having medical coverage through a spouse was positively linked to a person's decision to pursue self-employment.[54] Adopting a healthcare policy that would take away the anxiety of leaving an incumbent position's employer-provided healthcare plan to start a new business might have had a positive effect on entrepreneurship by reducing the costs of job mobility, but instead of creating automatic health coverage that follows the individual, Congress opted for a complicated mandated coverage approach. Some people will have to buy their own insurance; others will have it provided by their employer. Someone who is employed by an employer that provides generous coverage will still confront a dilemma when considering the jump to a start-up.[55] The effect on businesses generally will be to pick up part of the cost of the insurance or pay the penalty. For many firms it is a cost they've been paying all along, but for others it will be a new obligation. For entrepreneurs contemplating the decision to start a new business, it will be a cost to take into account not only for themselves, but also as a crucial piece of attracting a quality workforce.[56]

---

[52]   *See* David Leonhardt, *Ignoring Failure's Real Cost,* N.Y. TIMES, Dec. 16, 2009 at B1 (quoting Eric Schmidt, Google's chief executive, as saying, "There clearly are people who choose to stay in their jobs due to the fact that they don't have insurance portability.").

[53]   Although the pre-reform regime provided limited insurance portability through COBRA, that law had significant drawbacks and largely failed to address the gap in insurance for workers who lost their jobs. *See* Jackson, *supra* note 51 at 124–25 (summarizing research on COBRA).

[54]   *Id.* at 120 (citing prior literature on spousal coverage).

[55]   The shared responsibility payments by businesses do not apply to businesses with fewer than 50 employees. Patient Protection and Affordable Care Act, Pub. L. No: 111-148, §1513, 124 Stat. 119 (2010), so most start-ups will be unaffected by the possible requirement to provide or contribute to the cost of healthcare insurance, in which case the would-be entrepreneur would have to provide his or her own coverage.

[56]   *See* Leonhardt, *supra* note 52 (reporting that the CEO of a Silicon Valley tech firm fields questions about health care "in almost every interview" with job applicants); see also Jackson, *supra* note 51 at 121 (citing research showing that providing health insurance was a major factor in recruiting and retaining employees).

Healthcare reform was a missed opportunity for Congress to change policy to remove obstacles possibly standing in the way of a would-be entrepreneur who is contemplating leaving an existing employer to start a new venture. A little more imagination and a little less demagoguery might have produced a healthcare system more accommodating to the typical middle-aged would-be entrepreneur who is a spouse and a parent and leery of unnecessary risks. In a short chapter, it is not possible to provide a complete survey of public policy that impedes the decision of the typical entrepreneur to leave an existing job to form a new business, but another common problem may prove illustrative.

Pro-business groups frequently decry the scourge of runaway litigation. In his State of the Union message in 2005, President Bush targeted the good guys—small business—and the bad guys—unscrupulous lawyers— in the same passage, saying:

> To make our economy stronger and more competitive, America must reward, not punish, the efforts and dreams of entrepreneurs. Small business is the path of advancement, especially for women and minorities, so we must free small businesses from needless regulation and protect honest job creators from junk lawsuits. Justice is distorted, and our economy is held back, by irresponsible class actions and frivolous asbestos claims—and I urge Congress to pass legal reforms this year.[57]

The passage nicely illustrates the disconnect between "entrepreneurship" policy and "small business" policy. The types of litigation cited by the President—class actions and asbestos claims—seem unlikely to affect the decision of a would-be entrepreneur to form a business. Those types of litigation do matter, however, to existing small businesses and, all things being equal, business owners would probably prefer to strip the right of redress for defective products from consumers. This is another illustration of a policy touted as being pro-entrepreneur that is really primarily just pro-business, as it seems unlikely that this kind of litigation influences the initial decision to form a business.

That being said, there is some litigation that does weigh heavily on the minds of would-be entrepreneurs: lawsuits for violating non-competition clauses and from allegedly appropriating an incumbent firm's intellectual property. Because the typical entrepreneur is employed in an organization before deciding to start a new business, the legal implications of departing from the incumbent position are an important consideration for the entrepreneur.

---

[57] George W. Bush, State of the Union Address (Feb. 2, 2005), *available at* http://millercenter.org/scripps/archive/speeches/detail/4464.

Many employers routinely bind their employees to non-competition agreements as a condition of continued employment. When the employee leaves the organization, the scope of what he or she can do is often an open question that might be costly to resolve. Non-competition agreements have legitimate applications, but, in general, they have a negative effect on worker mobility and entrepreneurial activity.

California law prohibits non-competition agreements[58] and its Supreme Court takes a dim view of the agreements in general.[59] If policy makers wish to create an environment that encourages business formation they ought to follow California's lead and recognize that entrepreneurs often start out somewhere else—in somebody else's organization. If a state has law that makes it difficult for workers to leave an employer and start something new, that is going to dampen entrepreneurship.

Innovative people sometimes find themselves working for employers who are not interested in new ideas. They want to leave, but find themselves potentially embroiled in litigation over a non-compete, confidentiality clause, or intellectual property agreement. Businesses have a legitimate concern to ensure that departing employees do not leave with intellectual property that belongs to the employer, and, even in California, intellectual property law provides a remedy for employers who can prove that a departing employee has appropriated trade secrets.[60] If policy makers could craft intellectual property laws to balance the reasonable expectations of employers and the innovative aspirations of would-be entrepreneurs, society would be better off.[61]

Changing the substance of these rules to make life easier for would-be entrepreneurs comes at a cost to the rights that existing small businesses believe protect their interests, illustrating again the situation that

---

[58]   CAL. BUS. & PROF. CODE § 16600 (West 1999) (providing that "Except as provided in this chapter, every contract by which anyone is restrained from engaging in a lawful profession, trade, or business of any kind is to that extent void.").

[59]   *See Edwards v. Arthur Andersen*, 44 Cal. 4th 937, 189 P.3d 285, 81 Cal. Rptr.3d 282 (2008) (finding there is no "narrow restraint" exception to general rule voiding non-competition agreements).

[60]   Michael Risch, *Comments on Trade Secret Sharing in High Velocity Labor Markets*, 12 EMP. RTS. & EMP. POL'Y J., No. 2, p. 339 (2009) (arguing that trade secret law in California is strong when applied to valuable information, but that most "information sharing" is tangential to core technologies of the incumbent employer).

[61]   Karen A. Campbell, *IP Protection Games: Does Technology Type Matter For Entrepreneurial Behavior?* (2011), *available at* http://ssrn.com/abstract=1784863 (suggesting that different protections ought to apply depending on whether the venture idea (innovation) is production specific or a general purpose technology).

policy conducive to entrepreneurship might be inimical to small business. Defenders of the status quo—i.e. small businesses—will resist a change, even while promoters of entrepreneurship might think a change is justified.

CONCLUSION

The world is changing, and the driving forces behind that change are the entrepreneurial ventures started by every-day entrepreneurs. Those every-day entrepreneurs typically are not college dropouts hell-bent on shifting some paradigm, instead they are middle-aged, married folks who are already working in another business and who do not relish the risks involved in making the leap from employee to business owner. In order to encourage would-be entrepreneurs to make the decision to start a new business, policy makers ought to be attuned to the impediments that make it more difficult for entrepreneurs to move out of their existing employment relationship and into a start-up firm.

These impediments will arise in many contexts. Something that is perceived as an obstacle to an entrepreneur may be viewed as an important legal protection for existing small businesses. Given the dynamics of pro-business interest groups, however, policy makers may not have the political capital to make entrepreneurship-friendly choices when those policies come at the expense of existing small business interests. Considering the importance of start-ups in creating new jobs, however, putting pro-entrepreneurship policies in place may pay off in the long run.

4. Transforming professional services to build regional innovation ecosystems

Sean M. O'Connor

INTRODUCTION

As policymakers seek the right policies to help industrial, or even pre-industrial, regional economies evolve into knowledge-based ones, they increasingly focus on concepts of "innovation ecosystems," or "clusters."[1] Originating in its current form largely from Michael Porter's seminal *The Competitive Advantage of Nations*,[2] a growing literature seeks to unpack and suggest ways to operationalize these concepts. Porter has succinctly defined his notion of a cluster as a "geographic concentration[] of inter-connected companies, specialized suppliers, service providers, firms in related industries, and associated institutions (*e.g.,* universities, standards agencies, trade associations) in a particular field that compete but also cooperate."[3] The key components of a cluster or innovation ecosystem[4] have more recently been summarized by a leading policymaker as: "A talent pool that connects across disciplines; [a]n 'innovation infrastructure' with physical facilities; [a] skilled workforce; [a]ccess to capital; and [a] support system that can shepherd promising innovations through the so-called 'valley of death.'"[5] While the expanding literature has begun exploring the human capital components of innovation ecosystems, little

---

[1] *See, e.g.,* U.S. Dept. of Commerce, Remarks at Innovation Clusters Conference, the Brookings Institution (Sept. 23, 2010) (Prepared remarks of Sec'y of Commerce, Gary Locke).

[2] MICHAEL PORTER, THE COMPETITIVE ADVANTAGE OF NATIONS (New York, NY, U.S.A.: Free Press, 1990)

[3] Michael Porter, *Location, Competition, And Economic Development: Local Clusters In A Global Economy*, 14 ECON. DEV. Q. 15 (2000).

[4] This Chapter adopts the term "innovation ecosystem" rather than "cluster."

[5] Locke, *supra* note 1.

appears to have been done with the professional service providers included in Porter's model. Rather, the literature seems to have favored studies of entrepreneurs and their workforces—which makes sense as a starting point for studying human capital in innovation ecosystems.

This Chapter seeks to expand the innovation ecosystems literature to focus on three themes. First, that a broader and deeper account of professional services is required to understand successful innovation ecosystems. Second, that attorneys have a central, yet bifurcated, presence in innovation ecosystems as either specialists or "targeted generalists." And third, that regional professional schools can play a central role in transforming professional services in local economies to provide the necessary innovation ecosystem that will allow (pre)industrial economies to evolve into knowledge economies.

THE ROLE OF PROFESSIONAL SERVICES IN INNOVATION ECOSYSTEMS

Porter's account of clusters actually focuses a bit more narrowly than the innovation ecosystem concept is currently used. He aims for something between a single industry and a high-level abstract grouping such as "high tech."[6] Notwithstanding his admonitions in this regard, his clusters do seem to form around a particular industry; for example, wine or computer chips. But his point may be that even as one industry is the organizing point, the cluster includes the firms and institutions that supply, service, or otherwise support that industry. This may be particularly the case where firms and institutions customize their products and services to support the industry. For vendors of, say, custom bottles for a regional wine industry, it should be intuitively obvious that those vendors would be counted as part of the cluster.

But what about professional service providers such as lawyers and accountants—can they be considered part of a cluster? For Porter, the answer would seem to lie in a determination of how much these professionals customize their services for a particular industry. In archetypal clusters such as Silicon Valley and Napa Valley, lawyers in particular have indeed developed specialized offerings and practices. Thus, even under Porter's stricter definitions, lawyers serving the original computer chip industry in Silicon Valley, and "wine lawyers" serving the one-time "upstart" wineries in Napa Valley, are part of their respective clusters.

---

[6] *See* Porter, *supra* note 3.

Yet, the well-documented "start-up lawyers" in Silicon Valley are not limited to chip manufacturers.[7] In fact, they are equally or more tailored to software and web-based ventures. Accordingly, Silicon Valley start-up lawyers seem instead to be part of a broader sense of a "cluster" focused on information technology (IT) start-ups. Leaving the particulars of Porter's clusters and broadening out to the concept of innovation ecosystems that this Chapter and many policymakers adopt allows us to simply observe and assert the phenomenon of start-up lawyers as integral to the IT-wide innovation ecosystem of Silicon Valley. Arguably, other professional service sectors, such as accountants, brand consultants, etc., have also tailored their services and proven integral to innovation ecosystems such as Silicon Valley. Thus, more needs to be done to study the role of professional service providers in innovation ecosystems.

To begin understanding and then studying the role of professional service providers in innovation ecosystems, one must first consider how the Silicon Valley style of technology entrepreneurship has spread. Those who work in or study this type of entrepreneurship are well aware of the standard path of entrepreneurs forming a corporation around an idea they developed or licensed in (often from a research university), securing angel and venture capital (VC) private financing, moving through proof of concept and then some delivery of the product or service, and finally "exiting" through sale or initial public offering (IPO) of the venture. But while successful "serial entrepreneurs" know how to navigate this path, first time entrepreneurs often do not. Further, much of the details and know-how integral to the pathway itself—as separate from the idea to be developed—are held by professional service providers, not the entrepreneurs. Thus, experienced professional service providers create a critical part of the infrastructure that allows first time entrepreneurs to "get into the game." At the same time, successful serial entrepreneurs rely just as much, if not more, on trusted professional service providers such as lawyers, because they believe it is more efficient to "outsource" the know-how for navigating the system, deals, etc. This allows the entrepreneur to focus on developing the business idea and vision into a marketable product or service.

While lawyers are increasingly understood to play a central role in

---

[7] *See, e.g.*, Mark C. Suchman, *Dealmakers and Counselors: Law Firms as Intermediaries in the Development of Silicon Valley, in* UNDERSTANDING SILICON VALLEY: THE ANATOMY OF AN ENTREPRENEURIAL REGION 71-97, Martin Kenney, (ed.), (Stanford, California, U.S.A.: Stanford University Press, 2000); Mark C. Suchman & Mia L. Cahill, *The Hired-Gun as Facilitator: The Case of Lawyers in Silicon Valley*, 21 LAW & SOC. INQUIRY 679 (1996).

Silicon Valley style innovation ecosystems, there are many other professional services that are important as well. Accountants must have knowledge of particular kinds of preferred stock valuations, stock option pricing, and tax issues associated with the foregoing that are customarily used in the VC-backed start-up model. Management consultants have to be experienced at focusing on risky growth ventures as opposed to large, mature organizations. Marketing and branding consultants in this space focus on creating stories and brands for not only cutting-edge products and services, but also for entirely new *kinds* of goods or services that indeed may generate whole new industries. In lab-based innovation ecosystems such as biotechnology, architects need a special focus on the kinds of wet labs needed for experimental new kinds of drugs, biologics, and devices. Finally, even designers, software coders, engineers, and others whom we often think of as playing the role of entrepreneur or employee will, in many cases, develop freelance consultancies that serve or support the new venture as professional service providers.

In sum, professional service providers with customized knowledge and experience related to the ways in which particular innovation ecosystems develop and commercialize products provide critical coordination and guideposts for new and experienced entrepreneurs in that ecosystem. In this way, they become as integral to the success of an innovation ecosystem as access to capital, human talent, and skilled workers. Therefore, as research continues on innovation ecosystems, more explicit attention needs to be paid to the various professional services providers. The remainder of this Chapter discusses the distinctive type of practice that start-up lawyers in technology hubs across the country developed, which vary quite a bit from the standard accounts of lawyers.

THE SPECIAL ROLE OF LAWYERS IN INNOVATION ECOSYSTEMS

While the common perception of lawyers is that they are litigation oriented and risk averse, those that practice successfully in technology hubs, such as Silicon Valley, Boston, Seattle, etc., are primarily transactional attorneys specializing in corporation and securities laws. They also often have some familiarity with intellectual property (IP), tax law, and employment law. But, these "start-up lawyers" not only have particular areas of substantive law knowledge, they also have a different approach to lawyering. By acting as dealmakers, connection brokers (especially between promising entrepreneurs and VCs), strategists, general facilitators, and trusted confidantes, they partner with their clients—sometimes even taking equity stakes—and act as the coordinator and guide for the planning, structure, and execution of the venture.[8]

Yet, before delving more deeply into this type of attorney, it is also important to note that legal specialists, such as patent attorneys, are a critical part of innovation ecosystems as well. In fact, many entrepreneurs have a relationship with a patent attorney or patent agent[9] before retaining a start-up lawyer. For heavily regulated technology industries such as biotechnology, attorneys with specialized expertise in food and drug law will also be critical. These various specialists may, but need not, tailor the nature of their practice to entrepreneurs in an innovation ecosystem. Simply being available in their normal capacities can be enough.

Accordingly, the "technology law firm" model has emerged in innovation ecosystems across the country. Typified by Wilson Sonsini in Silicon Valley, it is simply a twist on an industry-focused firm. Thus, rather than, say, a construction industry focused firm, these firms organize their practice around serving VC-backed technology start-ups. Distinct from traditional practice boutiques that limit their practice to one area of law, but then serve all comers who need that specialty, the technology law firms are full-service, general practice (GP) firms that can deliver essentially all areas of law that their clients need. Some, like Wilson Sonsini and Gunderson Dettmer, appear to have been formed expressly to deliver this model. Others, like Wilmer Hale, were long standing GP firms—often with strong litigation practices—that then built technology law practices because they were located in major technology hubs, such as Boston with its 128 beltway innovation ecosystem.[10] But these firms are not merely GP

---

[8] *See, e.g.*, Suchman, and Suchman and Cahill, *supra* note 7.

[9] The term "patent attorney" is usually, although not always, reserved for those admitted to practice at the U.S. Patent & Trademark Office (USPTO) and to obtain patents on behalf of clients. However, this "patent prosecution" work is only one kind of lawyering that is central to patents. The other kinds are patent litigation and transactions such as assignments and licensing. Attorneys regularly admitted to practice in a state need not be admitted to the USPTO to litigate patent matters or represent clients in patent transactional matters. The term "patent agent," by contrast, is used for those individuals who are admitted to practice before the USPTO but are *not* admitted to practice in a state as a general attorney. Therefore, they may not engage in any kind of legal services for clients other than patent prosecution before the USPTO. Further, patent agents need not hold a juris doctor degree or have attended any kind of law school or legal training program. Instead, the only prerequisite to sit for the USPTO patent bar is the equivalent of a four-year degree in a listed scientific or technical field.

[10] Route 128 is a beltway around Boston that was home to the original technology hub in the United States. Companies like Raytheon and MITRE clustered in towns on 128 including Lexington and Bedford because of the availability of

firms that target technology start-up clients. Instead, they ensure that all of their practice areas relevant to start-ups have lawyers who specialize in that field of law as it applies to technology start-ups. The bigger firms further break this down into specialists who focus on different fields of technology such as biotechnology or IT.

At the same time, these technology law firms are not simply aggregates of specialists focused on the technology field. Instead, they also include the targeted generalist start-up lawyer who can work as outside general counsel (GC) to start-up clients. This is crucial for two reasons. First, as will be discussed below, start-ups need general representation from outside counsel who can coordinate all of their legal affairs while integrating a comprehensive legal strategy into the start-up's business plan. Specialists are not in a good position to do this. Second, the technology law firm benefits because these start-up lawyers are usually those who own the client relationship and cross-sell the firm's specialty services. This is not meant to suggest anything insidious, because this cross-selling is often beneficial to the client: the start-up lawyer relationship partner acts as a guide to legal services for the start-up. If the start-up lawyer starts overselling or mis-selling her colleagues' services, the client will figure this out sooner or later and look for other counsel. To underscore this, "super lawyers" in this space such as Larry Sonsini have reputations for guiding clients through their legal affairs efficiently. Because this is the standard, other lawyers and firms in this space who seek to build long-term reputations and clients seem to serve their clients well in this regard, rather than seeking a short-term gain by over- or mis-selling the services of their firms.

The foregoing leads to the question of the nature and scope of representation of start-ups. Specialist attorneys will tend to enter into carefully limited engagement letters that specify the exact nature and scope of services. This makes sense because the attorney may not feel qualified to give advice outside of her specialty area. Further, specialists' services will usually not be needed on an ongoing basis by clients. And finally, if the lawyer does not expressly limit the engagement, then a client could assume the attorney was providing general representation and thus have liability for catching and addressing any legal issue that might arise for the client.

---

developable land close to Harvard and MIT in Cambridge. Silicon Valley essentially emulated this basic suburban cluster when technology start-ups began locating in the environs around Stanford in Palo Alto. *See, e.g.*, ANNALEE SAXENIAN, REGIONAL ADVANTAGE: CULTURE AND COMPETITION IN SILICON VALLEY AND ROUTE 128 (Cambridge, MA, U.S.A.: Harvard University Press, 1994), Ronald J. Gilson, *The Legal Infrastructure of High Technology Industrial Districts: Silicon Valley, Route 128, and Covenants Not to Compete*, 74 N.Y.U. L. REV. 575 (1999).

For example, if a patent attorney failed to catch a major securities law issue arising for a client out of a financing that the patent attorney had nothing to do with, and the client had no other counsel for the financing, the client could try to sue the patent attorney for malpractice if things went poorly. This seems bizarre—and it would be—but of course specialists avoid the problem by normally using limited engagement letters.

Two further questions from the start-up's perspective are then raised. First, do they understand the limited scope of the specialist's engagement letter? Second, does a patchwork of limited representations work for them? On the first question, there can be significant doubt, especially with regard to first-time entrepreneurs. They may not be sophisticated consumers of legal services and engagement letters are often written in the dense legalese that would require an attorney to interpret. Thus, while the attorney protects herself against a malpractice claim, the client is left with less coverage than they thought and may still assume the attorney is covering all of the start-up's legal issues. This flows directly to the second question, where the answer is likely "no"—an uncoordinated aggregation of specialists does not a comprehensive legal strategy make. The real issue is that with regard to both questions the start-up is in many cases unlikely to even be fully aware of the problems. This is compounded where the start-up's only interactions are with specialists who cannot show management how a comprehensive legal strategy works and benefits the venture.

But there is a further obstacle to a start-up securing adequate legal counsel. Legal services are often perceived as expensive and intimidating in the start-up community. There is a vague fear of meeting with a lawyer and then receiving a bill for thousands of dollars the next week. Further, entrepreneurs often do not understand the broad range of legal issues that will confront the venture and how serious legal issues down the road can be limited or prevented by bringing in appropriate counsel early on. Instead, start-ups with first time or inexperienced management tend to wait until a legal dispute arises, or until they realize they might have a patentable idea on their hands. By this point much remedial legal work may need to be done or, worse, the legal issue may prove fatal to the venture (*e.g.*, the IP rights may be lost or the lawsuit may sink the company financially). In the alternative, the venture might flourish even as some of the founders or other participants are harmed financially due to poor legal structures. After the release of the motion picture *The Social Network*,[11] it has become easier to get founders and their staff to take these issues seriously at the outset of the venture. But lawyers and their firms must themselves have the

---

[11]   THE SOCIAL NETWORK (Columbia Pictures 2010).

right structure and personnel to respond and deliver quality legal services in this space.

The technology law firms attempt to accommodate these issues by adopting flexible, hybrid models. They have specialists who can deliver limited engagement services as well as targeted generalists who can enter into general representation engagements on behalf of the firm. Discount or deferred fee arrangements are available for promising but cash-strapped start-ups. In many cases, the client will not be responsible for the accruing legal bills until and unless it secures a specified angel or VC round of financing. Flat fee packages for "routine" work such as incorporation, trademark registration, or even basic financing rounds are now offered by many of these firms. Some firms offer flat fee retainer packages for ongoing corporate "housekeeping" services such as acting as secretary of the corporation, attending board meetings, maintaining the stock ledger, etc. It must be stated that firms take on additional potential liability for all these services, as well as the broad potential liability for taking on a client in a general representation. But the value to the client and the firm appear to outweigh these concerns for the firms operating in this space.

Drilling down into the general representation models, there are more subtle distinctions among them. In one model, the firm simply designates one of the specialists with the role of coordinating or quarterbacking legal services for a particular client. This is the engagement or billing partner model prevalent in many professional services firms for a wide range of clients. It requires the engagement partners to have some familiarity with the different services the firm offers and to recognize when the client needs them; it does not require the engagement partner to be a targeted generalist. By contrast, the second model is based on having a number of attorneys in the firm who consciously do *not* practice as specialists of any kind. Instead, they have developed a broad legal knowledge and can provide basic services across a range of different specialties. Only when a particular issue becomes more complicated will the targeted generalist then call in her specialist colleagues from the firm.

The targeted generalist is not merely a jack-of-all-trades-master-of-none. Instead, she actually does have a specialized type of professional practice, but it is not defined by legal categories. Instead, her expertise is in understanding the business, finance, and basic technical aspects of a technology entrepreneurship field, as well as the core legal issues that are applicable to it. Her added value is in acting as a kind of *consigliere*[12] to

---

[12] The term *consigliere* originated from the Italian word *consiglio*, meaning "advice" or "counsel." This in turn, derived from the Latin word *consilium*.

the founders, and being consulted on all important decisions and strategizing of the venture. While other professionals can also play this role, lawyers in innovation ecosystems such as Silicon Valley have emerged as leading contenders for it based on a few possible reasons. First, as lawyers, they have legally enforceable, fiduciary and confidentiality obligations to their clients that other professionals such as accountants, VCs, and management consultants do not. Further, these obligations do not arise by contract alone, but by the simple act of entering into the attorney–client relationship. This also means that they are enforceable in ways that contracts are not (*e.g.*, no theory of efficient breach for an attorney breaching her client obligations). Second, attorneys have expert knowledge in the legal structures and regulatory aspects that undergird the entire business venture, acting as what has been termed an "enterprise architect."[13] They alone can offer legal advice on how to structure the entity; enter into enforceable and rights-altering arrangements; and navigate federal, state, and municipal regulatory or business licensing requirements.[14] They also can act as "transaction cost engineers," arguably reducing the overall

---

Consigliere has been in use since at least 1615, and has the broad generic meaning of "counselor" or "advisor." *See* MERRIAM-WEBSTER ONLINE DICTIONARY, *available at* http://www.merriam-webster.com/dictionary/consigliere (last visited Aug. 20, 2011). But over time it developed a primary meaning that signified the single most trusted advisor to a mob crime boss. *Id.*; THE NEW OXFORD ENGLISH DICTIONARY 366 (Oxford, UK: Oxford University Press, 2001); Wikipedia: Consigliere, http://en.wikipedia.org/wiki/Consigliere (last visited Aug. 20, 2011). While the Mafia may have brought the term to the United States, and it became popularized through books and movies including *The Godfather*, the term is now being used more broadly again for advisors in a number of "legitimate" professions. However, this new use seems to rely as much on the Mafia sense of the most highly trusted lieutenant or advisor of the boss and/or a private arbitrator who is authorized to settle disputes among underlings of that boss. Thus, a *consigliere* is not just any counselor or advisor, but the one to whom the boss will go for advice on all his most important decisions.

[13]   There is an evolving literature on the nature of business lawyers. *See* Anthony J. Luppino, *The Value of Lawyers as Members of Entrepreneurial Teams* in ROBERT E. LITAN ED., HANDBOOK ON LAW, INNOVATION AND GROWTH 300 (Cheltenham, UK, Northampton, MA, U.S.A.: Edward Elgar, 2011); George Dent, *Business Lawyers and Enterprise Architects*, 64 BUS. LAWYER 279 (2009); Stephen L. Schwarcz, *Explaining the Value of Transactional Lawyering*, 12 STAN. J. L., BUS. & FIN. 486 (2007); Ronald J. Gilson, *Value Creation by Business Lawyers: Legal Skills and Asset Pricing*, 94 YALE L.J. 239 (1984).

[14]   Other professionals can have knowledge of these things and arguably possess equivalent know-how to do these things, but they cannot render services as legal services or as legal advice unless they are also licensed at attorneys in that jurisdiction.

costs of transactions by making the parties aware of potential problems, regulations, and even time-saving customs or norms in a particular field or transaction type. Yet, while all of these things are what arguably give lawyers a preferential position to act as *consigliere*, if the attorney does not have the wisdom or ability to act in this role, the role will nonetheless go to someone else. Thus, the question is how attorneys can position themselves to act as *consigliere* to start-ups.

TRANSFORMING PROFESSIONAL SERVICES THROUGH NEW MODELS OF PROFESSIONAL SCHOOLS

The foregoing sections examined the "state of the art" for professional services—and law in particular—in major innovation ecosystems. But what about regions that have non-existent or underdeveloped innovation ecosystems? Should government policy focus only on access to capital, research and development funding or tax credits, the recruitment of entrepreneurs or skilled workers, or even the building of facilities? While those are all necessary, they seem to have been insufficient in regions where they have been tried. Accordingly, this Chapter suggests that an additional necessary component is the building of tailored professional services to make an innovation ecosystem a true cluster in the Porter sense. This final section outlines ways to accomplish this through regional professional schools.

Professional Schools' Special Challenges and Opportunities

Assuming a region does not have a cadre of professional service providers with tailored expertise for the desired innovation ecosystem, then policymakers confront something akin to the entrepreneur's own "make or buy" decision. They can either try to lure in experienced professionals from outside the region, or they can try to develop the right kind of professionals organically from local talent. Of course, these are not mutually exclusive. And, in fact, one strategy is to recruit experienced professionals to the region's professional schools on a full- or part-time basis so that local talent can be groomed by those with deep experience from a successful innovation ecosystem elsewhere. The remainder of this section follows this approach.

While the notion of recruiting experienced professionals to the professional school of a region that seeks to develop a particular innovation ecosystem seems quite intuitive, it is not without challenges. First, most or all professional schools have core faculty who must receive full-time academic appointments generally with specific scholarship requirements (especially if the position is tenure or tenure track). Many practicing professionals have little inclination toward spending significant portions of their time researching and writing. Second, faculties still exercise a fair degree of self-governance and the existing faculty of a professional school may not be willing to approve an offer of appointment to a non-academic professional—no matter how strongly the president, provost, or dean of the institution may feel, or local policymakers and political leaders may request or demand it. Third, the appointment of an outside practitioner to a regional professional school by no means guarantees that local professionals and their firms will support the outsider or welcome the inculcation of a different culture of practice in students studying the profession.

Despite these challenges, however, the prospects of recruiting seasoned professionals to a region's professional schools are not so bleak. There is anecdotal evidence of it occurring successfully. The bigger issue is instead the evolving nature of professional schools. Whereas many kinds of professional schools in the U.S. began outside the universities, what we perceive to be the core, prestigious professional schools—medicine, law, business, engineering, design, education, and architecture—largely migrated into universities. This helped both the schools and the universities. The schools increased in prestige (query whether what we think of as the prestigious professional schools are so because of something inherent to them or simply because they found their way into universities), and the universities absorbed some important potential (or actual) competitors for educational services. But these unions have not been without their conflicts. Like corporate mergers, the parties often minimize the risks of merging two different cultures ahead of time. Only after the integration of the two operations commences do significant culture clashes become glaringly obvious.

Of the many challenges that faced this integration of professional schools into the academy, only one is examined here: the mismatch of professional and academic objectives and careers. Debates over "theory versus practice" are quite heated within professional schools. Practitioners often view professional school faculty as "pointy-headed academics" with no clue about practice in the real world. Professional school academics often view practitioners as mere tradesmen engaged in ignoble commercial activities. By contrast, there seems to be less of this conflict with regard to schools and departments within the core colleges of arts and sciences (*i.e.*, non-professional schools). The difference, of course, is that many of the core academic departments unify their theory and practice components within the academy. In other words, graduate students in, for example, philosophy are primarily in training to become academic philosophers. If they do something else it is usually because they leave the field entirely. Even professional historians who work for non-academic institutions, or industry scientists, still by and large practice the same skill set that their academic instructors did. By contrast, the professional schools are supposed to be training practitioners who will engage in nonacademic activities, but the faculty in such schools have increasingly taken it upon themselves to engage in almost purely academic activities. Thus, for example, the kinds of scholarship in which law professors routinely now engage has little to nothing in common with the kinds of activities in which practicing lawyers engage. Likewise, business school faculty routinely engage in scholarship that has little to do with how a business person would start or manage a business. These issues have been treated elsewhere, especially with regard to law schools,[15] and so will not be treated in depth in this Chapter. Instead, the remainder of this section considers the example of how regional law schools can help develop targeted generalist/outside GC/*consigliere* kinds of lawyers who would support the development of innovation ecosystems in that region.

Regional Law Schools and the Training of Start-up Lawyers

As discussed above, the start-up lawyer who combines elements of an outside GC, targeted generalist, and *consigliere* is a well-established model among lawyers in major innovation ecosystems. However, at this point, a start-up lawyer only learns on the job—assuming the lawyer was lucky enough to have discovered this type of practice and been mentored by an existing start-up lawyer early in the lawyer's career. This timing and serendipity problem is compounded because law schools by and large still teach as if students will become litigators, or even, law professors. Business and transactional law generally are still relatively rare to find in law schools. Deeper, practice-oriented nuances like the skill sets of a start-up lawyer versus a securities law specialist are even rarer.

But this paucity of programs and faculty in law schools is also a disguised opportunity. Now that awareness is increasing about this issue, many law schools are seeking to build these types of programs and faculty. With a relatively clean slate to work on, it is an exciting time for law

---

[15] *See, generally*, WILLIAM M. SULLIVAN ET AL., EDUCATING LAWYERS: PREPARATION FOR THE PROFESSION OF LAW (Stanford, CA, U.S.A.: The Carnegie Foundation for the Advancement of Teaching, 2007); Report of the Task Force on Law Schools and the Profession (Chicago, IL, U.S.A.: American Bar Association, 1992) (generally known as the "MacCrate Report').

schools and their faculty to enter the game. The question then is what such programs should look like and what content and skills they should deliver. While this topic is beyond the scope of this Chapter, some summary thoughts are given below.

First, "innovation law" (including but not limited to IP) faculty have too often been drawn from litigation, regulatory, or purely academic backgrounds with no experience or deep understanding of actually building innovative ventures. Such faculties are often dismissive of practice, practitioners, and "skills training." They also tend to perceive the details of deal making and venture building as inscrutable "private ordering." But there is a high art, and even theory, to acting as a start-up lawyer that can be taught by demonstration. The issue is that in many ways the substantive law matters less than the way in which the start-up lawyer works with her client.[16] So, while solid grounding in the relevant substantive areas of law is a prerequisite, students must also be introduced to the nature of practice as a start-up lawyer as soon as possible. And because much of this can only be taught by example and practice, the students must have access to experienced start-up lawyers and experiential learning courses, such as clinics. Thus, the nature of faculties has to change to bring on professors with experience in this space. This does not mean that practitioners with no interest in academics or scholarship should replace existing faculty. Rather it means that individuals who combine practice experience with academic interest and aptitude must be sought. This is not as hard as it sounds, especially as the numbers of start-up lawyers continues to grow, and a significant number of them have an interest in becoming a law professor someday, with academic aspirations to match. Perhaps the bigger issue is to shepherd along the continued development of new kinds of legal scholarship that map better onto the things that start-up lawyers do and need to know. Thus, ideally, new law professors with the relevant start-up lawyer background can provide context and skills for students, as well as research platforms for understanding the emerging legal issues of innovation ecosystems.

Second, start-up lawyer programs must emphasize the role of business and financial knowledge. Ideally, the aspiring start-up lawyer would take MBA and other relevant, non-law courses on top of their law curriculum. But the heart of the training should be the "business first" simulations and/or clinic model; students must be trained to understand the business proposition first and then layer in legal strategy and tactics.[17]

---

[16] *See, e.g.*, Jeffrey M. Lipshaw, *Why the Law of Entrepreneurship Hardly Matters*, 31 WESTERN NEW ENGL. L. REV. 701 (2009).

[17] This is the model developed by the Author for the Entrepreneurial Law

Third, students must be trained in being able to envision and implement descending orders of "best" legal solutions, while being able to advise the client of the increasing risk as the legal solutions get weaker. For example, many entrepreneurs will need to disclose confidential information to potential partners, financiers, and others. The standard lawyer advice is for the entrepreneur to get a confidentiality or nondisclosure agreement (NDA) signed before disclosure. The "best" form of these can run to four pages of intimidating legalese. In the technology entrepreneurship space, many key players like VCs will not sign these. Law professors or practitioners with no experience in this space may simply throw up their hands and tell the entrepreneur she is out of luck and has to get the NDA signed or risk losing everything in the disclosure. But, this is not the case. Instead, those who practice in this space have at their disposal a descending set of options for their clients. If the full "bells and whistles" NDA is unacceptable, the start-up lawyer has a one-page form, with less legalese. It may not be as protective of the client as the long form, but it may be acceptable to the other party. In which case having *something* signed is a lot better than having nothing signed. In many cases, the opposite party might refuse to sign any form. In that case, the start-up lawyer may recommend that the client at least sends an email or other documented note before or after the disclosure, noting the confidentiality of the material. If for some reason even this is not possible, then advice for the entrepreneur to at least give verbal notice of the confidentiality of the material is still better than nothing. The extra benefits of this kind of counseling flexibility is that it reduces the instances of the lawyer as "deal-killer" and increases the trust and respect of clients, who are then more likely to bring in the lawyer more frequently as the kind of *consigliere* who helps with all facets of business planning and execution. This relationship ultimately benefits both parties in that the skilled *consigliere* steers the client away from potential legal and business land mines, and allows the venture to focus on delivering the best possible product to the market, with minimal interference of distracting legal issues.

By growing out programs in this manner, and recruiting in law professors with experience in respected innovation ecosystems, regional law schools can help develop the next generation of lawyers in that region who can act as start-up lawyers to support the emerging or desired innovation ecosystem. A number of law schools have in fact adopted this model and results seem to be promising.[18] As new scholarship models in this space

---

Clinic at the University of Washington School of Law in Seattle (http://www.law.washington.edu/clinics/entrepreneurial).

[18] *See, e.g.*, Michael Risch, *IP and Entrepreneurship in an Evolving Economy:*

continue to build out, these new kinds of legal academics will also be able to operate in their academic capacities as well to minimize the risk that they will instead be seen as non-academics jeopardizing the academic mission of the university-based law school.

CONCLUSION

Regions seeking innovation ecosystems need to focus on their professional services networks. The importance of tailored professional service providers to a particular innovation ecosystem is implicit in models such as that of Porter's clusters. But more needs to be done in fleshing out this part of research and policymaking on innovation ecosystems. At the same time, lawyers provide a central role in innovation ecosystems and may provide an excellent research object for those interested in the role of professional services generally. Further, the nature of legal practice in innovation ecosystems is varied and nuanced. At its heart is the fascinating start-up lawyer model. Beyond merely studying the role of professional service providers in innovation ecosystems, however, professional schools themselves can become a player in a region's bid to build an innovation ecosystem. By identifying the needs of the region, developing programs, and recruiting appropriate faculty from regions that have an established and successful version of the desired innovation ecosystem, regional professional schools can generate the next generation of professional service providers in their region to support the emerging innovation ecosystem. Law schools in particular have made some strides in this regard. But more can be done. And more must be done if we are to realize the promise of America's great innovators and entrepreneurs, who can come from anywhere, but need the right support system to build their dreams that benefit us all.

A Case Study, in EVOLVING ECONOMIES: THE ROLE OF LAW IN ENTREPRENEURSHIP AND INNOVATION (*infra*, Chapter 8); Patricia Lee, *The Role and Impact of Clinical Programs on Entrepreneurship and Economic Growth, in* EVOLVING ECONOMIES: THE ROLE OF LAW IN ENTREPRENEURSHIP AND INNOVATION (*infra*, Chapter 9).

5. The strategic lawyer

Shubha Ghosh

Entrepreneurism is the buzzword today. In the context of politics, the word stands for clever negotiations to maneuver hot-button political issues. In economics, the term often accompanies market-centered, anti-government intervention policies. Culturally, entrepreneurism captures the spirit of self-help and minimal civic engagement through the provision of services, such as the local restaurant, daycare service, nail salon, or bakery. Law schools reflect this entrepreneurial trend through the creation of Entrepreneurship Clinics and the call to students and faculty to be more "entrepreneurial" in their efforts for finding jobs or funding. With all this extramural and intramural buzz, one has to ask "are lawyers entrepreneurial?" and the broader question "are lawyers creative?"

This chapter addresses each of these questions, especially the second. In addressing the questions, I play off against the demonstrated lack of entrepreneurship and creativity within law schools. Certainly, law school administrators seem particularly entrepreneurial and creative in seeking out students, especially tuition-paying ones, in creating an effective profile for the rankings. Such creative endeavors extend to the ability to play faculty off each other to maintain the status quo enjoyed by specific deans and faculty members. But despite the expansion of clinical opportunities and alternative teaching methods (generically referred to as non-Socratic), law schools have been remarkably stable institutions.[1] A law dean, professor, or student from a century ago would walk into a contemporary law school and not see much changed, except for improved demographics. I know this because I have respected colleagues (at various schools) who have been around the block, so to speak, and have testified to this observation, sometimes with the bigoted aside that the demographic change has been for the worse. This chapter begins with what is at best a paradox

---

[1]   *See* ELIZABETH MERTZ, THE LANGUAGE OF LAW SCHOOL: LEARNING TO "THINK LIKE A LAWYER" 12–13 (New York, NY, U.S.A.: Oxford University Press, 2007) (describing the stability of law school environment).

and at worst an identified hypocrisy. How can law schools speak about entrepreneurship when they seem to exhibit little of this quality?

In examining these issues, I echo the challenges raised by Professors Gillian Hadfield and Larry Ribstein in their recent criticisms of legal education. Professor Hadfield poses the question where are the "garage guy" equivalents to start-up entrepreneurs among lawyers.[2] She suggests that law school education does not encourage or develop creative, problem-solving thinking among law students.[3] As a possible reform, she describes her own work in teaching transactional practice in law schools.[4] Her brand of teaching is to develop problem-solving skills that are responsive to client needs, as opposed to abstract policy making.[5] Professor Ribstein offers a different, but related, point. He points to the decline of big law firm practice, not simply as a result of the recent economic downturn, but also as the product of a stale business model.[6] He encourages a rethinking of how legal services are delivered in the marketplace and the role of law schools in training students to develop and work with new business models.[7] The ideas in this chapter reflect my support of these arguments, but with a slightly different focus. I seek to identify what is entrepreneurial and creative about lawyering. Identifying the entrepreneurial and creative aspects of lawyering provides a basis for reconstructing legal education to promote these virtues.

I use the phrase "the strategic lawyer" to signify the set of entrepreneurial and creative skills in lawyering. The phrase strategic can be criticized for being overused and for promoting the lawyering enterprise as an opportunistic one. My discussion carefully avoids these pitfalls. By strategic lawyer, I mean one who uses the law to serve a client's ends. The point is not to bend the law, but to use the law as tools to identify and reach certain goals defined by a client. Not to trivialize lawyering by any means, but I use the word strategic in the same way I would describe the task of a GPS system or a travel agent. Either is supplied with certain criteria (start point, end point, times, distances, modes of transport) and each presents an itinerary. Of course, what distinguishes lawyering from these two examples are the institutional contexts, the moral and ethical challenges,

---

[2]   *See* Gillian K. Hadfield, *Equipping the Garage Guys in Law*, 70 MD. L. REV. 484, 484 (2011).

[3]   *Id.* at 491.

[4]   *Id.* at 492-3.

[5]   *Id.*

[6]   *See* Larry E. Ribstein, *The Death of Big Law*, 2010 WISC. L. REV. 749 (2010).

[7]   *Id.* at 767.

and the complex, interactive environment within which strategies are made.

I like the term strategic lawyer primarily because of its implications for legal education. The term shifts attention from the internalization of rules and legal materials to their application. Professor Hadfield makes a distinction between real and phantom issues in advising clients and the need to teach law students how to make that distinction. The traditional issue-spotter exam, for example, often fails to distinguish between the two as students can often present any relevant issues to score the requisite points. What issues are real and what are phantom, I would argue, is a strategic choice, depending on the context. To recognize the lawyer's role as a strategic one reveals the practical and contextual nature of legal practice as well as the ways in which lawyers can be entrepreneurial and creative. This is the central argument of this chapter.

The argument develops in three parts. First, I examine what it means to be strategic. Second, I answer the question "Is lawyering a creative enterprise?" by considering both the affirmative and negative responses to this question. Finally, I present the implications for legal education and conclude.

THE MACHIAVELLIAN LAWYER

In an earlier presentation of the ideas in this chapter, I referred to the strategic lawyer as the Machiavellian lawyer. The invocation of Nicolo Machiavelli's *The Prince*, the encomium to the statecraft associated with the Florentine d'Medici family, was designed to highlight the pragmatic orientation of the strategic lawyer.[8] Machiavelli is associated with unscrupulous behavior directed towards the aggrandizement of power. I am certainly not touting this interpretation as a role model for lawyering. Instead, I am espousing Machiavelli as a realist, who was writing in opposition to Plato's view of the ideal Republic where virtue and good defined public behavior.[9] The point is not to promote non-virtuous behavior, but to recognize that there is a pragmatic dimension to even virtuous ideals. Lawyering is about this pragmatic dimension, rather than abstract virtues of justice and correct behavior.

To develop this last thought, I refer to a book chapter I wrote in which

---

[8] NICOLO MACHIEVELLI, THE PRINCE (Peter Constantine trans., New York, NY, U.S.A.: Modern Library, 2008) (1532).

[9] Albert Russel Ascoli, *Introduction* to MACHIEVELLI, *supra* note 8 at viii.

I make the argument that law should not be understood in purely instrumental terms. I was writing in response to the view that intellectual property laws incentivize creativity, a view that ignores that there may be many incentives for creativity independent of the law. Instead of interpreting law in such instrumental terms, I was suggesting that the policies of intellectual property law be understood in the context of how authors and inventors actually create. However, to say that specific laws should not be interpreted purely in instrumental terms does not mean that lawyers should not be instrumental in practice. In fact in practice, law is purely instrumental, a set of tools that are used to reach a particular result for a client. Legal education should be training students to become strategic lawyers, Machiavellian in a pragmatic sense, rather than in the negative sense.

Current education models are antithetical to the development of the strategic lawyer. To establish this point, I will point to three sets of dichotomies that define the continuing debates over legal education. These dichotomies highlight trends and norms in legal education both among traditionalists and reformers. My overarching argument is that contemporary debates in legal education miss the need for strategic lawyering as the critical focus for legal education. The three dichotomies are: (1) theory versus practice; (2) autonomy versus interdisciplinary; and (3) normative versus empirical.

The theory-practice divide is often demarcated along lines of disciplinarity. Critics of law as being too theoretical point to the influence of "law and" schools of thought that ignore practical training.[10] I frame that debate, however, in terms of autonomy versus interdisciplinary, the second dichotomy. The criticism that law is too theoretical is rooted in the view that law is a science through which legal materials (statutes, cases) are understood and structured. The Socratic Method when used to promote the law as science notion is an example of law as theory. Counter to this view is the teaching of actual legal practices, often as a substitute for or imitation of a legal apprenticeship. The legal construct of contract is replaced by actual legal documents, and abstract predictions of the outcome of a dispute are ignored in favor of practical negotiation and procedures for dispute resolution.

My goal is not to take sides in the theory–practice debate. Instead, I make the point that both sides ignore the strategic lawyer as the role for students. The theoretical approach to law often ignores how the law actually can be used as an instrument, often masking this instrumentalism

---

[10]   *See, e.g.*, Harry T. Edwards, *The Growing Disjunction Between Legal Education and the Legal Profession*, 91 MICH. L. REV. 34, 36 (1992).

with a feigned logic. Teachers of legal practice provide useful institutional detail, but can fail to teach what factors go into particular legal decisions in light of a client's specific needs and questions.

Of course, what I present here is a caricature of two positions. But this characterization moves from caricature and becomes responsive to actual needs when the strategic view of lawyering is introduced. Socratic probing aimed at fact analysis and gathering and identification of gaps in the law can serve the role of legal strategizing. Similarly, framing legal practice in concrete problem solving is a critical movement toward recognizing the role of lawyer as strategist. The theory–practice divide in debates over legal education with its well-worn and readily recognized arguments can be bridged with the understanding of the strategic role of lawyering.

A similar point flows from the autonomy–interdisciplinary debate. Advocates of the autonomy of law point to the role of law as an independent discipline, consisting of a body of knowledge and practices that need to be passed on to students who intend to pursue law as a profession.[11] By contrast, advocates of interdisciplinary work in law point to the discipline's dependence of other fields, such as the social sciences, psychology, mathematics, and the natural sciences.[12] Interdisciplinarity in law may reflect the fluidity of disciplines and the interconnectedness of knowledge. At a more practical level, advocates of interdisciplinary approaches to legal education point to the need for effective attorneys to understand where law touches upon other fields. A successful environmental or patent attorney needs, in many instances, to have a good understanding of chemistry or biology. An effective litigator should understand economics, at least in assessing the damages phase of a trial. Those who emphasize the autonomy of law point to the role of experts from other fields to supplement the attorney's arsenal, which legal education should fill through a focus on legal practice, method, and institutions as opposed to a potentially diluted blend of law and other disciplines.

But neither approach fully appreciates the need for the strategic lawyer. Arguably, integrating strategic thinking in legal education is a potential bridge between the view that law is autonomous and the view that law is situated in a network of disciplines and approaches. The point is that not only is law an instrument, but so is knowledge. As an attorney, one needs to know many things including knowing the gaps in one's

---

[11] *See* Yishai Blank, *The Reenchantment of Law*, 96 CORNELL L. REV. 633, 645 (2011) (describing legal formalism and view that law is an autonomous discipline).
[12] *See* Douglas W. Vick, *Interdisciplinarity and the Discipline of Law*, 31 J.L. & SOC'Y 163, 189–90 (2004) (explaining role of interdisciplinarity in legal theory).

understanding and the need for disciplines external to law to resolve factual and legal policy lacunae. The danger in treating knowledge as an instrument is dilettantism and superficial application of difficult concepts to provide quick fixes. The phenomenon of expert for hire is an example of this danger. I am of course not suggesting dilettantism. Instead, a successful strategic lawyer will understand this danger and factor it into the instrumentalism I propose. With appropriate rules of evidence and legal policy making in the background, a strategic lawyer can gauge when an area of knowledge is sufficiently developed to support a legal case and when the gaps may not be fully filled. In this way, law is recognized as a body of independent knowledge that may rely upon other areas in a strategic manner.

Finally, current debates in legal education fall along the fault line between law's role in implementing a normative ideal universe and in developing an empirical understanding of practices to which legal rules respond. Those who pursue the former bemoan the slow progress in developing a complete empirical picture before acting. If one knows what needs to be done and how to resolve a problem, then empirical understanding may be duplicative or even unnecessary. Furthermore, facts are separate from values, and law ultimately is about making a value judgment based on normative understanding. Empiricists decry these assertions, emphasizing the practical point that law has consequences that are important to measure and gauge. Furthermore, while facts and values are separate, values can be deepened and better understood when held up to facts. Since individual behavior often is framed by the choices made possible by legal institutions, studying the law on the ground serves as a test for one's normative priors.

The strategic lawyer is both norm based and empirically grounded. While strategic lawyering is normatively plural, supporting ends that can be labeled conservative as well as those labeled as liberal or progressive, it also is informed by the pragmatic implications of actions within the legal system. A strategic lawyer may zealously advocate a specific normative position but also must test that position against reality. Does this lead to opportunism or fickleness? Perhaps, but the properly educated strategic lawyer will work within notions of socially acceptable behavior that can keep the legal strategist from going astray. The problem with the pure normative and pure empiricist positions is that each can lead to homogeneity. The normative view can create an identical set of advocates, each thinking and acting in unison. The empirical view can create a set of advocates who are unable to act, each caught in pursuing those additional set of facts that might provide clarity. Thinking strategically as an attorney bridges this divide by intermixing norms and facts.

This section has presented a picture of the strategic lawyer in a fairly abstract way through an engagement with recurring debates over the nature of legal education. In the remainder of this chapter, I flesh out the strategic lawyer through further details and examples. The first step is to address the question of whether a lawyer can be creative. Since the strategic lawyer is one who is entrepreneurial and creative, one test for the feasibility of a strategic lawyer is to explore the question whether creativity is really possible in any meaningful way in lawyering. Once I explain how lawyers are creative, I turn to the second step and show how legal education needs to develop a skill set that supports the strategic lawyer.

ARE LAWYERS CREATIVE?

What I am building toward in this chapter is an articulation of the skill set necessary to inculcate in the burgeoning strategic lawyer. The lawyer strategist, as described so far, works to guide a client to a particular result. Law, meaning the body of cases, statutes, regulations, and other materials that define and shape institutions, serves as tools for the legal strategist, defining strategies and avenues to achieve success. Lawyering is about acting and doing. Legal education, consequently, is about training students in recognizing possibilities.

Implicit in my argument is the notion of lawyering as a craft, a set of skills and values that define a profession. Of course that craft can be practiced in many ways, but to recognize lawyering as a craft is to provide the proper respect and place for attorneys in the professional realm. Sociologist Richard Sennett has written about the death of craft and its replacement with a deadening corporate culture within which the completion of narrowly proscribed tasks pushes out creative work.[13] Professor Anthony Kronman painted an equally dismal picture of the legal profession nearly two decades ago in *The Lost Lawyer*.[14] The landscape Professor Kronman surveyed was one in which the lawyer statesman, the broad thinker with civic engagement was pushed to the wall by narrow analytical thinkers who viewed the law and the profession in purely political terms. Within Professor Sennett's terms, the lawyer has become a drone, forced into repetitive, predictable tasks (document product, due

---

[13]   RICHARD SENNETT, THE CRAFTSMAN (London, UK: Penguin, 2009).
[14]   ANTHONY T. KRONMAN, THE LOST LAWYER: FAILING IDEALS OF THE LEGAL PROFESSION (Cambridge, MA. U.S.A.; Belknap Press of Harvard University Press, 1994).

diligence, review of records) made necessary for corporate entities to survive within a regulatory environment that is equally bureaucratic.

Since the strategic lawyer has been described as an instrumentalist, one might be tempted to subject my proposal to the kind of criticisms put forward by Professor Sennett and Kronman. But the strategic lawyer is not instrumentalist in the sense of gauging success in purely monetary terms or in terms of pursuing narrow corporate interests within a bureaucratic structure. My point is that lawyering is a craft, and one way to recognize the craft of lawyering is to recognize that much of the craft is exercised in strategic terms, moving the client's interests by identifying issues and legal pressure points. Legal education needs to push the craft of lawyering by restructuring the types of skills that develop the lawyer strategist.

In a recent Supreme Court opinion, Chief Justice Roberts examined the difference in meaning between a noun and its adjectival form. The Court's focus was on the words "person" and "personal."[15] Similarly, there is a big difference between the words "craft" and "crafty." Culturally and historically, the craft of lawyering has often been thought of as the art of being crafty. The craftiness of lawyers has obvious anti-Semitic roots and is grounded in a cynical view of the law and what attorneys accomplish. But, of course, the noun does not track the adjective in terms of meaning and implication for legal practice. The lawyer's craft consists of a set of skills that allow for the creative use of legal instruments to meet a client's needs, not just the manipulation of law for short-term, opportunistic gains.

But does the lawyer's craft allow for creativity? There are several reasons to respond "no." The lawyer's craft is rule bound. Even if the law is in many instances fuzzy, underdetermined in places, over-determined in others, there often are few degrees of freedom within which to act. Legal practice has its rule as set by the institutions of law firms, legislatures, or courts. Success as a lawyer is often gauged by the ability to comply with these rules. "Creative lawyering" may sound too much like "creative accounting," an indication of "cooking the books" or manipulating the rules.

Furthermore, a lawyer has accountability to one's client, to other lawyers, and to the public at large, which may limit the play of creativity. Accountability is codified and captured in the rules that govern the conduct of lawyers. But accountability may also be associated with a sense of social responsibility and connection to the community granted by professional status. There is a quid pro quo between the status of being a lawyer and obligations to society, a quid pro quo realized through pro

---

[15]   *See FCC v. AT&T, Inc.*, 131 S. Ct. 1177 (2011).

bono activity, community involvement, and civic engagement in cultural, educational, and social institutions. The artist Edgar Degas famously proclaimed: "A painting calls for as much cunning, roguishness, and wickedness as the committing of a crime."[16] Degas is also attributed as saying that an artist approaches his creative work as a criminal, meaning the point is to break rules through creative expression. Needless to say, a lawyer is not a creative genius in the sense described by Degas. If anything, a lawyer embodies civic virtue in a way that resembles complacency and conformism, rather than a challenge to convention.

Encapsulating these arguments against creative lawyering is the manner in which lawyers are institutionally constrained. Not only are they rule bound and socially accountable, the identity of a lawyer is situated within a particular set of institutions. If courts did not exist, if legislatures were disbanded (as some seem to desire), if governmental power was a nullity, would there be a need for lawyers? Even if all power were private, and lawyers were deemed as private agents or intermediaries, what would it mean to speak of a legal profession? Certainly there may be skills that we could still identify with the craft of lawyering—negotiation, mediation, deal-making. But would these constitute just individual skills, rather than representing the standards of a profession? The point is that to be a lawyer, to practice the lawyer's craft, requires a certain set of institutions, perhaps those associated with a liberal democracy, perhaps those with a regulated market economy. The institutional context of lawyering casts doubt on whether lawyers are creative agents, or actors whose roles are proscribed by very specific institutional contexts.

In a previous essay, I reported how a colleague expressed a healthy skepticism of describing lawyering as a creative activity.[17] My sense is that his argument reflected, in part, some of the arguments presented here. In that essay, I also reported, somewhat begrudgingly, that the lawyer's creative might be like that of Kafka's Hunger Artist, whose creativity lay in suffering and denying the self for the entertainment and benefit of others.[18]

---

[16] *See* Lorraine Gamman & Maziar Raien, *Reviewing the Art of Crime: What, If Anything, Do Criminals and Artists/Designers Have in Common?*, in David H. Cropley et al., (eds), THE DARK SIDE OF CREATIVITY 155, 159 (New York, NY, U.S.A.: Cambridge University Press, 2010).

[17] Shubha Ghosh, *Introduction: can we incentivize creativity and entrepreneurship?*, in Shubha Ghosh & Robin Paul Malloy, (eds), CREATIVITY, LAW, AND ENTREPRENEURSHIP 1, 2 (Cheltenham, UK and Northampton, MA, U.S.A.: Edward Elgar Publishing 2011).

[18] FRANZ KAFKA, A HUNGER ARTIST (1922). http://www.manybooks.net/titles/ kafkafraother05hunger_artist.html Also published as a book in 2010 by , Las Vegas, NV, U.S.A.: IAP, 2010.

The Hunger Artist's aesthetics surfaced in a performance that was self-abnegating, denying one's own pleasure to enhance those of others. My analogy to the Hunger Artist was motivated by the drudgery of the lawyer's task, the ennui of billable hours, the dread of endless forms and documents to be constructed impeccably. Lawyerly craft entails lawyerly tasks, which involve much self-denial. That total involvement in tasks can embody a certain type of creativity.

But lawyerly creativity goes beyond the imagined joys of drudgery. Although a lawyer is certainly bound by rules, by social accountability, and by institutions, there are identifiable ways in which lawyers are creative beyond their commitment to work. Lawyers engage with epistemic shifts, both in the large and the small. Civil rights and constitutional attorneys must navigate among conflicting visions of the good and creatively construct compromises that balance these conflicting visions within a textually and institutionally defined set of conventions. In the small, lawyers often guide clients to recognize their true interests and to fashion compromises among conflicting and conflicted parties in business disputes, in family disintegration, and in the creation of new enterprises. In working these epistemic shifts, lawyers must work within a set of market and political shifts, recognizing when change is occurring and how to make use of these changes in order to further a client's ends. Working within this fabric, lawyers often create new institutions, fashion new precedents, draft new legislation, and create new contractual and property instruments that function within ever-changing environments. When understood in these ways, lawyering does entail creative activities.

The contrasting visions of lawyerly creativity (or its absence) rest on differing descriptions of the environments within which lawyers work. The arguments against creativity presume a static environment defined by a well-defined and unchanging set of lawyerly skills. The arguments in favor of creativity presume a dynamic environment with which lawyers interact. Needless to say, the world has both static and dynamic elements. The lawyer's craft, I would dare say its creativity, requires recognition of what elements of the environment are fixed and what are changing. In this way, a lawyer's craft is no different than that of other fields, whether medicine or more ancient artisanal crafts. Members of any profession must recognize its traditions, but also be prepared to play within these rules in order for the profession to move forward. To the extent that law is a craft, these tensions play within the practice of law in order to maintain the innovativeness of the profession, which translates into the progress of society's conventions and norms.

The relationship between craft and creativity is a contested one within intellectual property law. The difficulties in extending intellectual property laws, to the extent needed, to traditional crafts reflects the limits on individual creativity within crafts, such as glassblowing, fashion, traditional music, folklore, and traditional medicines. In contemporary contexts, courts attempt to identify the individually creative elements within a craft and apply intellectual property protection to instances of individual creativity. This strategy reflects the presumption of intellectual property rights as individual legal rights, rather than ones assigned to particular groups. In addition, the strategy prevents the individual appropriate of practices shred within a craft. For example, copyright law does not protect a style or genre of work. Similarly, patent law does not protect abstract ideas that include high-level principles (such as scientific laws) that practitioners of a field rely upon for their craft. This legal strategy implicitly recognizes that individual creativity exists within a professional context of artistic and scientific practices. Creativity coexists with craft, and each develop sympathetically, if not harmoniously.

In short, the craft of lawyering is no different from other professions. Creativity can be an important dimension of the practice of lawyering even if such practice is constrained by rules, social accountability, and institutions. The next section explores how legal education can be redesigned to accommodate the creativity of the lawyer's craft.

IMPLICATIONS FOR LEGAL EDUCATION

I have made the case for identifying lawyering as a strategic activity. The lawyer strategist, I argue, practices a craft, within which creativity is possible. In this section, I turn to the implications of these propositions for legal education.

My focus will be on identifying the skill set that legal education provides for starting attorneys to facilitate an understanding of the craft of lawyering. The skill set follows from the central tasks of the strategic lawyer. As described above, the strategic lawyer accomplishes three tasks: (1) the identification of a client's interests; (2) the identification of the paths permitted by legal institutions to fulfill these interests; and (3) the identification of missing institutions, or legal reforms, that might be necessary to satisfy the second task. These tasks are dynamic ones, requiring the strategic lawyer to recognize that interests and the environment in which these interests arise might change. Starting from these tasks, broadly identified, we can turn to the requisite skill set to support the strategic lawyer.

Current legal education, starting with its roots in the scientific approach proposed by Langdell and continuing with variants in clinical education and interdisciplinary study, inculcates three skills. The first is the identification of law, whether through the reading of cases or through the analyses of statutes, regulations, and other texts. The second is the distillation of facts, whether through an examination of a trial or appellate record or through the testimony or background that supports new legislation. The third is the prediction of the resolution of a particular legal problem based on an understanding of the law and facts. Although this characterization is highly stylized and arguably simplistic, the distillation of current legal education into this skill set provides a foil against which to understand and think about reform of legal education. My contention is that these three characterize not only traditional legal education, but also variants. For example, clinical legal education tracks these three quite well in the context of actual and ongoing legal problems as opposed to abstracted appellate opinions. Similarly, interdisciplinary approaches, such as law and economics or law and social science, presume these three skills as the goal of law school, with each specific skill nuanced by the relevant disciplinary perspective. So, for example, a law and social science approach would view fact distillation in terms of social facts, such as the description of a marketplace or of an organization, as well as more traditional facts, such as admissible evidence.

The problem with the existing skill set is that it does not necessarily encourage strategic theory, which I have argued is the principal mindset of the practicing attorney. The three skills are static, decontextualized, and turn the craft of lawyering into a rote exercise of applying identified law to identified facts to obtain a clear set of predictions of possible outcomes for a dispute. In short, the existing skill set neither grooms the strategic lawyer nor fosters creative thinking.

I am not proposing abandoning this skill set, but rethinking it with emphasis on the goals and traits of the strategic lawyer. After all, law and facts are the basic building blocks of lawyering. Although we can disagree on what constitutes law and what constitutes facts, one would be hard pressed to suggest that lawyering has nothing to do with both facts and laws. I propose to reconstitute these three, and the changes are not merely semantic ones.

The requisite skill set for the strategic lawyer consists of (1) legal instrumentalism; (2) fact exploration; and (3) the management of legal problems. Each of these skills enhances the skill set found within current legal education. As a result, the reforms build on what currently exists without necessarily radically altering the status quo. These gradualist reforms, however, can aid in rethinking what lawyers do and how lawyers are trained.

Legal instrumentalism builds on law distillation through an emphasis not only on identifying case holdings and rules in the traditional fashion, but also on identifying the implications of a particular law and how it effects the interests of parties. Viewed one way, legal instrumentalism entails recognizing the consequences of an identified law, who is benefitted, and who is hurt. Furthermore, identifying the consequences entails appreciating how the law might change over time and what forces might be unleashed to push the law in various directions. Of course, the purpose of this understanding is to aid clients in reaching their interests, specifically in recognizing the law as a tool that shapes those interests.

Fact exploration similarly goes beyond what I have called fact distillation. The problem with fact distillation is that it can give the impression that a trial record is given and not the creation of the parties to a dispute and the judges at both the trial and appellate levels in deciding what facts are relevant. Fact exploration requires, at one level, emphasizing the importance of how a record is created and the consequences of the record for the resolution of a dispute. Requisite skills for fact exploration include traditional ones, such as client interviewing and document review. But these skills need to be inculcated with an appreciation of the dynamic nature of facts and the official record.

Finally, management of legal problems echoes the theme of lawyer as strategist. Often lawyers are derided as poor managers. In some instances, this criticism points to the role of lawyers as problem creators rather than solvers. Of course, what some may call problem creation is just an example of zealous representation. The point is that lawyers should recognize their role as managers, not necessarily in the spirit of scientific management or of the profit maximizing CEO. As a counselor, the lawyer's job is to provide guidance—handholding in some instances and hardheadedness in others. Part of this role is to offer advice based on prediction of how a problem might be resolved. But prediction is often belied by the randomness of process, whether in the context of a trial or of a transaction. The lawyer as manager understands the law and the facts in a dynamic way in order to effectively manage a case. Legal education should support the training of the legal manager and not just the deductive predictor of case outcomes.

This newly defined skill set leads to several suggestions for curricular reform, many of which are already a part of how law schools have been experimenting with legal education. Problem solving has been integrated into many core courses, both in the first year and beyond. Some schools even have courses on problem solving, which focus on decision making and strategic thinking. In addition, courses on the business and social environment in which lawyers operate are valuable in providing more contextualized thinking for problem solving as well as a sense of where the

legal profession is headed. Finally, courses should emphasize the purpose
of legal doctrine and practices and the role of law as part of the tool kit of
lawyers as they aid clients in identifying and pursuing their interests.

FINAL THOUGHTS

I end this chapter with a reality check. After first presenting the ideas in
this chapter, a commentator said, quite blankly, that whenever he tried to
teach law as a set of tools, students hated it. Another colleague thanked
me for offering a defense of clinical legal education. I mention these comments to point out that the status quo is hard to change. Despite its identified flaws, there is a certain comfort and predictability to current legal
education that makes students (and faculty and administrators) resistant
to change. Furthermore, whatever the merits of these ideas, it is facile to
immediately use them in the ongoing battles between clinical and non-
clinical legal education. I am aware of the forces of resistance, and I also
do not take sides in the debate over clinics. My intention is to offer some
ideas and contribute to the ongoing discussion over legal education.

Beyond the rhetoric of entrepreneurism and reform, it appears there is a
crisis of confidence within legal education. As Professor Ribstein suggests,
this crisis stems from the economic challenges to the "Big Firm" model of
legal practice. What was once a pervasive model that often accommodated
students and schools at even the lowest ranks of the hierarchy is now
relegated to an elite few. Consequently, students need to rethink employment opportunities and schools need to rework the kind of preparation
provided to their students.

Even if the challenges to Big Law are temporary and the market returns
to the halcyon times of the Eighties (an unlikely turn of events), there
remains the issues provided by Professor Hadfield: does law school train
students for working with business clients and for developing an entrepreneurial, "garage guy" mentality? At one level, this question is moot if Big
Law re-emerges, and young associates can remain ensconced in document
review, protected from clients. But Professor Hadfield raises issues that
affect both Big Law and small law start-up law firms. What is it that we are
teaching law students? Are they gaining the broad set of skills necessary
for a climate defined by an entrepreneurial mentality?

The model of the strategic lawyer and the proposals for rethinking
legal education are modest responses to the crisis that presage ideas raised
by Professors Hadfield and Ribstein. As I have suggested, the proposals
build on the existing skill set taught by law schools and are consistent with
changes that are already occurring. The argument of this chapter provides

more context and analysis to existing reform efforts. If entrepreneurism is the new wave, then the strategic turn is to think deeply about how to invoke creativity in the training of lawyers. Such a turn can help to keep law schools honest about their efforts as well as restore some degree of optimism and vitality to the study of law.

6. A social justice perspective on intellectual property, innovation, and entrepreneurship

Steven D. Jamar and Lateef Mtima*

> Innovation is an unruly thing. There will be some ideas that don't get caught in your cup. But that is not what the game is about. The game is about what you catch, not what you spill.[1]
>
> Nathan Myhrvold

Myhrvold's point ties into our essential theme that care must be taken not to tie up ideas and not to bind up the rights in works of the intellect too tightly because if we do, the flow from the spigot of creativity will be reduced, producing a drought in innovation and development. Not only will the cup of innovation not overflow and spill some ideas that others catch and exploit, but the cup will have only a drop or two of value to its owner. Intellectual property law, policy, and administration must not constrict the flow of creativity in order to catch 100% of the flow from the pipe, but rather should be designed to release a gusher of creativity and innovation for the benefit of all.

---

* The authors wish to thank Megan Carpenter, Associate Professor of Law and Director of the Center for Law and Intellectual Property at Texas Wesleyan School of Law, for convening the conference on April 1, 2011 on *Evolving Economies: The Role of Law in Entrepreneurship and Innovation* and inviting their participation in the conference and to submit a chapter for the book. We also wish to thank the conference presenters and authors of chapters of the forthcoming book based on the conference for their valuable contributions and insights. We also wish to thank Bryant Young, IIPSJ Scholar in Residence, & Chair, Institute Development and Advancement for his research support for this chapter. Portions of this chapter are similar to portions of an article Steven D. Jamar was writing concurrently, *A Social Justice Perspective on the Role of Copyright in Realizing International Human Rights*, 24 PACIFIC MCGEORGE GLOBAL BUSINESS & DEVELOPMENT L.J., [page] (2011) (forthcoming).

[1] Nathan Myhrvold, quoted by Malcolm Gladwell, *Creation Myth: Xerox PARC, Apple, and the truth about innovation,* New Yorker 44 at 52 (May 16, 2011).

Innovation, the creating of new things or processes, is a core factor in development,[2] but it is not sufficient for development; the innovations must be exploited effectively in the marketplace. An intellectual property regime that favors too strongly one interest over another, as for example on the one hand by making the property holder's interests too strong thereby limiting the social utility of the work, or on the other hand by making the user's rights too strong thereby limiting the incentive for an inventor or writer to create, can lead to stagnation.

The development of a new method for exploiting protected works or inventions often engenders disputes as to who owns or controls (as well as debates over who *should* own or control) certain attendant property rights that arise in connection with the new methodology. The author or inventor of the subject intellectual property may seek to control all means for using and enjoying her creation. If she is successful in her efforts, however, she will likely discourage other innovators from working to develop such alternative uses and methods, and society will be denied the benefit of these aborted creative endeavors.

Thus properly balanced intellectual property laws can incentivize not only innovation, but also will enhance the incentive to commercially exploit those innovations, especially through entrepreneurial endeavor, often by individuals or small groups, thereby fostering development, broadly defined, and not incidentally fostering inclusion and empowerment of marginalized groups.

The *American Heritage Dictionary* defines an entrepreneur as "a person who organizes and manages any enterprise, especially a business, usually with considerable initiative and risk."[3] Wikipedia adds the idea of one who exploits innovation economically.[4] Not all development and not all

---

[2] Robert Cooter, Aaron Edlin, Robert E. Litan, and George L. Priest, *The Importance of Law in Promoting Innovation and Growth, in* KAUFFMAN TASKFORCE ON LAW, INNOVATION, AND GROWTH, RULES FOR GROWTH: PROMOTING INNOVATION AND GROWTH THROUGH LEGAL REFORM 3-4 (Kansas City, MO, U.S.A.: Ewing Marion Kauffman Foundation, 2011). Just what constitutes innovation or how we value various aspects of it is contestable. *See* Doris Estelle Long, *Crossing the Innovation Divide*, 81 TEMP. L. REV. 507 (2008). Nonetheless, we use a straightforward traditional understanding of the term as used in most western law and development literature, e.g., the Kauffman report.

[3] Dictionary.com, http://dictionary.reference.com/browse/entrepreneur (last visited July 10, 2011).

[4] "Entrepreneurship is the act of being an entrepreneur, which can be defined as 'one who undertakes innovations, finance and business acumen in an effort to transform innovations into economic goods'." http://en.wikipedia.org/wiki/Entrepreneurship (last visited July 10, 2011).

entrepreneurial work involves innovation that involves intellectual property such as copyright, patent, trade secrets, or trademarks, or even innovation more generally involving non-protectable know-how. Indeed, much development can arise from doing very standard, well-established things such as building power plants and roads or engaging in micro-financing such as under the Grameen Bank model.[5] The Grameen Bank engages in micro-financing to individuals to help them develop extremely small businesses to help lift themselves and their communities out of poverty. In heavy industry, well-known processes are also still subject to innovation with respect to increasing efficiency and reducing environmental impacts.[6] Innovation plays a role in development at all levels from small shops to massive heavy industrial projects.

Within this broader context, our focus is on intellectual property, particularly copyright, and its effects on innovation and development with respect to entrepreneurs, particularly when viewed from a social justice perspective.[7] Thus this chapter addresses the social justice aspects of fostering entrepreneurship through copyright law, policies, and administration. It focuses on how copyright and, to a more limited extent, how other forms of intellectual property can either foster or inhibit access to, creation of, dissemination of, and use of works to empower marginalized individuals and groups and to advance societal development collectively.[8] Although this chapter is more normative than empirical, it does rely on the seminal empirical work of Robert Sherwood[9] and more recent analytic work of the Kauffman Foundation.[10]

---

[5]   ALEX COUNTS, GIVE US CREDIT (New York, NY, U.S.A.: Times Books, 1996).
[6]   *E.g.*, Joel Kirkland, *China's Ambitious, High-Growth 5-Year Plan Stirs a Climate Debate*, N.Y. Times, Apr. 12, 2011, *available at* http://www.nytimes.com/cwire/2011/04/12/12climatewire-chinas-ambitious-high-growth-5-year-plan-sti-12439.html.
[7]   Lateef Mtima, *Copyright Social Utility and Social Justice Interdependence: A Paradigm for Intellectual Property Empowerment and Digital Entrepreneurship*, 112 W. VA. L. REV. 97 (2009).
[8]   Peter K. Yu, *The Copyright Divide*, 25 CARDOZO L. REV. 331 (2003) (exposing the disconnect between expectations and practices of copyright holders and users); Christine Steiner, *Intellectual Property and the Right to Culture*, 43, 44-45, 53-55, Intellectual Property and Human Rights, WIPO Publication No. 762(E) (Geneva, Switzerland: WIPO, June 2006).
[9]   ROBERT M. SHERWOOD, INTELLECTUAL PROPERTY AND ECONOMIC DEVELOPMENT 191 (Boulder, CO, U.S.A.: Westview Press 1990) (hereinafter "Sherwood"); Robert M. Sherwood, *Intellectual Property Syste ms and Investment Stimulation: The Ratings of Systems in Eighteen Developing Countries*, 337 IDEA 261 (1997) (hereinafter "Sherwood, Rating").
[10]   KAUFFMAN TASKFORCE ON LAW, INNOVATION, AND GROWTH, RULES FOR

Not only law proper matters, but also how the law is administered in practice can significantly affect innovation and development. If the law is strict, but the policy and administrative practice is to ignore minor infractions, that matters. If the law is administered capriciously, it loses predictability and that matters. If the law is fine, but the costs of compliance (e.g., obtaining and defending a patent) are steep, that too matters.[11] Consequently, when we refer to "copyright" or "intellectual property," the terms should be understood throughout as including not only law, but also policy and administration, unless the context requires a narrower construction.

We are not iconoclasts. We believe that intellectual property can serve the cause of inclusion and empowerment, and thus social justice, if it is properly balanced and tailored to appropriate ends.[12] Indeed, in light of the advancements in equal access to justice and opportunities for social advancement and economic empowerment for marginalized groups, societies, and nations, strong intellectual property rights can finally be used as tools for inclusion and empowerment, as opposed to weapons for mass oppression and exploitation. Thus, we do not buy into the radical perspective exemplified by the slogan that "information wants to be free,"[13] nor into a sort of mindset toward intellectual property that seeks to tie up information too tightly in order to capture the last morsel of value available, as exemplified metaphorically by the seagulls' refrain of "mine, mine,

---

GROWTH: PROMOTING INNOVATION AND GROWTH THROUGH LEGAL REFORM (Kansas City, MO, U.S.A.: Ewing Marion Kauffman Foundation, 2011) (hereinafter "Kauffman").

[11] *See* Shubha Ghosh, *The Strategic Lawyer, in* ENTREPRENEURSHIP AND INNOVATION IN EVOLVING ECONOMIES (*infra*, Chapter 5) (discussing lawyering in practice as more than doctrinal facility); *see also* Steven D. Jamar, *A Lawyering Approach to Law and Development*, 27 N.C. J. INT'L L. & COM. REG. 31, 34–35 (2001) (discussing the need for lawyers in the field to use lawyering skills of problem solving to create laws appropriate to particular problems on the ground rather than a Weberian top-down approach to law and development).

[12] *See* Ruth Okediji, *Givers, Takers, and Other Kinds of Users: A Fair Use Doctrine for Cyberspace*, 53 FLA. L. REV. 107 (2001); Ruth Gana Okediji, *Copyright and Public Welfare in Global Perspective*, 7 IND. J. GLOBAL LEGAL STUD. 117 (1999) (arguing "that the harmonized rules of intellectual property are unlikely to produce net welfare gains either domestically for the United States or globally.").

[13] Attributed to Steven Brand, Information Wants to be Free, http://en.wikipedia.org/wiki/Information_wants_to_be_free (last visited July 20, 2011); Peter Drahos, *The Universality of Intellectual Property Rights: Origins and Development*, 13, 23–34, Intellectual Property and Human Rights, WIPO Publication No. 762(E) (Geneva, Switzerland: WIPO, June 2006).

mine" in the Disney/Pixar movie *Finding Nemo*.[14] If one uses a balanced
approach that takes into account social justice concerns of inclusion and
empowerment, the interests of all affected parties, local conditions, and
the specific attributes of the particular type of work at issue, copyright law,
policy, and administration will be an engine of development, not a brake
on innovation.

A basic background on copyright law helps inform the discussion of
how copyright law, policy, and administration can affect innovation and
entrepreneurship from a social justice perspective. The grounding in copyright includes the theoretical underpinnings of it, the content of the law
itself, and some aspects of its administration.

The underlying justification for copyright can inform our assessment
of appropriate balances to strike. The two primary theoretical justifica-
tions for copyright are a natural law or natural rights approach[15] and
a utilitarian approach.[16] In practice, in most instances the theoretical
underpinnings give way to practical considerations without much regard
to theory. For our purposes, we will emphasize the utilitarian approach,
but a few words about the impact of natural rights approach will help
illustrate that the natural rights theory is not antithetical to limits on
intellectual property rights and indeed can be supportive of social justice
perspectives.

The natural rights theory is in essence that the act of creating something
(including a play or musical composition or work of art, etc.) gives one

[14] FINDING NEMO (Pixar 2003); FINDING NEMO—MINE (YouTube), http://
www.youtube.com/watch?v=H4BNbHBcnDI&feature=related (last visited May
14, 2010); FINDING NEMO—SEAGULL SCENE HQ CLIP (YouTube), http://
www.youtube.com/watch?v=1AdSn_YE0VQ&feature=related (last visited May
14, 2010); *See* WILLIAM PATRY, MORAL PANICS AND THE COPYRIGHT WARS (New
York, U.SA,: Oxford University Press, 2009); LAWRENCE LESSIG, REMIX: MAKING
ART AND COMMERCE THRIVE IN THE HYBRID ECONOMY (U.S.A.: Avery Pub., 2008).

[15] Generally in the United States the natural rights position is traced to JOHN
LOCKE, TWO TREATISES ON GOVERNMENT, Book II, Ch. V (1690). *See* Jane C.
Ginsburg, *A Tale of Two Copyrights: Literary Property in Revolutionary France and
America*, 64 TUL. L. REV. 991 (1990); Megan Carpenter, *Trademarks and Human
Rights: Oil and Water? Or Chocolate and Peanut Butter?*, 99 TRADEMARK REP. 892
(2009); Laurence R. Helfer, *Toward a Human Rights Framework for Intellectual
Property*, 40 U.C. DAVIS L. REV. 971 (2007); Mary W. S. Wong, *Toward an
Alternative Normative Framework for Copyright: From Private Property to Human
Rights*, 26 CARDOZO ARTS & ENT. L.J. 775 (2009).

[16] *See* JEREMY BENTHAM, THE PRINCIPLES OF MORALS AND LEGISLATION (1789)
available online at http://www.econlib.org/library/Enc/bios/Bentham.html; and
JOHN STUART MILL, UTILITARIANISM (1863) available online at http://www.utilitar
ianism.com/mill1.htm.

rights in it as a matter of natural law or rights.[17] At its core the natural rights theory does not focus on giving property rights in the created works for the good of society, but rather it has more of an egocentric focus on the creator. In many ways, intellectual property can be regarded as the ultimate personal property, as the fruit of an individual's ideas, dreams, feelings, and personal inspirations. As such, it seems appropriate to concede to individual creators absolute dominion over the manifestations of their individual identity.

On the other hand, an individual's intellectual product usually has limited value absent society's protection and exploitation. More so than most forms of tangible property, intellectual property is extremely difficult to protect, and perhaps even to complete, without the intervention and participation of an organized society. While there are those creators who are fully satiated by the mere act of creation, many authors and inventors find their incentive and recompense in the critical response and/or commercial benefits received as a result of society's exposure to and use of their creative works.

Moreover, natural rights, including human rights like free speech and real property rights, are subject to limitations for the overall public good[18]—indeed, serving the public good is an obligation under the social contract between a society and its citizens. Individual human civil and political rights are subject to various limitations such as protecting the rights of others and protecting morals and national security.[19] With respect to property, the power of eminent domain, zoning, nuisance, and other limitations for the public good are commonplace.[20] Intellectual property, even if founded on natural law, is properly subject to similar limitations for the public good.[21]

As with core human rights like freedom of expression, intellectual

---

[17] *See generally*, Wendy J. Gordon, *A Property Right in Self-Expression: Equality and Individualism in the Natural Law of Intellectual Property*, 102 YALE L.J. 1533, 1544–45 (1993).

[18] *See* International Convention on Civil and Political Rights Art. 19, ¶ 3 (discussing freedom of expression limitations).

[19] *Id.*

[20] The Takings Clause of the United States constitution permits private property to be taken for a public purpose provided only that just compensation is made. U.S. CONST. amend. V; Under the incorporation doctrine, the Due Process Clause of the 14th Amendment has been held to impose the same limits on states. *Kelo v. City of New London*, 545 U.S. 469 (2005).

[21] *See* Gregory S. Alexander, *The Social-Obligation Norm in American Property Law*, 94 CORNELL L. REV. 745 (2009); Daniel Benoliel, *Copyright Distributive Injustice*, 10 YALE J.L. & TECH. 45 (2007).

property rights cannot be so absolute as to unduly impinge on other rights such as free speech or such as to undermine the public good. The natural rights theory also supports moral rights of attribution and integrity of the work. These too do not unduly limit the appropriate constraints on intellectual property rights for the public good or social justice purposes. Finally, the granting of intellectual property rights themselves regardless of the underlying theory can serve the interests of social justice and the public good. Thus a natural rights perspective is not necessarily antithetical to crafting intellectual property law, policy, and administration to encourage innovation and entrepreneurship; balancing interests is the key.[22]

The other foundational theory is utilitarian. Under a utilitarian theory, one needs to decide on what is to be accomplished and then give rights and provide limitations on and exceptions to those rights, as appropriate, to accomplish the desired ends. Under this theory, intellectual property is granted in certain works because doing so helps promote progress in society.[23] By granting the rights, people will be encouraged to create works.[24] Thus the utilitarian theory goes hand-in-hand with incentivizing the creation of new works.[25] In the United States intellectual property is explicitly built on a utilitarian premise. Congress is given power under the U.S. Constitution to create copyright laws explicitly for the good of society; copyright is to serve the utilitarian goal of progress.[26] Thus under copyright we have fair use[27] and a host of other limitations[28] of the rights granted.

---

[22]   *E.g., New York Times Co. v. Tasini*, 533 U.S. 483 (2001); *See also* Lateef Mtima, *Tasini and Its Progeny: The New Exclusive Right or Fair Use on the Electronic Publishing Frontier?*, 14 FORDHAM INTELL. PROP. MEDIA & ENT. L.J. 369 (2004).

[23]   *Sony Corp. of Am. v. Universal City Studios, Inc.*, 464 U.S. 417, 429 (1984); *See* Neil Weinstock Netanel, *Copyright and a Democratic Civil Society*, 106 YALE L.J. 283 (1996).

[24]   *Sony Corp. of Am. v. Universal City Studios, Inc.,* 464 U.S. 417, 429 (1984); *Twentieth Century Music Corp. v. Aiken*, 422 U.S. 151, 156 (1975); *Mazer v. Stein*, 347 U.S. 201, 219 (1954).

[25]   *Sony Corp. of Am. v. Universal City Studios, Inc.*, 464 U.S. 417, 429 (1984); *Campbell v. Acuff-Rose Music, Inc.*, 510 U.S. 569, 599(1994) (Kennedy, J. concurring). *See* Trotter Hardy, *Property (and Copyright) in Cyberspace*, 1996 U. CHI. LEGAL F. 217, 220–228 (1996).

[26]   Congress is empowered "[t]o promote the progress of science and the useful arts, by securing for limited times to authors and inventors the exclusive rights to their respective writings and discoveries." U.S. CONST. art. I, § 8.

[27]   17 U.S.C. § 107.

[28]   17 U.S.C. §§ 108–122 (e.g., first sale doctrine, compulsory licenses, making archival copies, etc.).

The substance of copyright, including both the rights granted and the limits on those rights, can affect innovation and entrepreneurship and so a brief summary of copyright law follows to provide context for our analysis. First and foremost, copyright does not protect ideas; ideas are free for the taking.[29] Nor does copyright protect processes or facts or scientific principles per se,[30] e.g., how to bake a pie,[31] the fact that the Internet has changed many people's lives,[32] and $E=mc^2$.[33] Copyright protects the expression of ideas or processes or facts, but not those things themselves.[34] William Kamkwamba learned information from books that were protected by copyright, but the copyright in those books extended only to the way the ideas were explained; the ideas, methods, and processes themselves were free for him to use as he did to make a windmill to generate electricity.[35]

Copyright protects literature, poetry, music, photographs, paintings, sculptures, plays, movies, video games, software, web pages, and more.[36] Copyright holders have exclusive rights to reproduce and distribute the works, to create derivative works, to perform and display the works, and to authorize others to do these things.[37] But the copyright holders' rights are limited in various ways including duration[38] and by the rights of others to use the works without permission in limited circumstances.[39]

---

[29] 17 U.S.C. § 102(b).

[30] *Id.*

[31] How to Bake a Pie from Scratch, http://www.wikihow.com/Bake-an-Apple-Pie-from-Scratch (last visited Aug. 24, 2011).

[32] *See, e.g.*, Matt Richtel, *Attached to Technology and Paying a Price*, N.Y. Times, June 6, 2010.

[33] Einstein Exhibit, http://www.aip.org/history/einstein/emc1.htm (last visited July 10, 2011).

[34] 17 U.S.C. §102(a); *Nichols v. Universal Pictures Corp.*, 45 F.2d 119 (2d Cir. 1930) (Abbie's Irish Rose) (Judge Learned Hand's opinion in this case is a work of literary art itself).

[35] William Kamkwamba as told to Bryan Mealer, THE BOY WHO HARNESSED THE WIND (U.S.A,: William Morrow, 2009) (see below at text accompanying footnote 74 for a more complete summary of Kamkwamba's experience.).

[36] 17 U.S.C. §§ 102-103; Berne Convention for the Protection of Literary and Artistic Works, *available at* http://www.wipo.int/treaties/en/ip/berne/index.html.

[37] 17 U.S.C. §106; Berne Convention for the Protection of Literary and Artistic Works, *available at* http://www.wipo.int/treaties/en/ip/berne/index.html.

[38] *E.g.*, 17 U.S.C. § 302.

[39] 17 U.S.C. §§ 107-122 (including among others, fair use (§107) and compulsory licensing for performing musical compositions (§115)); Berne Convention Art. 11*bis*(2) and Art. 13(1).

These limits generally help realize the utilitarian function of copyright of advancing culture and society.[40]

The particulars of copyright law matter, but so does the overarching effect of the law in general, including administration of it. Care must be taken not only with respect to the particular balance of any particular provision of the law in a particular context, but, especially in the dynamic cyberspace context, the law must also "accept the chaotic, complex, open nature of a system that has been important to innovation and growth [and] not try to make [too much] order with law."[41] The point is developed more fully by Yochai Benkler[42] as follows:

> Freedom to operate is more important than power to appropriate. Appropriation of the benefits of one's investment is critical *ex post*, and there is no question that at root, its anticipation drives investment in commercialized applications, services, and cultural goods. But in a globally connected, networked world, the level of uncertainty and the rapid changes in modes of appropriation of the benefits of innovation are so great that agility and continuous updating for responses to actual practices and technical, social, or behavioral opportunities is more important than the ability to plan clearly for a release schedule and a well-specified model in advance, and then execute reliably in a predictable environment. The benefits of crisply defined and enforced appropriation models are outweighed by the fact that in order to secure that appropriability, the law has set up a set of rules that, in protecting yesterday's actors, limits to too great an extent the freedom of new innovators to operate today.[43]

While one must acknowledge, as Benkler does, that industry-sponsored studies are to be treated with some degree of skepticism,[44] there is certainly

---

[40]   *See, e.g., Eldred v. Ashcroft*, 537 U.S. 186 (2003) (holding fair use and non-protection for ideas protects First Amendment rights of free expression).

[41]   Robert Cooter, Aaron Edlin, Robert E. Litan, and George L. Priest, *The Importance of Law in Promoting Innovation and Growth, supra* note 4 at 20, in *Kauffman* ch. 1, pp. 1–22 (2011).

[42]   Jack N. and Lillian R. Berkman Professor of Entrepreneurial Legal Studies, Harvard Law School; Faculty co-Director, Berkman Center for Internet and Society, Harvard University.

[43]   Yochai Benkler, *Growth-Oriented Law for the Networked Information Economy: Emphasizing Freedom to Operate Over Power to Appropriate*, in Kauffman 313, 314 (Hereinafter "Benkler").

[44]   *See* Patry's exposure of the utterly speculative nature of the copyright industry's claims of billions of dollars lost to improper use of their copyrighted works. WILLIAM PATRY, MORAL PANICS AND THE COPYRIGHT WARS, 30–36 (New York, NY, U.S.A,: Oxford University Press 2009). The Government Accounting Office agrees with Patry:

> While experts and literature we reviewed provided different examples of effects on the U.S. economy, most observed that despite significant efforts, it is difficult,

much more than a grain of truth in the claim of the Computer and Communications Industry Association (CCIA) that

> industries that depend on and benefit from limitations to copyright, rather than its extension, account for \$4.7 trillion, with a value added of \$2.7 trillion, or about one-sixth of U.S. GDP, employing about 17.5 million employees with a per-employee productivity that was over 25 percent higher than economy-wide average productivity.[45]

The point is not that copyright should have no effect in cyberspace-related business and technology and works of authorship—it does and should—but rather that even given the aims of incentivizing creation of new works to benefit the commonwealth, the rules that apply in cyber-space and the application of even the same copyright rules might well be different than they are for certain established and less agile copyright and IP-dependent industries like the Hollywood film industry, old-business-model music moguls, and even traditional software companies. The way we address copyright issues with respect to Google Books, YouTube, and Facebook probably should not be the same as how we address a movie, a vinyl LP 33 1/3 rpm music recording, an oil painting, or a sculpture.[46] We should protect innovative platforms and the ability of users and

---

if not impossible, to quantify the net effect of counterfeiting and piracy on the economy as a whole. For example, as previously discussed, OECD attempted to develop an estimate of the economic impact of counterfeiting and concluded that an acceptable overall estimate of counterfeit goods could not be developed. OECD further stated that information that can be obtained, such as data on enforcement and information developed through surveys, "has significant limitations, however, and falls far short of what is needed to develop a robust overall estimate." One expert characterized the attempt to quantify the overall economic impact of counterfeiting as "fruitless," while another stated that any estimate is highly suspect since this is covert trade and the numbers are all "guesstimates."

U.S. Gov't Accountability Office, GAO-10-423, REPORT TO CONGRESSIONAL COMMITTEES, OBSERVATIONS ON EFFORTS TO QUANTIFY THE ECONOMIC EFFECTS OF COUNTERFEIT AND PIRATED GOODS, 27 (2010).

[45] *Id.*, citing Computer & Communications Industry Association, *Fair Use in the U.S. Economy: Economic Contribution of Industries Relying on Fair Use* (Washington, DC, U.S.A.: CCIA, 2007), http://www.ccianet.org/CCIA/files/cc LibraryFiles/Filename/000000000085/FairUseStudy-Sep12.pdf; CCIA, Fair Use in the U.S. Economy (Washington, DC, U.S.A.: CCIA 2010), http://www.ccianet. org/CCIA/files/ccLibraryFiles/Filename/000000000354/fair-use-study-final.pdf (last visited Aug. 24, 2011).

[46] Steven D. Jamar, *Crafting Copyright to Encourage and Protect User Generated Content in the Internet Social Networking Context*, 19 WIDENER L.J. 843 (2010) (discussing copyright in the social networking context).

downstream creators to exploit them, erring on the side of innovation and entrepreneurial "chaos" rather than on extracting the last dollar of value from any intellectual property contained in them.[47] In particular, if we want to encourage innovation and entrepreneurship we should be careful to allow *de minimis* impacts, limited copying, and the creation of new value in the form of derivative works without imposing high transaction costs through increasingly burdensome protection.[48] Rights should be granted sufficient to incentivize the creation and dissemination of works, but should not be so restrictive as to stymie others building on those works.

For this reason, the "all or nothing" attitude toward unauthorized use of copyrighted works in cyberspace is socially counterproductive. It ignores the social and legal reality that all unauthorized digital use cannot and should not be regarded as piracy. Such extremist positions not only inhibit progressive initiatives to recalibrate the IP rights holder/public interest balance so as to better exploit the full benefits of digital information technology, but they also undermine efforts to develop reasonable and effective measures to preserve legitimate IP property interests and incentives.

Copyright administration, like the law itself, should be efficient and balanced. While copyright holders' rights must be recognized and enforceable, the enforcement burden and mechanisms must not be such that *in terrorum* tactics employed in the service of improper assertions of rights or even of barely colorable rights are enough to dissuade creators from creating and disseminating works. The abuse of take-down notices under the Digital Millennium Copyright Act (DMCA) to effect the removal of properly and legally posted items,[49] the overly aggressive intrusion into private information, the abuse of contract terms to expand copyrights,[50] the avoidance of the first sale doctrine,[51] and more are all problematic insofar as they can be, have been, and are used to the detriment of users and weaker parties.

Perhaps most important to innovation and developing economies,

---

[47]   Benkler, *supra* note 45 at 313–314.

[48]   *See* Benkler, *supra* note 45 at 316–317.

[49]   *Lenz v. Universal Music Corp.*, 572 F. Supp. 2d 1150 (N.D. Cal. 2008), ("Let's Go Crazy" #1 is a home video of toddler bopping to a barely audible, twenty-second portion of a recording of Prince's "Let's Go Crazy," *available at* "LET'S GO CRAZY" #1 (YouTube), http://www.youtube.com/watch?v=N1KfJHFWlhQ (last visited May 14, 2010)).

[50]   Ariel Katz, What Antitrust Law Can (and Cannot) Teach About the First Sale Doctrine, (2011), *available at* http://ssrn.com/paper=1845842 (examining first sale and exhaustion doctrines).

[51]   *Vernor v. Autodesk, Inc.*, 621 F.3d 1102 (9th Cir. 2010).

remedies such as injunctions are not always needed to vindicate rights.[52] As the United States Supreme Court held in *eBay vs. Mercexchange, LLC.*,[53] once an IP plaintiff has advanced a prima facie case, the court should carefully consider whether there are any societal social utility or social justice interests that would be advanced by allowing the unauthorized use to continue. Where important societal interests are at stake, the court should proceed to weigh the relevant equities in deciding whether the unauthorized use should be allowed. Thus, a weighing of the equities in many cases will not preclude an unauthorized use of intellectual property but rather, will only assure the rights holder a portion of the revenues generated by the unauthorized use.

The role of innovation in development is massive and the role of intellectual property protection in facilitating innovation (or debilitating it) has been demonstrated to be of significant importance. Economies develop from several important "inputs:" physical capital, human work, and what is generally considered the most important one, innovation.[54] Of course other factors are critical as well, such as the rule of law,[55] access to financial capital,[56] education level of the workforce, infrastructure, and political and economic stability.[57] But, if you will, from a reductionist accounting sort of perspective, only three things go in—physical capital, human effort, and innovation—and one thing comes out—economic growth. Regardless of how one parcels out the factors involved in development and growth, innovation is critical.

A leading proponent of the role of intellectual property in facilitating innovation and development is Robert M. Sherwood. He demonstrated that legal protection of intellectual property is part of the infrastructure needed for innovation and technology transfer, and hence development.[58] In some circumstances effective legal protection for intellectual property

[52]   *eBay Inc. v. MercExchange, L.L.C.*, 547 U.S. 388 (2006); *New York Times Co. v. Tasini*, 533 U.S. 483 (2001). *See also* Benkler at 333–38.
[53]   *eBay vs. Mercexchange, LLC.*,126 S. Ct. 1837, 1840 (2006).
[54]   Robert Cooter, Aaron Edlin, Robert E. Litan, and George L. Priest, *The Importance of Law in Promoting Innovation and Growth*, *supra* note 4, Kauffman at 3–4.
[55]   Andrea L. Johnson, *The Rule of Law, Privatization, and the Promise of Transborder Licensing*, in ENTREPRENEURSHIP AND INNOVATION IN EVOLVING ECONOMIES (*infra*, Chapter 10).
[56]   Brian Krumm, *State Legislative Efforts to improve Access to Venture Capital*, in ENTREPRENEURSHIP AND INNOVATION IN EVOLVING ECONOMIES (*infra*, Chapter 2).
[57]   *See generally*, Sherwood *supra* note 11; Sherwood, Rating *supra* note 11.
[58]   Sherwood *supra* note 11; Margaret Chon, *Intellectual Property and the Development Divide*, 27 CARDOZO L. REV. 2821 (2006).

may play a positive role in economic development in part by encouraging the creation of indigenous businesses based on economic exploitation of the protected information owned by others.[59] Entrepreneurship can involve marketing the works of others, and typically does. Sherwood's analysis can extend beyond mainstream participants such that protecting IP will sometimes encourage marginalized members of society to engage in creative endeavors as a means of social advancement; in other situations, intellectual property protection may open the door for such groups to exploit someone else's IP commercially. Protecting IP in such settings facilitates confidence in sharing the information or works with less concern about it being expropriated without compensation. Provided the system is set up so that license fees are not so high as to result in unacceptably few distributions and so that underserved communities are not excluded, this sort of protection for this purpose can be valuable. But social justice requirements of inclusion and empowerment must also be taken into account.

Current law and policy debates regarding state law publicity rights provide an excellent example of the potential for intellectual property protection as a tool for economic empowerment and development, particularly in the digital information context.

> The right of publicity is an intellectual property right of recent origin which has been defined as the inherent right of every human being to control the commercial use of his or her identity. . . . [It] is a creature of state law and its violation gives rise to a cause of action for the commercial tort of unfair competition.[60]

The right of publicity assures individuals the right to determine the instances under which others may utilize or exploit their personas, and also the right to participate in the commercial benefits that might be derived from such uses. In addition to protecting individual privacy and personal dignity, the right further provides incentive to individuals to

---

[59]   Sherwood, *supra* note 11 at 5–7. Sherwood's work is persuasive in part due to the detail of the studies. Sherwood has demonstrated at least that protection of intellectual property can be part of a program to encourage development. We are here concerned with attaching a social justice component to the calculus.

[60]   *ETW Corp. v. Jireh Pub., Inc.*, 332 F. 3d 915, 928 (6th Cir. 2003). The right was first recognized by the Second Circuit in *Haelan Labs., Inc. v. Topps Chewing Gum, Inc.*, 202 F.2d 866 (2nd Cir. 1953), cert. denied, 346 U.S. 816, 98 L. Ed. 343, 74 S. Ct. 26 (1953) ("[I]n addition to and independent of [the] right of privacy . . . a man has a right in the publicity value of his photograph, i.e., the right to grant the exclusive privilege of publishing his picture. . . . This right might be called a 'right of publicity.'").

invest effort and resources in the development and stylization of personal attributes and innovations, and to pursue activities and accomplishments of public and popular interest, with the possibility of celebrity, public renown, and attendant commercial reward. Resourceful ingenuity and creativity exercised under challenging conditions often spurs the development, refinement, and stylization of personal attributes and individual innovations, which sometimes engender enormous popular culture interest and concomitant commercial potential.

At the same time, however, proper identification of right of publicity social utility objectives necessitates recognition of competing social objectives that help to define the limits of these intellectual property rights. Just as is the case with the copyright, the law seeks to promote right of publicity social utility objectives up to the point that they interfere with other, equally important or even superior objectives. For example, society has an interest in promoting the accurate discourse of historical and public events, including the roles of individuals in such events.[61]

Right of publicity law and policy debates provide a particularly interesting opportunity for evaluating the role of IP protection in the digital society because in recent years, it has often been the entrenched IP-owner establishment that has opposed its recognition and expansion. Because of institutionalized barriers to information, financial capital, and legal support, many members of marginalized communities have been unable to commercially develop and exploit their publicity rights, while majority enterprises have proven quite adept at exploiting these properties, such as in digital video games and in the entertainment industry, and have often done so *without authorization*. In defense of their actions, IP conglomerates have pointed to the countervailing social utility concerns regarding First Amendment rights, as well as society's interest in stimulation expressive discourse. However, these counter considerations are often raised not in the defense of genuine innovation and/or social progress, but rather to disguise protectionism for entrenched conglomerates and business models. Here the concern is not that the recognition of IP rights will impede innovation, but rather, will spur development by new players and thereby threaten entrenched positions of commercial dominance. Thus where broader IP rights could perform the intended task of spurring innovation,

---

[61] "[T]he right of publicity cannot be used to prevent someone's name or picture in news reporting. It cannot be used to prevent the use of identity in an unauthorized biography. It cannot prevent use of identity in an entertainment parody or satire, such as that of Rich Little or Saturday Night Live." J. Thomas McCarthy, *The Human Persona as Commercial Property: The Right of Publicity*, 19 COLUM.-VLA J.L. & Arts 129, 130–31 (1995).

innovation (and inclusion) is sacrificed in favor of initiatives for which dominant commercial actors can see—and reap—ready profit.[62]

Consequently in many cases, an "either/or" First Amendment/publicity right categorization will inadequately assess the societal and constituent interests implicated in digital right of publicity disputes. In addition to those circumstances in which the purpose of an unauthorized use of a persona is undertaken solely to market or promote a product or expressive work, there may be instances in which the purpose or impact of an unauthorized use is "mixed", i.e., both promotional and expressive, such that any pertinent societal interest (i.e. First Amendment, historical accuracy, etc.) may be limited or even minimal. In such cases it seems more consistent with the social utility objectives that underlie the right of publicity, as well as its potential to foster innovation and inclusion, to weigh the relevant equities as between the rights holder and the user in deciding whether the unauthorized use should be permitted and, if so, what kind of royalty requirement would further society's interests.[63] In these situations, the issue is not so much a question of the plaintiff's compensatory interests

---

[62]   Although the *Brown* court invokes appropriate mechanisms in assessing the plaintiff's intellectual property claims, its application of said mechanisms could be more in tune with the social utility/social justice interests implicated in the dispute. For one thing, the court's "knee-jerk" emphasis on the historical significance of Brown's "legendary" accomplishments to support its finding of "First Amendment relevance" under the first prong of *Rogers* is somewhat circular, in that notable athletic or other achievements will almost always have some historical value. Under the *Brown* analysis it therefore becomes difficult to conceive of any notable achievement that would be "irrelevant" to any expressive work concerning the same subject matter. A more socially cognizant application of the *Rogers* test recognizes that although Jim Brown's exploits are indeed a part of football history, not every invocation of Brown and his accomplishments or attributes are exclusively or even principally historical in purpose or effect. The inclusion of "Brown attributes" in a commercial expressive work might be for reasons of historical accuracy and experience authenticity, or merely for reasons of marketing appeal, *or for a combination of these purposes.*

[63]   *See, e.g. Zacchini v. Scripps-Howard Broadcasting Co.*, 433 U.S. 562 (1977). (First Amendment interests do not support the unauthorized rebroadcast of performer's entire act.) The *Brown* assessment of the second *Rogers* prong also seemed unduly conservative; in some cases, an individual may be identifiable (and her persona exploited) notwithstanding the fact that her name or precise image are not used. "[T]he common law right of publicity . . . is not limited to the appropriation of name or likeness. Infringement is triggered by the use of any indicia by which the plaintiff is identifiable." J. Thomas McCarthy, *The Human Persona as Commercial Property: The Right of Publicity*, 19 COLUM.-VLA J.L. & ARTS at 136. Again, where the question of persona recognition is factually complicated, a weighing of the relevant equities seems appropriate.

being at odds with an important societal interest, but rather, more that of deciding as between the plaintiff and the defendant, how should the fruits of commercial exploitation of the subject persona or persona attributes be allocated.

In short, appropriate protection of intellectual property can foster innovation, entrepreneurship and development. Marginalized entrepreneurs can develop and exploit their own creations, or they can deploy the creations of others (who otherwise may not license it absent some assurance of protection of that technology).[64]

A second reason to protect intellectual property is that protection is part of international legal norms through the Paris Convention, the Berne Convention, and the WTO. Conformity to international standards has value separate from instrumental domestic affects, including particularly for Internet-related businesses the potential of a worldwide market.[65] Playing by the rules, or at least core aspects of the rules, makes good sense. But, as the international rules themselves become tighter, especially with the creation of increasingly oppressive and intrusive enforcement mechanisms,[66] those rules may need to be modified in light of principles of social justice and in light of the concerns expressed in the Kauffman study.[67]

Sherwood concedes that "[t]he role of effective intellectual property protection is little understood in developing countries."[68] This has not changed. A problem in developing any IP regime is to avoid having it be solely a wealth transfer system from the target state to the multinational corporation. The aim is to create a structure that encourages real internal

[64] *Intellectual Property: U.S. Companies Reluctant to Sign Technology Contracts Without Stronger Protection Law*, 4 INT'L TRADE REP. 276 (BNA Feb. 25, 1987). *See* Alan S. Gutterman, *The North-South Debate Regarding the Protection of Intellectual Property Rights*, 28 WAKE FOREST L. REV. 89 (1993); Richard T. Rapp & Richard P. Rozek, *Benefits and Costs of Intellectual Property Protection in Developing Countries*, 24 J. WORLD TRADE 75 Oct. 1990.

[65] *But see,* Ruth Gana Okediji, *Copyright and Public Welfare in Global Perspective*, 7 IND. J. GLOBAL LEGAL STUD. 117 (1999) (arguing "that the harmonized rules of intellectual property are unlikely to produce net welfare gains either domestically for the United States or globally.").

[66] *E.g.,* Office of the U.S. Trade Representative, Anti-Counterfeiting Trade Agreement, (2010), *available at* http://www.ustr.gov/webfm_send/2417.

[67] *See generally* Benkler. For an example of these ideas in action in part see Michael Risch, *IP and Entrepreneurship in an Evolving Economy: A Case Study, in,* ENTREPRENEURSHIP AND INNOVATION IN EVOLVING ECONOMIES (*infra,* Chapter 8).

[68] Sherwood, Rating, *supra* note 11, at 357. *See also,* Jerome H. Reichman, *Intellectual Property in the Twenty-first Century: Will the Developing Countries Lead or Follow?*, 46 HOUS. L. REV. 1115 (2009).

innovation and development.[69] To do this, one of us (Jamar) has previously advocated that a problem-solving, lawyering approach rather than a normative approach be used.[70] Benkler and the Kauffman study as a whole support this approach, going even further to argue that whatever system is put in place needs to have maximum flexibility and indeed needs to be somewhat chaotic. A rights regime that is too protective or rigid will limit or even eliminate the very thing it seeks to enhance.

Despite the similarity in the legal norms, which are likely to result from both the traditional law and development top-down-one-size-fits-all approach and the lawyering approach, the effectiveness of the solution is likely to be different because an essential element of the lawyering problem-solving approach is the active engagement of the interested parties. In typical transactional lawyering, if a client buys into the solution in a deeper way, then the solution is likely to be effective. In the bigger context of development, if the interested parties buy in, the solutions are likely to be better implemented, respected, and effective. The difference in process is thus an important one; mere normative change in the laws is not sufficient. Not only the substance of copyright law matters, but also how it is arrived at and administered also matters.

The ongoing explosion of information technologies relating to creation, dissemination, and use of information in all its forms, including copyrightable works, creates challenges and opportunities different from ever before. Because copyright can affect the creation and dissemination of information, the leading role of information for innovation and development today concomitantly makes the impact of copyright law more important across a broader swath of the economy and society than it may have been historically. Accordingly, the objectives and boundaries

---

[69] Margaret Chon, Intellectual Property and the Development Divide, 27 CARDOZO L. REV. 2821 (2006). *See also,* CARLOS M. CORREA, INTELLECTUAL PROPERTY RIGHTS, THE WTO AND DEVELOPING COUNTRIES: THE TRIPS AGREEMENT AND POLICY OPTIONS 5–6 (London, UK: Zed Books, 2000); Paul J. Heald, *Mowing the Playing Field: Addressing Information Distortion and Asymmetry in the TRIPS Game,* 88 MINN. L. REV. 249 (2003).

[70] Steven D. Jamar, *A Lawyering Approach to Law and Development,* 27 N.C. J. INT'L L. & COM. REG. 31 (2001). *See also* Patricia H. Lee, *The Role and Impact of Clinical Programs on Entrepreneurship and Economic Growth,* in ENTREPRENEURSHIP AND INNOVATION IN EVOLVING ECONOMIES Chapter. 9 – (demonstrating the value of hands-on practical lawyering training in clinical programs for innovation and entrepreneurship); Peter Drahos, *When the Weak Bargain with the Strong: Negotiations in the WTO,* 8 INT'L NEGOTIATION 79 (2003) (arguing that developing countries need to communicate and coordinate when negotiating with more powerful developed countries over IP rights).

of copyright protection must be reconsidered in the context of promoting social progress, such that they accommodate the benefits that can be derived from digital advances, and otherwise assure that technological options and opportunities are not stunted by legal canons which may (initially) appear inhospitable to these new uses of intellectual property.

Three examples illustrate the value of information and the role of copyright in innovation, entrepreneurship, and development, particularly with respect to inclusion and empowerment of marginalized groups. Each example illuminates the role of copyright from a different perspective. The first example is of William Kamkwamba and illustrates most directly and powerfully the use of information effectively in a remote location, but copyright is not of direct central importance. The second example is of the Grameen Bank and exemplifies non-technological information affecting lives dramatically, particularly for those in the lowest ranks of economic scale, and copyright plays no role. The third example, Google Books, is more hypothetical and forward-looking and is used as a partial stand-in for the role technology can play in making information available and helps illustrate how copyright law and administration of it can affect the availability of information both positively and adversely. Indeed, copyright is at the center the Google Books example and that case provides a negative illustration of what happens when Benkler's point about treating copyright in cyberspace differently with a careful eye on enhancing, not undercutting, innovation and development is not heeded.[71]

William Kamkwamba's experience illustrates the availability of information having a direct, beneficial effect on economic development. Kamkwamba grew up in Masitala, Malawi, a small rural town without electricity.[72] When he was fourteen, he saw a windmill electric generator in a textbook and set to work building one. He ultimately built several, which provide power to his home and community for charging cell phones, pumping water from the village well, and powering electric lights, radio, and television. All this from a picture and a couple of books on electricity and physics in a tiny American-stocked library. Though the books he used were copyrighted, it was the ideas in them that mattered and copyright

---

[71] *The Authors Guild v. Google, Inc.,* 05 Civ. 8136 (DC) (Opinion and Order denying the Amended Settlement Agreement, Mar. 22, 2011), *available at* http://www.nysd.uscourts.gov/cases/show.php?db=special&id=115.

[72] William Kamkwamba as told to Bryan Mealer, THE BOY WHO HARNESSED THE WIND (2009), *available at* http://www.wired.com/wiredscience/2009/10/kamwamba-windmill/, http://www.youtube.com/watch?v=arD374MFk4w&feature=player_embedded, and http://www.thedailyshow.com/watch/wed-october-7-2009/william-kamkwamba.

played little role in what followed. Kamkwamba's efforts also illustrate that innovation and entrepreneurship do not necessarily mean the development of cutting-edge technology or new online applications, but instead often involve the creative, industrious application of existing technology long out of patent.

The second example, the Grameen Bank, also shows non-protectable information making a difference.[73] The Grameen Bank engages in micro-financing to individuals to help them develop extremely small businesses to help lift themselves and their communities out of poverty. The loans have had dramatic positive impacts on many lives.[74] Engaging in Grameen Bank micro-financing depends not upon technology or copyright, but rather upon social support networks and some modest funding. A small entrepreneur such as Kamkwamba could be supported by micro-financing as could a person or small company providing Internet-related services, but the essence of micro-financing is not related to technology or the Internet or copyright.

The third example, Google Books,[75] is directly related to the Internet, technology, and copyright, and is certainly not an instance of micro-financing. The Google Books Project aims to put all of the world's text-based material online, in multiple languages, accessible to anyone with a computer and access to the Internet.[76] Google Books will make available public domain works for no cost to the user beyond the cost of a computer and internet access.[77] Books still in copyright for whom the copyright holder can be identified will be compensated when users buy the books.

---

[73]   ALEX COUNTS, GIVE US CREDIT (New York, NY, U.S.A.: Times Books,1996) (Grameen Bank in Bangladesh). Though perhaps in the U.S., but not in India and many other countries, the methods and the implementation of the ideas could have been subject to a business patent, with most untoward results.

[74]   *Id.* There has been some controversy as the Grameen bank model has expanded and inevitable abuses have arisen. Rama Lakshmi, *Indian Micro-Credit Crisis Puts Women in Bind,* Washington Post, Apr. 26, 2011, *available at* http://www.washingtonpost.com/world/indian-micro-credit-crisis-puts-poor-women-in-a-bind/2011/04/21/AFpckbsE_story.html.

[75]   Google has partnered with libraries and publishers working toward its "ultimate goal [of] creat[ing] a comprehensive, searchable, virtual card catalog of all books in all languages." Google Books Library Project, Google Books, http://books.google.com/ (last visited May 31, 2011).

[76]   *Id.*

[77]   The need for Internet service and an Internet device (including smartphones and tablets, as well as computers today) is itself a significant bar to access, especially in the developing world, but that aspect of the broader problem of providing effective access to information is not part of the core focus of this chapter.

Important aspects of the relationship of copyright, innovation, and inclusion and empowerment at play in the Google Books Project include (1) how access to information can affect inclusion and empowerment; (2) how technology can affect access to information; and (3) how copyright improperly construed and applied in a novel context can limit or at least delay access to that information.

Information is power. William Kamkwamba's story illustrates that. Kamkwamba's response to using Google Search on the Internet for the first time underscores the point of the power of making information available and inexpensive.[78] We cannot predict what access to the world's books will mean to hundreds of thousands or even millions of people, but if only one-tenth of one percent of the world's almost seven billion people seeks and finds useful information from Google Books, on anything, including perhaps even on innovation and development and the role of copyright in it, that would still be seven million people. And if only an average of 100 people per country found the information useful, that would still be about 20,000 people equipped with information to help make a difference in their communities. Google and the Grameen Bank both started small.

Technology obviously affects access to information. The printing press meant people did not need to reproduce books by hand. Removable type meant that many more books, pamphlets, newspapers, and all sorts of information could be created, reproduced, and distributed much more quickly than having to carve (and then discard) a separate plate for each new page. Photocopiers changed things again. And now with digital documents and the internet, the ease of creation of information and the cost of distribution of it have been reduced dramatically, even as the dissemination has become easier and cheaper. It is much easier and less expensive to send bits and bytes through the ether to someone's computer than to print a book, pack it, and ship it. It gets there faster, cheaper, and more reliably. The ability to make information available to those seeking it is unparalleled in history—nothing like this has ever existed before. Even a modest site dedicated to a single topic like *Brown v. Board of Education* has, in seven years, had approximately 700,000 visitors from more than 120 countries and is used as resource by thousands of secondary students in the United States each year.[79]

When Google Books becomes fully operational, not only will the

---

[78] *The Daily Show*, interview with Jon Stewart, *available at* http://www.the dailyshow.com/watch/wed-october-7-2009/william-kamkwamba, Oct. 7, 2009.

[79] Brown at 50, http://brownat50.org (last visited Aug. 24, 2011).

seemingly endless informational websites still be available,[80] but scholarly, inspirational, speculative, and informative books—books of all sorts—will become readily available. Not just books in print or books that vendors like Amazon.com or Borders carry, but all books in every language, published everywhere. That is a big step toward fulfilling the promise of the digital age.

Google Books not only will empower by disseminating existing information, but also will spur the creation and dissemination of new information and thus new voices will be heard. The cost of producing and posting for sale an electronic version of a book is vastly less than making a hardcopy version.

Given the opportunity to get their works to a worldwide audience, if the works meet a receptive audience, the authors may be able to build a business on them. That is, anyone who is literate, has a computer, and access to the Internet would be able to write a book and try to sell it to anyone in the world. While most of the works would likely still not be worth reading, some would be and some people would develop a sufficient following to make a living. Still, it would be the informational aspect that would likely be most valuable—sharing a success or failure will help others. Kamkwamba's full story is in a book. If it is available online in electronic form in addition to hardcopy, with affordable access to it, it could reach and inspire many more than the hard copy alone can.

The third aspect concerning empowerment exemplified by Google Books relates to the role of copyright in the ability of Google Books to reach its potential. Google Books project is affected by copyright in several ways. First, and simplest, a copyright in a work is granted for a limited time and thus many works that were copyrighted are now in the public domain—their copyrights having expired—and are therefore available for inclusion in Google Books for copying and distribution without permission from authors or former copyright holders. Unfortunately, the current duration of copyright in the United States and in many countries is now so long[81] that many relevant works will not be entering the public domain for many years or even decades.

A second way in which copyright matters for Google Books is that it

---

[80]   E.g., WebMD (medical information), http://www.webmd.com; DIY (Do It Yourself) Network, http://www.diynetwork.com; Guitar Instructor, guitar lessons online, http://www.guitarinstructor.com; and, of course, Wikipedia.

[81]   Life plus 70 years for natural authors, 95 years from publication for institutional authors. In some countries the span is shorter—life plus 50 years—but not in a meaningful way for the fast-paced change and development of new information in the world today. 17 U.S.C. § 302; *See Eldred v. Ashcroft*, 537 U.S. 186 (2003).

provides a means for known copyright holders of books included in the online library to get paid for their works.[82] For many works that have long been out of print, this could give them a new life and result in new revenues for publishers and authors. For new authors it can provide a new outlet for works, bypassing traditional publishers.

The third way in which copyright affects Google Books is that copyright can be a drag on digitizing books and on creating new works in at least two ways. First, and this has already happened, copyright can be interpreted strictly rather than creatively, in such a manner that important developments like digitizing books get delayed significantly. Too cramped a reading of copyright with insufficient weighting of society interests, of the new practicalities, and of the importance of facilitating, not restricting chaotic change,[83] can lead to exactly what happened to the Google Books Project Proposed Settlement—it can be rejected based on reasoning that fits in an older world no longer in existence. By rejecting the class action settlement of the lawsuit designed to insure that Google and users world-wide would have broad access to books now largely hidden away in inaccessible major research libraries at elite educational institutions, the Court has delayed, probably by many years, getting useful information to those who could use it.[84] Requiring opt-in processes ignores digital realities. If such antediluvian interpretations of the copyright law continue to prevail so as to impede mass-digitization initiatives, the public will continue to be denied access to millions of works, and not because the unidentified copyright holders have objected to their digital distribution, but because of an irrational presumption that these authors would prefer that their ideas not be disseminated, nor any remuneration be paid to them or their successors and assigns until it can be positively confirmed that this is their preference. Even if this could somehow be construed as a rational presumption of copyright behavior, to encourage it would be the copyright policy choice that turns American copyright on its head. In the past, courts have found ways to make copyright work in the face of new technologies like video tape recorders, recorded music, excessive transactional costs for licensing musical performances, application of copyright to computers and video games, and more. It is more than a little disappointing that Judge Chin did not apply that same progressive attitude to the Google Books Project.

The second way in which a project like Google Books is impacted by

---

[82] The special problem of orphan works is beyond the scope of this chapter. *See* Brianna Dahlberg, *The Orphan Works Problem: Preserving Access to the Cultural History of Disadvantaged Groups*, 20 S. CAL. REV. L. & SOC. JUST. 1 (2011).
[83] *Id.*
[84] *The Authors Guild v. Google, Inc.*, 05 Civ. 8136, *supra* note 73.

an inadequately flexible copyright law concerns the creation and dissemination of new works. If the ability of users of the copyrighted works, in
this instance books or literary works, are too restricted in their ability to
create derivative works, i.e., new works based on the existing work, or too
restricted in their ability to quote and reference works without obtaining
permission, the flow and dynamism of the digital world can be slowed
significantly.[85]

Google Books, and the innovation that it represents and that it could
trigger in others in the future, is affected by copyright. The court's denial
of the proposed class action settlement, which would have opened the way
for full implementation of this forward-looking development, illustrates
how the failure to recognize that copyright should be interpreted and
applied flexibly and creatively to encourage innovation and development
can block developments that even the court and opponents of the settlement regard as good things[86] and as even inevitable. Judge Chin wrote:

> The benefits of Google's book project are many. Books will become more
> accessible. Libraries, schools, researchers, and disadvantaged populations will
> gain access to far more books. Digitization will facilitate the conversion of
> books to Braille and audio formats, increasing access for individuals with dis-
> abilities. Authors and publishers will benefit as well, as new audiences will be
> generated and new sources of income created. Older books—particularly out-
> of-print books, many of which are falling apart buried in library stacks—will be
> preserved and given new life.[87]

While the first two examples, Kamkwamba's windmill and the Grameen
Bank, did not depend upon the availability of vast amounts of searchable information on the Internet for them to be disseminated, there is no
gainsaying that the unprecedented actual and potential access to information brought about by the Internet and its many information-mediating
platforms has a massive role to play in innovation, entrepreneurship, and
development. Kamkwamba himself instantly recognized the potential of
it. Some four years after Kamkwamba's first windmill, after his work had

---

[85] *See* Benkler at 316–317. The creation of *The Wind Done Gone* (New
York, NY, U.S.A.: Houghton Mifflin, 2001) by Alice Randall based on Margaret
Mitchell's classic, *Gone with the Wind* (New York, NY, U.S.A.: Scribner, 1936), is
an example of the value of giving space for creation of derivative works; *Suntrust
v. Houghton Mifflin Co.*, 268 F.3d 1257 (11th Cir. 2001) (settled after remand when
Mitchell's estate agreed to drop the suit in exchange for Houghton Mifflin making
a donation to Morehouse College in Atlanta, GA).
[86] *The Authors Guild v. Google, Inc.*, 05 Civ. 8136.
[87] *Id.* at 3.

A social justice perspective 101

been discovered by others and he was brought to a city for a conference on development, he was shown Google Search and the Internet. He Googled "windmill," pulled up all sorts of information, and his first thought was, "Where was this Google all this time?".[88]

We now move from providing background and examples to the prescriptive part of this chapter in which we address the question: From a social justice perspective, what are the most salient concerns regarding copyright law, policy, and administration to support innovation and entrepreneurship in transitioning from traditional, agrarian, or industrial economies to new information and technology-driven economies?

There are two overriding general observations: first, of foremost importance is that there is no single answer that fits every situation. Local conditions vary and copyright laws need to be tailored to local situations. Nonetheless, even though local conditions must be taken into account in devising and implementing any particular intellectual property scheme, there are some common features of an innovation-friendly copyright regime that we highlight below.

The second most important point is that made by Benkler: a certain amount of chaos, lack of clarity and certainty, and lack of pre-planning for all developments is a good thing.[89] Flexibility is the watchword, not tightly regulated and policed property rights.

With those two critically important, overriding points in mind, some contours of a copyright regime that would support innovation, inclusion, empowerment, and entrepreneurship can be sketched.

1. International norms of copyright should generally be respected as to subject matter and scope of copyright. But not all international norms are proper in all settings and certainly not all U.S. approaches make sense elsewhere (or necessarily in the U.S. for that matter). Protection of copyright under relatively uniform international standards enhances the ability of marginalized groups and individuals to exploit their copyrighted works by reducing their need to know the details of foreign laws and by having some confidence in their own copyrighted works being generally protected by copyright elsewhere.[90]

---

[88] The Daily Show, interview with Jon Stewart, *available at* http://www.the dailyshow.com/watch/wed-october-7-2009/william-kamkwamba, Oct. 7, 2009.

[89] Benkler at 317.

[90] *But see* Ruth Gana Okediji, *Copyright and Public Welfare in Global Perspective*, 7 IND. J. GLOBAL LEGAL STUD. 117 (1999) (arguing "that the harmonized rules of intellectual property are unlikely to produce net welfare gains either domestically for the United States or globally."); Jerome H. Reichman, *Intellectual*

2.   Derivative work rights should be limited or at least very concretely defined.[91] Derivative works are those that incorporate some or all of an existing work in a new work. One of the exclusive rights of a copyright holder in the United States is to make derivative works.[92] A number of problems arise in the derivative work context, particularly online, and particularly with respect to a number of common activities engaged in by many people.[93] If *de minimis* copying is held to violate copyright, then raw material for new works is limited by a too-expansive derivative work right. This has already happened in sampling where the use of miniscule portions of prior works remixed into new works has been held to violate the copyright in the sound recording.[94]

Other sorts of derivative works like fan fiction,[95] parodies,[96] satires,[97] and commentaries are found throughout the Internet. Some social interaction consists of building on each other's works.[98] One

---

Property in the Twenty-first Century: Will the Developing Countries Lead or Follow?, 46 Hous. L. Rev. 1115 (2009); and Peter K. Yu, *The Copyright Divide*, 25 Cardozo L. Rev. 331 (2003).

[91]   17 U.S.C. §§103, 106(2); Berne Convention Art. 12.

[92]   17 U.S.C. § 106(2).

[93]   *See* Edward Lee, *Developing Copyright Practices for User-Generated Content*, J. Internet L., July 2009, at 6, 12; Steven D. Jamar, *Crafting Copyright Law to Encourage and Protect User-Generated Content in the Internet Social Networking Context*, 19 Widener L.J. 843 (2010).

[94]   *Bridgeport Music, Inc. v. Dimension Films*, 410 F.3d 792 (6th Cir. 2005). *See generally*, K.J. Greene, *Copyright, Culture & Black Music: A Legacy of Unequal Protection*, 21 Hastings Comm. & Ent. L.J. 339 (1999); Neela Kartha, *Digital Sampling and Copyright Law in the Social Context: No More Colorblindness!!*, 14 U. Miami Ent. & Sports L. Rev. 218 (1997).

[95]   *See, e.g.*, Harry Potter Fan Fiction, http://www.harrypotterfanfiction.com/ (last visited May 14, 2010).

[96]   *E.g., Campbell v. Acuff-Rose Music, Inc.*, 510 U.S. 569 (1994).

[97]   The Onion—America's Finest News Source, http://www.theonion.com/ (last visited Aug. 24, 2011).

[98]   *See* News Release, Library of Congress, Michael Wesch to Discuss "The Anthropology of YouTube" at Library of Congress on June 23 (May 22, 2008), *available at* http://www.loc.gov/today/pr/2008/08-104.html; *see also* An Anthropological Introduction to YouTube (YouTube June 23, 2008), http://www.youtube.com/watch?v=TPAO-lZ4_hU; Numa Numa (YouTube Aug. 14, 2006), http://www.youtube.com/watch?v=60og9gwKh1o; Numa Numa, Dragostea Din Tei – South Park (YouTube Apr. 3, 2008), http://www.youtube.com/watch?v=9-MZEe-jvzY&feature=related; Soulja Boy Tell'Em – Crank That (YouTube 2007), http://www.youtube.com/watch?v=8UFIYGkROII [hereinafter Crank That]; *see also* Copyright Criminals (PBS 2009). For more information on the film, see Independent Lens, Copyright Criminals, http://www.pbs.org/independentlens/copyright-criminals/ (last visited May 14, 2010).

of us (Jamar) has proposed that for derivative works in the social networking context a broad right for users be created either through statutory amendment or interpretation and application of fair use. The proposal is:

1. Noncommercial social network users should be allowed to post links to and post portions of copyrighted works without permission.
2. A broad right to create and disseminate derivative works online for noncommercial purposes should be provided.
3. A right to create derivative works for commercial purposes should be given even where substantial portions of the original work are used, provided:
    (a) the new work is original;
    (b) the new work is (i) transformative or (ii) constitutes parody, satire, or commentary; and
    (c) the new work does not directly compete with the source work.[99]

The third part of this proposal essentially seeks a rethinking of the scope of the right to control the creation and distribution of derivative works in a number of situations involving digital forms of works.

We would extend this same sort of analysis to most sorts of derivative works online. Doing so would create the space necessary for innovation and development, thereby empowering people to create new things without undue fear of being shut down or sued by aggressive copyright holders. This is one implementation of Benkler's proposals for how to interpret the Copyright Act to make space for innovation. Benkler proposes:

> Courts and legislatures should consistently try to limit the extent to which existing players who own elements of systems that new players are building on use law to extract value from the new players by:
> • Emphasizing exemptions and narrow construction that create freedom to operate, such as narrow construction of copyright to exclude claims about linking or crawling, or expanding the definition of what use counts as *de minimis* in copyright. All are ways of creating zones of freedom to operate.[100]

An alternative or possibly in some ways complementary proposal would be to create a statutory Digital Compulsory License mechanism that would open digital works for others, much as the compulsory license opened musical compositions to all performers.

---

[99] Jamar, *Crafting, supra* note 48 at 848–49.
[100] Benkler at 316.

3. Enforcement mechanisms are a major concern.[101] Appropriate enforcement mechanisms for appropriate levels of rights are important. But balance is required and just as not all uses of copyrighted works should be deemed infringing, not all infringements should be met with dragon fire. As proposed by Benkler:

- Emphasizing freedom to operate and revenue sharing over forcing *ex ante* negotiation or creating deterrence. In the classic terms of liability versus property rules, this emphasizes liability systems, but a certain limited liability type: more on the model of disgorging a share of the profits than the torts or contracts model.
- Capping risks of liability, tying it to revenue from the new use, and providing an anchor for negotiations in the shadow not of exclusion or massive crippling damages, but of upside sharing among successful operations that choose a revenue-generating or profit-making model. Charges imposed as liability for access to existing information, standards, or elements, should be minimized. Courts should adopt *ex post* upside-sharing rules as quasi-liability rules, rather than either (a) *ex ante* property rules, which create risks of hold ups and high transactions costs, or (b) liability rules that are not tied to revenue or profit of the innovator, such as strict damages based on high statutory levels or hypothetical lost sales or similar mechanisms that courts in the past have used when driven by a property-protection model that conceived of follow-on innovation without permission as a species of theft or injustice.[102]

Not all infringements or potential infringements, or even as is too often the case non-infringements, need be met with threatening letters, injunctions, take-down notices, or lawsuits. Courts and other enforcement agencies should have built-in tools to limit enforcement abuses. Statutory and other remedies should have sufficient discretion built into them and sufficient defenses such as a modestly expanded version of copyright misuse[103] to insure that the fear of infringement does not stifle innovation and development.

---

[101]   Peter Yu, *The Graduated Response,* 62 FLA. L. REV. (2010), *available at* SSRN-id1579782.pdf.
[102]   Benkler at 316–17. *See also,* Jedediah Purdy, *A Freedom-Promoting Approach to Property: A Renewed Tradition for New Debates,* 72 U. CHI. L. REV. 1 (2005).
[103]   *See* Brett Frischmann & Dan Moylan, *The Evolving Common Law Doctrine of Copyright Misuse: A Unified Theory and its Application to Software,* 15 BERKELEY TECH. L.J. 865 (2000); Lydia Pallas Loren, *Slaying the Leather-Winged Demons in the Night: Copyright Misuse as a Tool for Reforming Copyright Owner Contracting Behavior,* 30 OHIO N.U. L. REV. 495 (2004).

Digital information technology presents the promise of democratization of access to information and knowledge, inclusive participation in the creative and inventive process, and more equitable opportunities for economic empowerment and social advancement. IP social justice strategies align IP user interests and author/owner property rights as mutually reinforcing assurances within the intellectual property regime. Accordingly, extreme care must be taken when seeking to redress the use of the Internet to sell and/or otherwise disseminate infringing material or products; when possible, IP enforcement should be undertaken with surgical precision and not blunderbuss indifference to the overarching social utility goals of the intellectual property law.

4. Procedural aspects of enacting, revising, and enforcing copyright law, policy, and administration must be inclusive. Procedurally, an effective program would include the following attributes:
   a. Use of a lawyering, problem-solving approach to develop and reform any legal system to be put into place.[104]
   b. Do not assume that what works in one place or one industry or what has worked in the past fits the particulars of the problem being addressed. Issues concerning cyberspace and software and music and movies and sculptures cannot all be generalized to each other.
   c. Take into account the core utilitarian aim of copyright—the advancement of society, especially through innovation and broad dissemination of information.
   d. Involve all interest groups affected by copyright in decision making at all levels, and to the maximum extent possible, implement the interests of all groups.[105]
5. Maintain flexibility and openness to support innovation and entrepreneurship.
6. Wherever possible, strengthen and clarify the well-established copyright principle of permitting *de minimis* uses to allow more use of works with more confidence in not being challenged by copyright holders.

---

[104] *See* Steven D. Jamar, *A Lawyering Approach to Law and Development*, 27 N.C. J. INT'L L. & COM. REG. 31, 34–35 (2001).
[105] *See* Peter K. Yu, *The Copyright Divide*, 25 CARDOZO L. REV. 331 (2003) (exposing the disconnect between expectations and practices of copyright holders and users).

7. Clarify exceptions and expand them as appropriate so as to avoid disputes over fair use when, as was decided in the case of parodies,[106] a particular set of activities can be defined and protected.

8. Develop, interpret, and apply the law with an eye not only to enforcement of rights, but also to the effect on innovation and development in general. For this we offer the theory of "digital entrepreneurship." Broadly defined, digital entrepreneurship involves the application of traditional entrepreneurial tenets and principles, which have long been utilized in the service of social uplift and advancement, to the cause of intellectual property empowerment in the digital context. Adapting these tenets and principles to the specific social utility/social justice function of the intellectual property law, digital entrepreneurship affirmatively seizes upon IP law as an instrument for economic empowerment and social advance.

    Implementation of digital entrepreneurship begins with the development of a program of grassroots intellectual property legal activism and community pedagogy, including education as to the commercial potential of fixed creative expression and the attendant significance of obtaining and enforcing comprehensive intellectual property protection for such work. Program design and instruction could be undertaken by practicing attorneys, law professors, and law students on a pro bono basis and, through collaboration with local civic, religious, and similar community leaders and institutions, these programs could successfully target marginalized and underserved groups and communities.

    While most laypersons readily appreciate the entrepreneurial significance of acquiring a trade skill or opening a small business, few routinely consider the development of intellectual property as a means toward socio-economic uplift. Certainly there are scores of amateur artists who see their talent as an avenue to fame and fortune, but even they often fail to place sufficient emphasis on intellectual property *ownership* in their long-term plans. Of course, even the most legally savvy unknown artist or inventor will lack the bargaining leverage to secure especially favorable terms in connection with the mass production, marketing, and distribution of her creative output, much the same as any unproven entrepreneur seeking start-up capital investment. Nonetheless, equipped with at least a working knowledge of the applicable intellectual property rights and protections, and of the intellectual property commoditization system as a whole, the

---

106   *Campbell v. Acuff-Rose Music, Inc.*, 510 U.S. 569 (1994).

marginalized amateur creator can negotiate her initial agreements more effectively, or at least negotiate *strategically* with respect to future agreements, when her bargaining position is likely to have improved.

In addition to understanding the commoditization potential of intellectual property endeavor, marginalized creators and communities must be thoroughly apprised as to the unique role that digital information technology can play in the development of original copyrightable expression and in offering alternative commercialization mechanisms to those controlled by the creative distribution conglomerates. To be sure, in many cases, traditional corporate licensing opportunities will provide the best development and marketing options for an undiscovered creator; however, digital exposure can create the kind of public following that can trigger a corporate licensing proposition, enhance creator bargaining leverage, or provide confirmation as to a market and revenue base worthy of the pursuit of an independent, entrepreneurial venture.

Equally important as education regarding the creation and protection of original copyrightable expression is knowledge of the public's rights and privileges to use preexisting creative material, both with respect to material in the public domain as well as the fair use and/or *de minimis* use of material under copyright. Many members of marginalized communities (indeed, many Americans period) are unaware of their entitlement to these "free" resources, or are skeptical of its reminiscence to the promise of forty acres and a mule. Nonetheless, from the musical *Wicked* to the film *Clueless* to the disco hit *A Fifth of Beethoven*, public domain material has been successfully exploited on a grade scale by those who are aware of its availability. Not only are members of marginalized communities equally entitled to profit from this bounty, but there is a sense of social gratification to be had in providing the descendants of victims of copyright injustice the opportunity to sip from the cup of communal creative works in the cause of their own socio-economic advancement.

Finally, in addition to the exploitation of the public domain and the legally sanctioned use of works in copyright, there is the matter of creative entrepreneurial use of protected material without the imprimatur of the copyright public use rights and privileges. There are cogent arguments to the affect that in light of past injustices, it is only fair that members of marginalized groups be allowed wide latitude in connection with the unauthorized use of copyrighted works. There is much merit to this position. As a pervasive intellectual property empowerment strategy, however, the efficacy of such an approach is limited. For one thing, the courts continue to hold firm that unauthorized digital use of copyrighted material, even in the absence of commercial exploitation, will be punished as copyright infringement.

Perhaps more to the point, such weakening of copyright property rights may not be in the long-term interests of the budding generation of digital entrepreneurs. Traditional entrepreneurial tenets contemplate long-term as well as immediate socio-economic advance through the development, ownership, and commercial exploitation of individual resources. In the context of digital entrepreneurship, this necessarily entails preservation of the copyright entrepreneur's traditional exclusive rights. Copyright social activists should therefore be wary of "digital free use" initiatives, given the American tradition of majority imitation of minority innovation. As many an African American rap artist has begun to appreciate, she who samples today shall herself be sampled tomorrow. Lest digital information technology be molded into a means for the repetition of past-institutionalized injustice, wholesale digital free use/reuse amendments to copyright property rights should be eschewed.

In sum, digital entrepreneurship strategies can promote intellectual property social utility and progress by way of the existing regime and not in defiance of it. Indeed, not only can lawyers, policy makers, and social activists play a critical role in furthering this agenda, but also courts should consider these factors in pertinent fair use cases. Creative albeit unauthorized entrepreneurial use of copyrighted material that inures to the benefit of copyright social utility/social justice interdependence, especially where it results in culturally unique creative expression, may well qualify as transformative use, and thus a digital entrepreneurialism bent on fair use could support a socially significant but otherwise limited intrusion upon the commercial market for a copyrighted work. Properly embraced by the bench and bar, digital entrepreneurship analyses and strategies can help to harvest the full copyright social utility/social justice potential of digital information technology.

9. Limit the use of contract and licensing to undo the statutory copyright balance,[107] e.g., do not allow licensing of mass-marketed works such as music and software to eliminate the first sale doctrine.[108]

---

[107] ARIEL KATZ, WHAT ANTITRUST LAW CAN (AND CANNOT) TEACH ABOUT THE FIRST SALE DOCTRINE, (2011), *available at* http://ssrn.com/paper=1845842 (examining first sale and exhaustion doctrines).

[108] *E.g., Vernor v. Autodesk, Inc.*, 621 F.3d 1102 (9th Cir. 2010).

As the foregoing analysis demonstrates, a balanced program of intellectual property protection to promote innovation includes putting most of Benkler's principles into action. Flexibility rather than rigidity; chaotic creativity rather than tightly regulated property rights; openness rather than closed-system; and recognition that in the fast-paced world of innovation online, careful planning and deliberate, controlled IP development and dissemination are almost impossible to corral. IP has a significant role to play, but it cannot be based on the heavy industry model or old-school Hollywood model.

Copyrights are given to induce the creation of works by giving limited property rights in the works for limited times for the benefit of society as a whole. Authors (and copyright holders) get compensated through the property rights regime and this compensation is the inducement for many works. A property rights regime is not necessary for the creation of works, though it may be the most efficient means for inducing the creation of certain kinds of works and incentivizing risk-taking. But, compensation can be accomplished through mechanisms other than direct licensing and sales. Indeed, some of the most important rights in copyright have complex compensation schemes based on compulsory licenses, site licenses, and so on, through copyright management organizations such as ASCAP, Harry Fox, and BMI.

Compensation for certain kinds of works can be accomplished through means other than copyright. For example, most academic writings are compensated by grants, salaries, or incentive payments from universities; the down-stream royalties are negligible for most scholarly articles. Governments publish vast quantities of information they pay to have written or produced. Advertising has long paid for magazines and newspapers and supports many online purveyors of information including blogs such as The Huffington Post.[109] The argument that copyright is needed to induce the creation of works through property rights-mediated compensation is not a complete defense of the property rights model. For various works in various settings other sorts of compensation schemes work better and will work better in the future. We need to look beyond received models and we need to creatively develop new models and to apply compensation models that are already tried and proven.[110]

---

[109] The Huffington Post—The Blog, http://www.huffingtonpost.com/theblog/ (last visited Aug. 24, 2011).

[110] *See generally*, Lateef Mtima & Steven D. Jamar, *Fulfilling the Copyright Social Justice Promise: Digitizing Textual Information*, 55 N.Y.L.S.L. REV. 77, 98–101 (2010).

Not all works are or should be treated the same way. Not all environments are or should be treated the same way. The Internet and new Internet-mediated technologies continue to challenge copyright. Youtube, Facebook, social networking in general create special and novel demands. Digitizing music, text, and video create new challenges. New forms of works including interactive video games, massive multi-player online games, and cloud computing all bring new challenges. These sorts of differences need to be accommodated in intellectual property. Music and software are not the same. Fan fiction has a different impact than derivative works of utilitarian software. *De minimis* sampling is simply using available raw material, not harmful infringing.

If the rights are too broad, too strong, too vigorously protected, then innovation, empowerment, and inclusion will suffer. The ability to make derivative works, to use works, to disseminate works, and even to create new works inspired by existing works will be chilled, even if they would otherwise still be lawful.

If the rights granted are too weak, then the incentive to create will be reduced, the powerful, moneyed interests will exploit the creative works of the weak, and the incentive to disseminate will be reduced. This too is not good for inclusion and empowerment.

Balance is what is required. Protect intellectual property, but do not tie up works so tightly that cultural participation and development are stymied.

7. Contrasts in innovation: Pittsburgh then and now

Michael J. Madison*

I INTRODUCTION

Discussion and analysis of law, public policy, and economic growth is often predictive, and often national or global. Tweak a rule or doctrine here, perhaps patent law or tax law or financial and securities regulation, and anticipate growth there—in the United States, or in India, or around the world. This chapter approaches the question of growth from a different angle, working backward from an example of economic development to understand, if possible, what accounted for it, and focusing on regional rather than national or global growth. My subject is Pittsburgh, Pennsylvania, U.S.A. I offer a descriptive account of one city's and region's work in progress in transitioning from Rust Belt collapse to Rust Belt chic,[1] or what President Barack Obama characterized as a "model for the future" in its transition to a diverse economy,[2] when he decided that the city would be the North American host of the September 2009 summit of the Group of 20 (G-20) finance ministers.[3]

---

* Portions of this chapter first appeared as a series of posts at Pittsblog 2.0, a weblog, at http://pittsblog.blogspot.com, over several days in September 2009. Thanks to Megan Carpenter for her interest in this work and to colleagues at the Evolving Economies conference at Texas Wesleyan University School of Law in April 2011, where a version of the work was presented.
[1] *See* Tod Newcombe, *The Rust Belt Has Arrived*, at GOVERNING: CONNECTING AMERICA'S LEADERS, Feb. 2011, *available at* http://www.governing.com/columns/urban-notebook/Rust-Belt-Arrived.html (last visited June 2, 2011).
[2] *See* Dan Malloy, *Obama calls Pittsburgh a model for the future*, PITTSBURGH POST-GAZETTE, Sept. 20, 2009, *available at* http://www.post-gazette.com/pg/09263/999493-482.stm (last visited June 2, 2011).
[3] *See* Kris Maher & James R. Hagerty, *Pittsburgh Scores the G-20 Summit*, WALL ST. J., May 29, 2009, at A3, *available at* http://online.wsj.com/article/SB124353544415163511.html. In the months leading up to the announcement in May 2009 of Pittsburgh's selection for the G-20, Pittsburgh had attracted impressive national media attention for its renewal. *See, e.g.,* David Streitfeld, *For*

I frame the description in terms supplied initially by the urban economist Benjamin Chinitz. Chinitz published a paper in 1961 titled "*Contrasts in Agglomeration: New York and Pittsburgh*," from which the title of this chapter is adapted.[4] Chinitz contrasted the respective "agglomeration economies" of two leading U.S. cities, New York, with its massive concentration of garment firms, and Pittsburgh, with its world-leading integrated steel producers. New York, Chinitz hypothesized, had the brighter economic future in the event that its leading industry declined, because of the heterogeneity of the suppliers that comprised that economy. Chinitz reasoned by examining supply side considerations, that is, the inputs into industrial production, rather than on demand- or consumer-side considerations. New York's garment business was defined by a plethora of small firms; that diversity of firms attracted a broad and complementary range of small, independent suppliers. Pittsburgh's steel industry, the anchor of a highly specialized manufacturing economy, was dominated by a small number of very large integrated firms; comparatively few ancillary firms served as suppliers. The two regions had different patterns of "agglomerated" or adjacent industries. If their specific architectures were to break down, Chinitz argued, the underlying components of New York—small-scale entrepreneurship, widely distributed labor, capital, and land—would serve New York well in supporting the reconstruction of new industry.

Pittsburgh is in many ways a test case for Chinitz's hypothesis, and not only because it was one of the cities that Chinitz reviewed in 1961. For most of the 20th century, Pittsburgh's steelmakers were leading examples worldwide of American economic prowess. Pittsburgh was so vibrant with industry that a late 19th-century travel writer called Pittsburgh "hell with the lid taken off," and he meant that as a compliment.[5] In the early 1980s, however, Pittsburgh's steel economy collapsed, a victim of changing worldwide demand for steel and the industry's inflexible commitment to a large-scale integrated production model.[6] As the steel industry collapsed,

Pittsburgh, There's Life After Steel, N.Y. TIMES, Jan. 8, 2009, at A1, *available at* http://www.nytimes.com/2009/01/08/business/economy/08collapse.html.

[4] Benjamin Chinitz, *Contrasts in Agglomeration: New York and Pittsburgh*, 51 AM. ECON. REV. PAPERS AND PROC. OF THE 73RD ANN. MTG. OF THE AM. ECON. ASS'N 279 (1961).

[5] *See* James Parton, *Pittsburg*, ATLANTIC MONTHLY, Jan. 1868, at 17, 21.

[6] The timing and causes of that collapse have been widely chronicled. *See* CLAYTON M. CHRISTENSEN, THE INNOVATOR'S DILEMMA: WHEN NEW TECHNOLOGIES CAUSE GREAT FIRMS TO FAIL 88-93 (Boston, MA, U.S.A.: Harvard Business School Press, 1997); JOHN P. HOERR, AND THE WOLF FINALLY CAME: THE DECLINE AND FALL OF THE AMERICAN STEEL INDUSTRY (Pittsburgh, PA, U.S.A.: Pittsburgh University Press, 1988).

the Pittsburgh region collapsed, too. Unemployment in some parts of the Pittsburgh region peaked at 20 percent. More than 100,000 manufacturing jobs disappeared. Tens of thousands of residents moved away—annually. Over the last thirty years, Pittsburgh has slowly recovered, building a new economy that balances limited manufacturing with a broad range of high-quality services. Most observers agree that Pittsburgh has managed an extraordinary transformation since then, evolving from a city and region dominated by heavy industry to a city dominated by what local leaders call "eds and meds": higher education (eds) and medical services (meds) and their spinoffs and spillovers. Forty years ago, manufacturing accounted for more than a quarter of all employment in Pittsburgh; today manufacturing accounts for well under ten percent of Pittsburgh employment. Forty years ago, medical services accounted for just over five percent of Pittsburgh employment. Today, health care contributes more than 15 percent of Pittsburgh's jobs. Teasing apart the causes and effects of that transformation yields some important insights into the accuracy of Chinitz's hypothesis, and relatedly, into the roles of law and the legal system in promoting and supporting regional rebirth.

II   THEORIZING ABOUT REGIONAL ECONOMICS

The Theoretical Challenge

"Innovation" is a buzzword of the 21st century. Countries, states, regions, cities, universities, and individuals all are urged to innovate—or fail. Innovation has its role in Chinitz's theory of regional growth, as I describe below, but innovation is only one part of the story to be told. Pittsburgh's emergence as a post-industrial city and region depends on elements of innovation, but the more significant story, and the one that has taken root locally, is not a story of finance and economics. It is a story of something akin to individual and collective well-being, measured largely by capacity and capability: the construction of a set of institutions and other social structures that supply opportunities and resources for individual and communal thriving.[7] Importantly, Pittsburghers know this, and see this. Many

---

[7]   The phrasing here is intentionally evocative of Amartya Sen's work on development and freedom. *See* AMARTYA SEN, DEVELOPMENT AS FREEDOM 3 (New York, NY, U.S.A.: Alfred A. Knopf, 1999) ("Development can be seen, it is argued here, as a process of expanding the real freedoms that people enjoy."); Amartya Sen, *Capability and Well-Being*, in Martha Nussbaum & Amartya Sen (eds), THE QUALITY OF LIFE 30, 30 (Oxford, UK: Oxford University Press, 1993).

of the objective metrics of Pittsburgh's economic performance (job creation, income, population) are stagnant or only modestly positive. The one
thing that Pittsburgh prides itself on is comparatively low unemployment.
It also has "livability," according to various published indices, which
is largely a product of ratings schemes that value low and slow-moving
residential real estate values—something that usually characterize a slug-
gish economy, rather than a vibrant one. A broader view of well-being
is needed simply because somewhat paradoxically, considering the data,
Pittsburgh has its mojo back.

Framing an analysis of that phenomenon in theoretical terms is, needless to say, a challenge. What explains relative communal well-being? The
question being asked is problematic for any number of reasons.

First is measurement. What I am after is not simply an explanation
for economic growth, even though growth considerations dominate most
narratives and analyses—even this one. Like many recovering industrial
regions, Pittsburgh has not experienced much growth in income or output
over the last thirty years. Instead, Pittsburgh has experienced a slowly
declining population, relative price stability, modestly increasing employment in the services sector and continued decline in the manufacturing
sector, and a sense of collective place-based satisfaction, if not always outright optimism. This combination clearly distinguishes Pittsburgh today
from Pittsburgh of fifteen or twenty-five years ago. Few Pittsburghers
would deny that in many significant respects, Pittsburgh is at least on its
way back to relative health. But the renewal of a place takes many forms,
and it is renewal relative to a specific moment in history, rather than an
altogether new beginning or growth in the abstract.

Second is scale. Pittsburgh's renewal has taken place against (and has
been grounded in) both local and global changes. At the local level, over
the last fifty years Pittsburgh has experienced an inside-out demographic
shift, a re-centering of regional population from urban core to suburban
periphery, that resembles that of many of similar regions. The historic
political boundaries of the city of Pittsburgh have not changed in many
decades. The city proper has long been and remains quite small in population and geographic terms. Roughly 300,000 souls call the city home
today, or roughly half of the city's population at its peak in the 1950s. The
population of the Pittsburgh region, taking account of Allegheny County
(Pittsburgh's location) and a surrounding ring of counties, is just more
than 2 million people; that overall total has declined only slightly over
the same period. That population shift from city to suburb is a familiar
one. But that shift masks the fact that much of Pittsburgh's legacy industrial communities are peripheral. Much of Pittsburgh's steel production
was located in the region's river valleys, well away from the urban core,

in communities that, unlike many modern suburbs, are poorly suited to being repurposed as centers of new business or as bedroom communities for commuters. The collapse of the steel industry emptied out both the city and the suburbs; the region, but not the city, has been repopulated. At the global level, Pittsburgh is, like all mid-sized American cities, connected to cities and communities worldwide by patterns of travel and commerce that simply did not exist even thirty years ago. Virtually every significant business enterprise in Pittsburgh today depends on global webs of suppliers and customers in ways that differ significantly from older patterns, when steel was sold globally but produced locally. Segregating the causes of Pittsburgh's renewal from larger demographic and economic trends may be difficult; in fact, those trends may be part of the story.

Third is the unit of analysis. Regional economics and regional renewal are sometimes assumed to be good in their own right. That perspective runs the risk of overlooking connections between regional and national outcomes and connections between regional and global outcomes. It is possible, for example, that regional policy initiatives directed at one region will produce positive or benign spillover effects on adjacent communities, but it is also possible that those spillovers will be negative. What is good for Pittsburgh may or may not be good for Cleveland, Ohio (a peer city, to its northwest) or Morgantown, West Virginia (a much smaller city, to its south). At the same time, it is unwise to focus analysis exclusively at the national level. National well-being depends in critical ways on local well-being. There must be some articulated relationship between the two.[8] Communal or collective analysis also runs the risk of interfering with achieving the goal of improving individual outcomes. Growth or well-being depends ultimately on improving the lives of individuals, wherever they live.

Fourth is the work that has been done already on regional innovation and prosperity, much of which I wish to distinguish, if briefly. Contemporary scholarship on public policy and legal solutions to regional innovation and growth dilemmas, with some salient exceptions, abstracts from the particular history of place and the particular characteristics of population and community. One cluster of explanations for growth, and related prescriptions, focuses on incentives and markets. Market demand shapes the growth and success of firms and therefore shapes the success (or failure) of the communities inhabited by those firms. Policymakers should emphasize fair and competitive market conditions,

---

[8]   Chinitz made this point long ago. *See* Benjamin Chinitz, *Appropriate Goals for Regional Economic Policy*, 3 URB. STUD. 1 (1966).

should ensure that firms and individuals have suitable incentives to participate in market transactions and are appropriately secure in their capital and other resource investments, and then should largely anticipate that demand will organize those resources in productive ways. For example, it is argued that inventing and patenting new technologies will structure research and development investments, both in the university sector and in the private sector, leading to additional public and private investment, new product development, new company formation, jobs, and income.[9] Gillian Hadfield suggests that laws and lawyers themselves should be freed from conventional and traditional organization in law firms and freed to migrate, via market demand, to better and more innovative uses.[10] Entrepreneurs and innovators would value basic legal advice supplied via forms available through low-cost legal information providers, rather than through high-cost law offices. A second cluster of related arguments is rather more "top down" and government-driven than "bottom-up" incentive-based approaches. Annalee Saxenian and Ronald Gilson, among others, have emphasized the relative openness of labor markets in high-velocity entrepreneurial communities, particularly the Silicon Valley in California,[11] and have contrasted those markets and outcomes favorably with counterparts elsewhere, notably Boston.[12] Labor mobility in California is higher than in other regions, particularly for skilled employees, because state law prohibits enforcement of most noncompetition agreements. Richard Florida and his colleagues are associated with research and related proposals to stimulate urban revitalization by attracting young creative professionals.[13] Land use and tax strategies have been developed to attract real estate development and/ or to concentrate real estate development, via Euclidean zoning (during much of the 20th century) and more recently through strategies grouped

---

[9]   *See generally* THE KAUFFMAN TASK FORCE ON LAW, INNOVATION, AND GROWTH RULES FOR GROWTH: PROMOTING INNOVATION AND GROWTH THROUGH LEGAL REFORM (Kansas City, MO, U.S.A.: Ewing Marion Kauffman Foundation, 2011) (hereinafter, "KAUFFMAN").

[10]   *See* Gillian Hadfield, *Producing Law for Innovation*, in KAUFFMAN, at 23.

[11]   *See* Ronald J. Gilson, *The Legal Infrastructure of High Technology Districts: Silicon Valley, Route 128, and Covenants Not to Compete*, 74 N.Y.U. L. REV. 575 (1999).

[12]   *See* ANNALEE SAXENIAN, REGIONAL ADVANTAGE: CULTURE AND COMPETITION IN SILICON VALLEY AND ROUTE 128 (Cambridge, MA, U.S.A.: Harvard University Press, 1994).

[13]   *See* RICHARD FLORIDA, THE RISE OF THE CREATIVE CLASS (New York, NY, U.S.A.: Basic Books, 2002).

under "New Urbanist" models[14] and "Edge City" models, particularly
with respect to populations, industries, and firms that are thought to have
demographic and other locational advantages relative to existing natural
or other regional resources, that is, that are thought to represent demand
for one form of infrastructure or another. Public/private partnerships or
governance arrangements combine these approaches.

Each of these strategies is, in one respect or another, largely "demand"
driven rather than "supply" driven. The assumption is that a region or
community can use law and policy to create or shape a set of demand
curves for resources and for human, financial, and cultural capital. Once
demand is specified—or stimulated, by importing young "creatives," for
example—then markets and structures will evolve to supply needed and
desired goods and services. These may be both tangible and intangible—
jobs, income, wealth, happiness—and they will emerge roughly in response
to signals processed through those markets. All markets are subject to a
broad variety of imperfections, and public policy advises that governments (among other institutions) should not only set in motion the processes of ensuring the relatively smooth functioning of these markets but
also should step in to minimize the harms of flawed markets (inequality
of capability and opportunity, for example, such as limited educational
options) and to maximize their benefits (wealth generation, for example,
or opportunities for self-determination through educational attainment
and career development).

The Chinitz Framework

The foregoing summary paints with a broad brush. My point for the
balance of this chapter is that the brush does not paint broadly enough. I
am not an economist and therefore do not confine my thinking or analysis to economic questions. But I am interested in economics, just as I am
interested in history, culture, geography, and politics. All of those bear
on how the law influences regional renewal, just as law influences each
of these disciplines separately. And a "demand" side account of regional
economics, policy, history, and law is incomplete. One should also look
at the "supply" side. That perspective was the distinct contribution of
Benjamin Chinitz. One of my goals in this chapter is to introduce Chinitz

---

[14] *See, e.g.,* Brian W. Ohm & Robert J. Sitkowski, *The Influence of New
Urbanism on Local Ordinances: The Twilight of Zoning?*, 35 URB. LAW. 783 (2003)
(describing impact of "New Urbanist" policy initiatives). Perhaps the most notori-
ous of these strategies has been using low-cost public financing to subsidize the
construction of stadiums and arenas for professional sports teams.

to a contemporary generation of scholars, particularly legal scholars, who are not acquainted with his work.

Chinitz recognized and agreed upon the communal ends of regional economic analysis: knowledge and innovation spillovers in markets for labor and capital, leading to formation of firms, creation of jobs, rising income, greater equality of opportunity and access to communal resources. The question he considered was the extent to which performance of one industry affects performance of other industries in the same region. He contended that existing analyses did not pay enough attention to supply-side considerations, precisely because demand-driven models paid too much attention to contemporary considerations (static effects) and too little attention to the future (dynamic effects). Noting that diversified "agglomeration" economies (characterized by smaller independent firms, such as New York in the 1950s) grow more quickly than non-diverse economies (such as Pittsburgh during the same period), Chinitz wrote:

> Suppose we project a sharp decline in the dominant industries along with a modest decline in the region's minor industries. True, the dominant industries will retard the growth of the region but in the process they will also decline in relative importance. The region will then become more diversified in its old age, so to speak. What then? Do we correct for the increased diversification? Does it open up new opportunities to the region? [¶] The need to understand the whys and wherefores of diversification should therefore be quite apparent.[15]

Chinitz expressed his basic hypothesis this way: "[A]gglomeration is nourished more by the availability of a wide range of goods and services created in the first instance by the growth of the dominant industries."[16] The question was why? He identified the challenge of specifying where the sources and supply of that diversification—more new firms—might come from, looking at four traditional sources: entrepreneurship, labor, capital, and land. The supply of each of these, he argued, varied across regions, for reasons having to do with history and culture as much as with incentives and markets.

Of entrepreneurship, Chinitz wrote that regions might vary in their supplies of entrepreneurship, not only because entrepreneurs might migrate to some regions rather than others but also because the culture of risk-taking might vary from place to place. Chinitz called this the "entrepreneurial birth rate"[17]:

---

15   Chinitz, *supra* note 4, at 281.
16   *Id.* at 288.
17   *Id.* at 285.

An industry which is competitively organized–in the neoclassical sense of the term "competition"—has more entrepreneurs per dollar of output than an industry which is organized along oligopolistic lines. The average establishment in the apparel industry, for example, has one-sixth as many employees as the average establishment in primary metals. Furthermore, multi-unit firms account for 82 per cent of the employment in primary metals, while they account for only 28 per cent of employment in apparel. Now you may have as much management per dollar of output in primary metals as you have in apparel, but you certainly do not have as many managers who are also risk-takers and this is my definition of an entrepreneur. [¶] What is the consequence of this? My feeling is that you do not breed as many entrepreneurs per capita in families allied with steel as you do in families allied with apparel, using these two industries for illustrative purposes only.[18]

That entrepreneurial "birth rate" would be coupled, Chinitz hypothesized, with a corresponding lack of cultural receptivity to in-migration of entrepreneurs.

Of capital, Chinitz suggested that it is less mobile inter-regionally than might be supposed. New firms were and are far more likely to find investors locally and regionally than elsewhere, and in regions dominated by large firms, surplus capital was far more likely to be distributed internally, inside the firm, than externally, to new firms, because profits were returned to shareholders and key employees. Bankers in diverse economies are more likely to spread their investments across a range of firms and industries than they are in oligopolistic economies, out of self-interest as well as necessity. Banks require a certain level of return to maintain profitability, and risk diversification is an explicit strategy supporting that goal. Chinitz used a regional economy dominated by US Steel and Westinghouse, two of Pittsburgh's leading firms of the time, to make his point.

Of labor, Chinitz suggested that regional differences in costs attributable to distinctions between diverse and less diverse economies could be traced in part to wage scales offered by oligopolistic firms. Pittsburgh's steelworkers were extremely well-paid and therefore had little financial incentive to explore different opportunities. Chinitz also noted that wage scales and the demands of twenty-four-hour manufacturing cycles depressed the participation of women in the workforce. Finally, he contrasted the confluence of Pittsburgh's hilly topography and distribution of integrated manufacturing across a broad area with the concentration of small firms in New York's garment district. Labor costs in the latter were considerably lower.

As to land, Chinitz's concern was with spillover environmental effects

---

[18]   *Id.* at 284.

of the widespread industrialization that he associated with the Pittsburgh region, and particularly with Pittsburgh's notoriously dirty air, and with the associated reputation impact of environmental quality on firms' willingness to locate in that region. By the time Chinitz was writing, however, Pittsburgh's historic air quality problem was already well on its way to resolution.

Chinitz's account of labor costs and natural resources has an anachronistic feel, but in sum his argument resonates with the following proposition: growth-oriented economies rely on a culture of entrepreneurship and investment that feeds and builds upon a heterogeneous field of small and smaller independent firms. In Chinitz's framework these are "agglomeration" economies, in which firms in one industry attract firms in other industries. In modern terms these are "innovation" economies, in which innovation in one field leads to firm growth and to innovation and growth in adjacent fields. That parallel is drawn today in the work of Harvard economist Edward Glaeser. Glaeser has written:

> All over the country, urban growth depends upon urban entrepreneurship—though measuring that entrepreneurship is easier said than done. There are at least three plausible, widely available statistical measures of entrepreneurial activity: average firm size, the entry rate of new unaffiliated establishments, and the self-employment rate. Average firm size distinguishes between places like Detroit, dominated by a few large employers, and places like Brooklyn, with an abundance of smaller, nimbler firms. The smaller a city's average firm, the thinking goes, the more entrepreneurial the city. The entry rate of new unaffiliated establishments, probably the most direct measure of entrepreneurial activity, refers to the percentage of employees in a metropolitan area who are working in new firms that don't share ownership with preexisting ones. As for the self-employment rate, it is a considerably less popular measure among economists, since it doesn't capture many important forms of entrepreneurship—hedge-fund managers, for example, rarely work for themselves—and is swamped by very modest entrepreneurs.
>
> None of the three measures is a perfect barometer of that hard-to-define quantity that we call entrepreneurship. But the good news is that all three usually move together. That is, places with smaller firms tend to have a high entry rate of new unaffiliated establishments, and they also tend to have high self-employment rates. The three measures suggest that levels of entrepreneurship differ substantially across regions of the country. [19]

Glaeser translates that account into a basic policy prescription that aligns with Chinitz's hypothesis: "Since important innovation is inherently

---

[19]   Edward L. Glaeser, *Start-Up City*, 20 CITY JOURNAL No. 4 (Autumn 2010), *available at* http://www.city-journal.org/2010/20_4_urban-entrepreneurship.html (last visited June 2, 2011).

unpredictable, the best economic-development policy may be to attract entrepreneurial people and get out of their way."[20]

How to do that—how to attract and keep entrepreneurs, build entrepreneurship, and sustain an innovation economy and an "agglomeration" economy of entrepreneurs attracting entrepreneurs and related service providers across industries—becomes the question that challenges policymakers everywhere. Is it the right question? The evidence from Pittsburgh goes to that point. As I turn from this account of theory to a narrative of Pittsburgh's recent revival, the theme to bear in mind is the extent to which Pittsburgh's relative prosperity today is due to features of the region that are designed to attract entry by new independent firms—that is, entrepreneurship—or at least, in Chinitz's framework, tend to enable entry.

III   THE STORY BEHIND PITTSBURGH'S REVITALIZATION

The following account of Pittsburgh today is somewhat impressionistic, just as Chinitz's account was in 1961. I have been observing Pittsburgh's progress for the last thirteen years as a resident of the region, and since 2003 I have been writing about the region, with a focus on economic development topics, at a weblog titled "Pittsblog."[21] The core of what follows is adapted from a long series of blog posts that I wrote over the summer of 2009, leading up to the G-20 summit held in Pittsburgh in late September

---

[20]   *Id.* Glaeser's research is summed up in a recent book. *See* EDWARD L. GLAESER, TRIUMPH OF THE CITY: HOW OUR GREATEST INVENTION MAKES US RICHER, SMARTER, GREENER, HEALTHIER, AND HAPPIER (New York, NY, U.S.A.: Penguin Press, 2011). *See also* Edward L. Glaeser, *The New Economics of Urban and Regional Growth,* in THE OXFORD HANDBOOK OF ECONOMIC GEOGRAPHY (Gordon L. Clark et al., (eds), Oxford, UK: Oxford University Press, 2003), at 83 (emphasizing the role of human capital); Edward L. Glaeser & William R. Kerr, Local Industrial Conditions and Entrepreneurship: How Much of the Spatial Distribution Can We Explain?, 18 J. ECON. & MAN. STRAT. 623 (2009) (summarizing data consistent with Chinitz's thesis that new manufacturing entrants are associated with regions with many smaller suppliers). Glaeser's work is echoed in the writing of urbanists who resist the prescription of Richard Florida, who argues that cities should attract young "creatives." *See* JOEL KOTKIN, THE CITY: A GLOBAL HISTORY (New York, NY, U.S.A.: Modern Library, 2005) (focusing broadly on the role of human capital in cities, and arguing that public policy should address three goals: keeping cities safe, busy (or vital), and sacred (filled with lives authentically lived).

[21]   *See* PITTSBLOG 2.0, http://pittsblog.blogspot.com (last visited June 2, 2011).

2009, which aimed to moderate some of the boosterish storyline that the leaders of the city and the region were feeding to the press.[22]

Background and History

How did Pittsburgh do it? How did Pittsburgh "revitalize" and achieve the renewal that justified its selection as the site of a global financial summit?

I start with a modestly contrarian premise. Did Pittsburgh revitalize itself? No. Cities do not "revitalize" themselves, at least not if one assumes that "cities" or "a city" can decide to do such a thing. Has Pittsburgh been revitalized? In some superficial (though nonetheless important) respects, yes. In many structural ways, no. Some, including the current mayor of Pittsburgh, take their case a step farther, arguing that the city is undergoing a renaissance, the third in a series that dates back to the mid-1950s (the first Pittsburgh renaissance, of which more below) and to the early 1980s (the second renaissance, of which more below, as well). Is there a renaissance underway in Pittsburgh as the second decade of the 21st century dawns? Not really.

There is no doubt that the tone of the city and the region is different and sunnier now than it was a decade ago, and that both psychic and economic conditions are vastly improved over conditions in the mid-1980s. Pittsburgh's growing international reputation as a successful post-industrial city is not altogether undeserved. As I argue below, a key factor has been that the cost of living in Pittsburgh has remained extremely low relative to the growing range and depth of its urban amenities. As Pittsburgh's business climate has improved and as its economy has gotten more diverse, the benefits from those changes have not been diverted into sustaining fast-growing, ever more expensive markets for real estate and other resources. But why has the region evolved in this way?

A tale of post-industrial beginnings, at any scale, begins in part with a tale of industrial endings. In many significant respects, Pittsburgh's current success begins with Pittsburgh's massive failure. As almost everyone in the world knows, for the first half of the 20th century Pittsburgh was the home of an extraordinary and extraordinarily successful confluence of industry and finance. Pittsburgh built the world. The steel industry and its related manufacturing and financial industries were so successful, wealthy, and powerful in the Pittsburgh region that they largely interfered with processes of entrepreneurship that might have diversified the economy. The

---

[22]   *See, e.g., The Revival of Pittsburgh: Lessons for the G20,* THE ECONOMIST, Sept. 17, 2009, *available at* http://www.economist.com/node/14460542.

demise of steel in the 1970s and 1980s was not a surprise to those paying careful attention. It was foreseen by economists and planners,[23] and its effects—which were dramatic and traumatic—might have been mitigated.[24] But in significant respects, planning for the transition—planning for a transition to an economy not based on large-scale, high-wage employment by integrated industrial manufacturers—was not done. When the steel industry collapsed in the early 1980s, the city and region collapsed with it. More than one hundred thousand of steel-related jobs disappeared (high-paying jobs, to boot, thanks to the effective work of strong labor unions).[25] Hundreds of thousands of people moved out of the region, and with them and their jobs went a significant amount of local income. Not only did the mills close, but neighborhood economies and entire mill towns all but closed, too.

What Pittsburgh was left with was little more than its legacy social infrastructure, a Downtown neighborhood dedicated to the financial institutions and law firms that supported the steel industry and the corporate headquarters of other major local manufacturers, the dozens of

---

[23] *See* PITTSBURGH REGIONAL PLANNING ASSOCIATION, ECONOMIC STUDY OF THE PITTSBURGH REGION, vols. 1–4 (1963–1964) (hereinafter, "ESPR"). The four volumes of the ESPR had different titles: Region in Transition (vol. 1); Portrait of a Region (vol. 2), Region with a Future (vol. 3), and Summary (vol. 4.) The authors of the ESPR, associated with the University of Pittsburgh, noted that Pittsburgh's overall economic success masked severe deficiencies in how the region treated human resources – its people. The region was characterized by slow population growth, a net outmigration of population, a lag in employment opportunities compared to other metropolitan areas, a low proportion of women in the labor force, a below-average rise in per capita income compared to the nation; above-average unemployment, an underrepresentation of small firms in the economy, an excessive income spread between high and low wage sectors, an excess of residents in non-productive age groups, and a proportion of blue-collar workers above average for the nation, urban areas, and large metropolitan communities. Benjamin Chinitz was a member of the team that produced the ESPR, and his *Contrasts in Agglomeration* paper was published mid-way through the study's completion.

[24] The authors of the ESPR specifically encouraged adoption of public policies in the region that would address the needs of its workers, particularly in the areas of education, training, job mobility, and health. Ironically, but not coincidentally, many of the same recommendations emerged from the pioneering Pittsburgh Study of 1907–08, a comprehensive sociological account of the city's turn-of-the-century urban living conditions. *See* Maurine W. Greenwald & Margo Anderson, PITTSBURGH SURVEYED: SOCIAL SCIENCE AND SOCIAL REFORM IN THE EARLY TWENTIETH CENTURY (Pittsburgh, PA, U.S.A.: University of Pittsburgh Press, 1996).

[25] *See* Mary E. Deily, *Wages in the Steel Industry: Take the Money and Run?*, 37 INDUS. REL.: J. ECON. & SOC. 153 (1998).

neighborhoods that make up the city of Pittsburgh and the many small towns around the region that had grown up and grown wealthy around the mills. Many of those neighborhoods and towns were anchored by the descendants of the Eastern and Southern European immigrants who populated Pittsburgh in the late 19th century and the descendants of the Scots-Irish immigrants to Appalachia, who populated Pittsburgh a century earlier.[26] Pittsburgh's many small communities were and are strong in cultural terms. Even as many of them struggled economically they provided an important social fabric for the city's remaining population; I refer to them as a "lattice" that supports new growth over time. But those communities did not provide the energy that has begun to restore the area.

Paradoxically, much of that energy has come from many of the same legacy institutions that were ineffective in planting the seeds for a smoother transition to a post-steel economy. Three of these deserve special note. Beginning in the 1950s, Pittsburgh's business and government leaders worked together on what was and remains known as "Renaissance I."[27] This was an unusual public–private partnership to move the city forward by improving the quality of life across a wide spectrum of class and community, particularly via physical improvements. Among other things, private real estate investment was channeled through public authorities. The most visible of these efforts were those of the Allegheny Conference on Community Development (the ACCD), a private group of civic leaders founded in the 1940s. The ACCD's membership was drawn mostly from the business community, including some leading bankers, led by Richard King Mellon, and a department store magnate, Edgar Kaufmann, who partnered with the city of Pittsburgh, led by Mayor David Lawrence, and Allegheny County. Its mission was to address some of the region's most pressing environmental and infrastructure issues. The ACCD led efforts to clear Downtown Pittsburgh of the relics of its industrial past. The Downtown neighborhood in Pittsburgh constitutes what is sometimes called the "Golden Triangle," because it occupies land defined by the confluence of the Monongahela River (rising from Pittsburgh's south) and the Allegheny River (descending from Pittsburgh's north), which join in Pittsburgh to form the head of the great Ohio River (giving rise to one of the city's nicknames: the City of Three Rivers). The tip of the Golden Triangle is known as the Point, and in the 1950s train sheds that had occu-

---

[26]   *See* FRANKLIN TOKER, PITTSBURGH: A NEW Portrait (Pittsburgh, PA, U.S.A.: University of Pittsburgh Press, 2009).
[27]   Its formal name, originally, was the Pittsburgh Renaissance Project.

pied the Point for decades, because of its location as an obvious transportation node, were replaced beginning in 1952 by the Gateway Center office and apartment towers.[28]

Renaissance I was about more than real estate development. Via local ordinances banning the burning of soft coal in residential furnaces, Pittsburgh's skies were largely cleared of their legendary smoke. During the 1950s and into the 1960s, the ACCD supported development of modern, regional water and sewer systems, supported the integration of a host of local transit systems into a county-wide Port Authority, renovated the remaining land at the Point into a showcase "Point State Park," and pushed for construction of new cultural amenities that would attract and retain businessmen and their families who might have been tempted to locate in larger cities. In 1961, a "Civic Auditorium" (soon, the "Civic Arena") opened. The steel-domed building, later nicknamed "The Igloo" because of its inverted-bowl appearance and its primary association with the Pittsburgh Penguins of the National Hockey League, was originally conceived as a concert venue and particularly as a home for the Pittsburgh Civic Light Opera. A minor-league ice hockey team competed there. The Penguins arrived later, in 1967.

Renaissance I and the ACCD have long been widely recognized for sowing seeds that paid off in the short term. The developments identified above have paid off over the longer term as well, even if Pittsburgh's contemporary political leaders and the modern ACCD itself no longer operate collaboratively in the *noblesse oblige* mode that helped accomplish so much fifty years ago. Had Renaissance I not taken place, it is difficult to imagine Pittsburgh looking as relatively bright as it does today. Renaissance II, a renewed public–private partnership initiated under the leadership of Mayor Richard Caligiuri in the late 1970s, witnessed the construction of a number of modern office towers and hotels in Downtown Pittsburgh, the most striking of which is the complex of glass-sided buildings designed by the modernist architect Philip Johnson and called PPG Place, after its principal tenant PPG Industries, and a new convention center. Renaissance II modestly extended the impact of Renaissance I on Pittsburgh's landscape, and it broadened the scope of public/private efforts by addressing interests of Pittsburgh's substantial not-for-profit community, its universities, and a broader array of residents. In the mid-1980s, three hospitals affiliated with the University of Pittsburgh became part

---

[28] Still in good condition more than fifty years later, these were unusually successful examples of urban redevelopment inspired by the "Towers in a Park" vision of the modernist architect Le Corbusier.

of a single organization that evolved into Pittsburgh's modern medical behemoth, the University of Pittsburgh Medical Center, now UPMC Health Systems. But Renaissance II lacked the momentum of Renaissance I; new skyscrapers in Downtown Pittsburgh could not offset the dramatic events unfolding along Pittsburgh's rivers, the demise of steel.

In addition to the ACCD and Renaissance I, the second major institutional development of fifty years ago was one that attracted far less notice at the time and had relatively modest short-term implications for Pittsburgh. It was a move that in time has made a world of difference to the modern city and region. In the 1950s, various wings of the Mellon family, scions of the banking empire that bore that name, donated more than $50 million to the University of Pittsburgh (known as Pitt) to finance the construction of a new medical school and to endow the program. For the first time, Pitt and Pittsburgh were in a position to operate a world-class medical research institution. Jonas Salk was a young researcher at Pitt in the early 1950s, and in Pittsburgh he researched and tested what became the polio vaccine.[29]

The long-term payoff of the 1950s investment in Pitt's medical school and research program has been profound, however. The clinical program at what grew into the University of Pittsburgh Medical Center benefited from enormous publicity surrounding its transplantation practice in the 1980s and 1990s, and today is recognized as among the world's best. UPMC, now an autonomous enterprise with clinical, hospital, and insurance divisions, has become one of the largest and most economically influential institutions in the region and the leading presence among the area's "meds," or medical services providers. On the research side, UPMC and the University of Pittsburgh together account for close to $1 billion in federal research funds annually, a result of strategic decisions made over the last fifteen years to build considerably on the region's biomedical research foundation. That figure has gone up dramatically over the last ten years. Among other things, the increase represents a significant and strategic decision by contemporary leaders at Pitt and UPMC to build on a regional asset that was first identified when steel still ruled the city. Pitt's share alone puts it in elite company, with Harvard, John Hopkins, and the University of California San Diego as its peers.

---

[29]   In a preview of what has become a complex local, national, and international debate about universities' pursuit of patents and profits at the expense of the public interest, Salk famously refused to patent his work, so that it could be distributed as broadly and inexpensively as possible. The University of Pittsburgh, at least initially, wanted to pursue a patent. Salk left Pittsburgh and established the Salk Institute in La Jolla, California, near San Diego.

The Mellon investments in Pitt's medical school are emblematic of a third and final major institutional force at work today: Pittsburgh's philanthropic community. The industrial era in Pittsburgh enabled the accumulation of enormous wealth. Much of that wealth was concentrated in a small number of Pittsburgh families that, fortunately, had the wisdom and foresight to direct much of it to philanthropy. That wealth remains at work in the region, distributed via foundations (many of them family-based), and that funding has been essential to sustaining much of Pittsburgh's cultural infrastructure, even as the collapse of steel undermined the region's economy in other critical ways. Pittsburgh's Downtown Cultural District and the city's traditional cultural institutions—the Symphony Orchestra, the Carnegie Library, and the Carnegie Museums of Pittsburgh among them—now have diversified income sources, if not always stable income sources, but they are here today in no small part because of support that is a legacy of Pittsburgh's industrial heritage.

Pittsburgh philanthropy has changed in recent years, and that change (like Pitt's strategic decision to grow its portfolio of federally-funded biomedical research) has contributed in a significant way to the recent brightening of the city. A dozen years ago, cultural philanthropy gave the outward appearance of Pittsburgh's older *noblesse oblige*. When Pittsburgh celebrated its arts and cultural communities, what it celebrated were the elite institutions that the philanthropic community and the upper tier of Pittsburgh society had long valued. Over the last decade Pittsburgh's foundations have started to take a broader and more forward-looking view of their role in the region, sometimes quite aggressively investing in artists and arts organizations that do not fit the elite model, investing in not-for-profit enterprises with missions defined by broad community impact, including neighborhood redevelopment and environmental advocacy and protection, and even occasionally investing in infrastructure for economic development throughout the region—this last being a role that in Pittsburgh was long reserved primarily for the ACCD. The philanthropic community is a long-standing Pittsburgh player that has taken on a new role.

Living

That summary demonstrates that Pittsburgh's present depends mightily on its history, as Chinitz predicted it would, and that the relevant history extends back much farther in time than the crisis in the steel industry with which Pittsburgh is popularly associated. Looking beyond Chinitz, however, the relevant history is cultural as well as economic. The spillover effects of that history are felt throughout the region. This section and the sections that follow address those spillovers, beginning with the now-vaunted "livability" of Pittsburgh.

Public relations information published by the region's official G-20 "partnership" sums up the recent news this way:

> Chosen as the most livable city in the United States for the fifth year in a row – and the 29th most livable city worldwide by The Economist, Pittsburgh offers economic stability, culture, educational opportunities and natural beauty to residents. Forbes.com also named Pittsburgh as one of the most livable cities in America, noting the city's low cost of living, crime rates and unemployment.[30]

Pittsburgh's reputation for livability depends on two key, related factors: its "economic stability" and its "low cost of living." I put those phrases in quotation marks because they are quotations, not because they are not true. They are true. Pittsburgh's unemployment rate over the last decade has consistently trailed the national unemployment rate. The average price of a house in the Pittsburgh region is less than $150,000 for a 3-bedroom, 2-bath home. That data is important. But those features are weaknesses at the same time that they are strengths. Livability is a great thing. Pittsburghers are justly proud of how recognition of the city and region as "livable" measures just how far both have recovered since the collapse of steel. But "livability" based on "economic stability" carries some big drawbacks.

That is partly because Pittsburgh shines today in contrast to its peer cities, which in many cases continue to suffer badly. By comparison with places like Buffalo, Cleveland, Detroit, Milwaukee, and St. Louis, Pittsburgh is doing pretty well overall, and by comparison it was doing pretty well overall even before the recession that began in 2008. Pittsburgh's proud place is partly a version of the old joke in which a volunteer is called to step forward from a line of candidates, and all but one member of the line takes a large step backward. Pittsburgh took its big step backward back in the 1970s and early 1980s and since then has crept forward—perceptibly but ever so slightly. In the main, its peers have taken those big backward steps more recently. Detroit, troubled most recently

[30] PITTSBURGH LIVABILITY AND AFFORDABILITY, *available at* http://www.g20pittsburghsummit.org/quality-of-life/livability-affordability/. Pittsburgh's "livability" first attracted notice in 1985 when the city was named "the most livable city in America" by a publication titled "Placed Rated Almanac." Over the last decade Pittsburgh has landed atop a number of related surveys. *See* Dan Majors, *Pittsburgh rated 'most livable' once again,* PITTSBURGH POST-GAZETTE, Apr. 26, 2007, *available at* http://www.post-gazette.com/pg/07116/781162-53.stm.

by the collapse of its automobile industry, is the salient recent example. Pittsburgh has yet to make a substantial move forward.

This is partly, also, because "livability" depends significantly on stable property values, and Pittsburgh's status owes much to the relative lack of dynamism in the local real estate market over the last several decades. While markets in places like Southern California, the desert Southwest, and Florida have gone through repeated boom and bust cycles, much of Pittsburgh's property market has motored steadily and quietly on. Western Pennsylvania does not smile on speculators, on the whole. Mortgage lending in the region never got out of hand in the early years of the 21st century. Foreclosure rates in Western Pennsylvania are lower than they are in much of the rest of the country. From the perspective of real estate values, many homeowners in Pittsburgh are reaping the benefit of the region's inherent modesty.

Low and slowly moving real estate values also owe their stability to the fact that demand for real estate is relatively low, and relatively fixed. In this second sense, "livability" means that Pittsburgh is highly livable for the people who already live there, because not that many people are moving in. Pittsburgh's foreign-born and non-native English-speaking populations are among the lowest in the United States among the top forty regions in total population. Close to 90 percent of the region's population were born in Pennsylvania, and fewer than 50,000 people move to Pittsburgh each year from outside Pennsylvania, on average. These statistics make Pittsburgh among the least transient cities in the country, a status that, one plausibly suspects, is linked historically to Pittsburgh's large-firm industrial history. Stable neighborhoods and communities complemented stable steel mills and factories. It was common for successive generations of boys and men to take the places of their fathers and grandfathers in the steel mills and, before that, in the coal mines. It was expected.

If demand for real estate were higher, values overall would move higher, and Pittsburgh's livability ratings might decline. Business Week magazine recently ranked the nation's cheapest real estate markets, places where it may be cheaper to own than rent.[31] Pittsburgh was ranked number 2. Number 1? Detroit. Low real estate values are not necessarily indicators of economic vitality. (There are signs that this may be starting to change. Real estate values in Pittsburgh are rising, from their generally low levels,

---

[31] *See* Prashant Gopal, *Why Rent When You Can Buy?*, BUSINESS WEEK, Aug. 20, 2009, *available at* http://www.businessweek.com/lifestyle/content/aug2009/bw20090819_413146.htm.

in contrast with falling real estate values in most of the United States.[32]) To the extent that there is meaningful demand for real estate in Pittsburgh, that demand is distributed unevenly across the region. Like most urban areas, Pittsburgh features its share of upscale, even outright rich communities. And some communities in the city and the region feature real estate that is astonishingly cheap by local as well as by national standards—detached single-family houses that can be had for as little as $20,000—partly because the surrounding economies are all but defunct and partly because of punitive real estate tax laws that discourage sale and redevelopment of adjacent abandoned properties. (More on tax systems below.) In this context, "livability" is not necessarily a good thing, because the structure of Pennsylvania's statewide property tax system means that cheap real estate translates into low local tax revenue and then into poor public services. Unsurprisingly, property-rich communities get wealthier. Property-poor communities lose ground.[33]

The bottom line is that "livability" is of limited value as a measure of Pittsburgh's revitalization. Many of Pittsburgh's neighborhoods are livelier than they have been in a long time. Downtown Pittsburgh, to pick one salient Pittsburgh neighborhood, is relatively safe and walkable and full of far more interesting things to do, places to live, and sights to see than it was ten or twenty or thirty years ago. As a venue for jobs, however, Downtown Pittsburgh has not changed much. Roughly 100,000 people are employed in Downtown Pittsburgh today, roughly the same number as were employed in Downtown Pittsburgh in 1960. Downtown Pittsburgh has not evaporated into the suburbs, as many American downtowns have done over the last 50 years. But neither has Downtown pushed Pittsburgh forward. Low demand is a symptom of things that are worrisome: demand is linked to growth, to wealth creation, and ultimately to the other (expensive) things—infrastructure reconstruction, for example—on which the region's continued "revitalization" depends. Even stability, staying the way that Pittsburgh is now, requires change. It requires money; it requires investment; it requires new people and new capital to replenish the well as other people and capital leave, as they will and do.

---

[32]   *See* Erich Schwartzel, *Home prices rose in region in first quarter*, PITTSBURGH POST-GAZETTE, May 31, 2011, available at http://www.post-gazette.com/pg/11151/1150398-100.stm; Chris Briem, *I'm shocked, shocked to find that housing appreciation is going on here!*, NULL SPACE, June 1, 2011, *available at* http://nullspace2.blogspot.com/2011/06/im-shocked-shocked-to-find-that-housing.html (last visited June 2, 2011).

[33]   Tim Grant, *'House rich' got richer, poor got poorer*, PITTSBURGH POST-GAZETTE, Aug. 29, 2009, *available at* http://www.post-gazette.com/pg/09241/993996-28.stm.

The Environment

Pittsburgh has acquired a reputation for embracing green-ness, or, in the jargon of the moment, for sustainability. The city and region are environmentally sensible, and perhaps even environmentally hip. Sustainability and clean energy were themes in President Obama's selection of Pittsburgh as the 2009 G-20 summit venue.[34] And in fact, Pittsburgh has come quite a long way since Chinitz noted the city's progress in 1961 to escape its "Smoky City" heritage.

Architecture

The green meme in Pittsburgh got started with the new David L. Lawrence Convention Center, completed in 2003 and site of the G-20 meeting, which was and remains among the largest LEED-certified (Leadership in Energy and Environmental Design) buildings anywhere.[35] It helps that the building is not only green, but cool—hip, neat, its giant white sail of a roof offering a truly distinctive addition to Pittsburgh's Allegheny River waterfront and to the view from the baseball stadium across the river, PNC Park. There are dozens of LEED-certified buildings in the region and more on the way. The recently-completed Consol Energy Center, a modern arena and home to the Pittsburgh Penguins ice hockey team, has been certified LEED Gold. City of Pittsburgh legislation requires that all publicly-financed development in Pittsburgh be certified "green." The LEED-driven, build green movement is gathering steam. Even local high school renovation projects are pitched to residents and taxpayers as LEED-friendly.

Air

It sometimes seems like every time a "livability" survey puts Pittsburgh at the top of the chart, an "air quality" survey puts Pittsburgh somewhere near the bottom. In 2008, long after coal smoke disappeared from Pittsburgh's skies, an American Lung Association (ALA) survey named Pittsburgh as home of the worst levels of short-term particle air pollution in the United States. Critics of the ALA study pointed out that measurements in Pittsburgh studied air quality not far from the huge US Steel coke plant in Clairton, Pennsylvania, nearly twenty miles from Downtown Pittsburgh and in the heart of the former "Steel Valley." Measurements in the Downtown

---

[34] *See* Malloy, *supra* note 2.
[35] *See* Union of Concerned Scientists, *Reinventing Pittsburgh as a Green City: Solutions in Action from the Climate 2030 Blueprint, available at* http://www.ucsusa. org/global_warming/solutions/big_picture_solutions/reinventing-pittsburgh.html (last visited June 2, 2011).

neighborhood or in more heavily populated areas would, they argued, show Pittsburgh in a better light. But Pittsburgh struggles to shed its dirty reputation, and how clean Pittsburgh's air seems today depends a lot on the relevant baseline. Compared to Pittsburgh's air in the middle of the 20th century, Pittsburgh's air now shines as day compares to night. (Literally.) But compared to what might reasonably be expected in a modern metropolitan area, the air in Pittsburgh is adequate at best and fragile, at worst. In 2003, when a massive power outage across much of the Northeast United States stilled coal-fired power plants in the Ohio River Valley, upwind from Downtown Pittsburgh, the skies above Pittsburgh were noticeably clearer.

Water
Pittsburgh's riverfront location is the source of enormous pride, and all three of its principal rivers today are marvelous multi-use sites. Recreation and industry share the space. Even after the collapse of the steel industry cleared the riverfronts of most of the region's large steel works, Pittsburgh's rivers long remained almost exclusively "working" rivers, too polluted and crowded with barge traffic for recreational boating or fishing, and with limited access for the general public. The riverfronts were dedicated largely to industrial use, lined by railroad rights of way, highways, abandoned industrial sites, and some legacy building materials suppliers. In 1995, Pittsburgh missed an opportunity to expand access to its rivers when it built a new Allegheny County Jail on a prime parcel of riverfront property near Downtown. Real estate development still reflected older industrial sensibilities. But the region's view of its rivers has changed dramatically over the last fifteen years. Partnerships among local government (including former Mayor Tom Murphy), real estate developers, and river access advocates have produced recreational trails along much of the riverfront Downtown, with more in development. The Great Allegheny Passage, a hiking and biking trail that connects Downtown Pittsburgh and the Georgetown neighborhood of Washington, DC, is essentially complete. Summer weekends and home football games at Heinz Field (one of Pittsburgh's new sports stadiums, described below) bring out large flotillas of recreational boaters. Fishing on the rivers is so good that in recent years Pittsburgh has twice played host to major bass fishing tournaments. On the North Side, a neighborhood just across the Allegheny River from Downtown, riverside development, including Heinz Field, PNC Park, and the Carnegie Science Center, have given a major visual and economic shot in the arm to the city. (Virtually all of this development was subsidized with public financing, discussed below.) Offices, educational facilities, and light industrial and research and development space have brightened the site of the former J&L Steel Works along the Monongahela River in the

Hazelwood neighborhood, which counts the city's main university neighborhood, Oakland, as its other boundary. The South Side Works shopping mall and condominium and office development has done the same on the opposite shore, on another reclaimed brownfield (steel mill) site.

Energy production

Coal is king in Western Pennsylvania even today, which reflects a basic truth about Pittsburgh's steel and (earlier) iron industries. There is a lot of coal in the region, even after more than a century of mining. Pittsburgh's new hockey and concert arena was christened the "Consol Energy Center" after the region's largest coal producer. That development recognizes the ongoing importance of coal to the region. But a host of clean energy alternatives are being explored here, too; Pittsburgh has a legitimate claim to being a center of 21st century energy research. Meanwhile, as I write Pittsburgh is the principal city in the middle of the Marcellus Shale, an underground shale formation that extends from western New York to Kentucky and that apparently holds an extraordinary amount of recoverable shale gas. Western Pennsylvania was home to the first oil well drilled in the United States, in the 1850s. With shale gas, a different kind of carbon-based energy is bringing new wealth to the region.

Waste and sewage

Water and waste have long been acute problems in Pittsburgh, partly due to the age of the region's infrastructure and partly due to its inescapably hilly terrain. The Pittsburgh Water & Sewer Authority regulates water and sewer systems in the City of Pittsburgh, and the Allegheny County Sanitary Authority (ALCOSAN). Despite modernization of both systems during Renaissance I, more often than it should today raw waste goes in its three rivers and down those rivers. Industrial pollution of the rivers is no longer a major problem in Pittsburgh, but untreated sewage is. Pittsburgh's sewer systems are antiquated and inadequate. Despite storm control in many part of the region, flash flooding during and after storms is common, leading to ugly and expensive backups in homes and some neighborhoods, and ugly and expensive deposits downstream (that is, down the Ohio River, towards West Virginia) from the Point. In 2007, ALCOSAN settled a claim by the United States Environmental Protection Agency over countywide untreated sewage discharges (billions of gallons per year), a settlement that obligates ALCOSAN to spend roughly $3 billion by 2026 to fix the problems and bring the Pittsburgh region into compliance with the federal Clean Water Act. That is $3 billion that the county's ratepayers will have to absorb over the next twenty years. Truly clean water in Pittsburgh is a long way off.

Transportation

Both public and private transit systems in Pittsburgh are creaking under the burdens of age, lack of public funds, and the pressure of politics that trump sensible planning. Unlike many American cities, Pittsburgh has no true freeway "beltway" for automobile traffic. That means that freeway traffic ("parkway" traffic to Pittsburghers) often travels from the periphery of the region into the heart of Downtown before making its way in a new direction. (Centering the parkway system in Downtown Pittsburgh, now part of the federal interstate highway system, is a legacy of Renaissance I.) Old and poorly engineered approaches to Pittsburgh's major bridges, inherently cautious Pittsburgh drivers, the lack of a grid system in the city (and the accompanying absence of easily accessed alternative routes, all attributable to the area's hills), and limited public funds for road and highway maintenance make rush-hour Pittsburgh traffic worse than its modest population otherwise might suggest. The public transit system is likewise fragile. The Port Authority, which now operates buses, the city's two remaining hillside Inclines (cable cars), and a single light rail line, was a product of Renaissance I; prior to its formation the region was served by a host of private transit companies. But declines in public support and tighter and tighter public budgets have produced successive rounds of service cuts. The light rail system is being extended from Downtown to the North Shore neighborhood at an extravagant cost, driven by rules associated with its federal funding source, while many Pittsburghers contend that better planning would have used the money to relieve congestion in the corridor between Downtown and the Uptown and Oakland neighborhoods, to the east of Downtown, where the region's three major universities and the bulk of its student population are located. The brightest spot in the local transit landscape today may be bicycles, which have found help in recent city administrations and among advocacy organizations. Between Pittsburgh's hilly landscape; narrow, old streets; and drivers and cyclists historically unused to sharing streets with each other, Pittsburgh is a notoriously bike-unfriendly place. But with new bike lanes being installed on some major city boulevards, and with the opening of additional riverfront bike and hiking paths, more cyclists are hitting Pittsburgh streets. Peaceful coexistence may be on the horizon. Slowly and awkwardly, Pittsburgh is getting greener.

Grit and Passion

This section challenges some Pittsburgh orthodoxy. The orthodox tale of Pittsburgh's revitalization is a simple tale of hard work. Pittsburgh owes its current success to the hard work and grit of Pittsburghers themselves, who stuck with their beloved city through thick and thin. Pittsburgh and Pittsburghers are the tortoise to the hare of places like Florida and Arizona. There is a native culture of hard work and modesty in Pittsburgh, combined with an unrivaled passion for and loyalty to the city, that was forged in the steel era and that drives the city forward today.

That theme, that "character" matters most of all and that Pittsburgh's gritty character, its passion for itself, has never really changed, dominated some media coverage of the G-20 meeting in 2009 (one column in Forbes. com, the online partner of Forbes magazine, is particularly evocative)[36] and pervades local culture. Yet I doubt very much that Pittsburgh's "character," whatever it might be, is the cause of Pittsburgh's current condition.

First, it is far from clear that Pittsburgh today has the "gritty" character so often associated with the place. Maybe it does, especially in some neighborhoods and communities, and especially among people and families who have lived in Pittsburgh for decades. I know a lot of "gritty" people in Pittsburgh. I also know a lot of enthusiastic and energetic movers and shakers, in the arts, in the neighborhoods, in politics, and in entrepreneurship, in wealthy towns and poor ones, who are not "gritty" at all. Many of them did not grow up in Pittsburgh, do not have family in Pittsburgh and would not know the inside of the region's steel history if they were hit on the head by a bust of Andrew Carnegie. Instead, these people have the same kind of passion and spirit and talent that one finds in arts advocates, neighborhood organizers, emerging political leaders, and entrepreneurs anywhere.

The "gritty character" story survives because it is a very American way of combining political, economic, and cultural success with a morality tale. Pittsburgh was once dominated by blue-collar workers and their families. The good people, the folks who put their heads down and planned for the future and avoided the flash and dash have come out on top. (And Pittsburghers, of course, are the good people, especially when Pittsburghers are contrasted with sporting rivals in other Rust Belt cities, particularly Cleveland and Baltimore.) Never mind that over the course

---

[36]   *See* Raquel Laneri, *Pittsburgh? Yes, Pittsburgh: Why the city on the Ohio River is the perfect G-20 host*, FORBES.COM, Sept. 2, 2009, *available at* http://www. forbes.com/2009/09/02/pittsburgh-g-20-economy-innovation-opinions-columnists-21-century-cities-09-pittsburgh.html ("But the thing Pittsburgh has done perhaps more brilliantly and unabashedly than any other American city—a philosophy Detroit and other suffering one-industry towns should consider—is stay true to its identity. Pittsburgh may have built one of the largest health centers in the U.S., but it has not tried to reinvent its character. [¶] Pittsburghers have a ferocious pride in their city . . .").

of the last 100 years in Pittsburgh, many of the people responsible for organizing and leading Pittsburgh's major successful economic, cultural, and political institutions either were not very nice (or even "gritty") and would struggle to achieve characterization as "the good people." Andrew Carnegie and his rival, Henry Clay Frick, come promptly to mind. In the morality tale, the workers and a small number of selfless capitalists and politicians are usually "the good people." Never mind that putting Pittsburghers' collective heads down and planning for the future and avoiding the flash and dash produced some important community milestones during the first Renaissance but ended up driving the city over an economic cliff in the early 1980s and did little to bring things back to life over the succeeding twenty-five years. I do not suggest that Pittsburghers are not good or hard working or that steelworker forebears did not struggle mightily to achieve success for their families and for the region. They are, and they did. But I am skeptical of the morality tale that says that Pittsburgh is where it is today because good people worked hard for it and cared passionately about where they live.

Second, it may be the case that Pittsburgh is succeeding today not *because* of its historic gritty character, assuming that this gritty character survives, but *despite* it. In truth, of course, some of both things is probably at work, but the *cause* part is already an element of the standard narrative. I want to focus briefly on the *effect* idea.

In the Forbes.com story I referred to above, Pittsburgh City Council Member Bill Peduto was quoted. In the wake of the steel industry's collapse, he said, "Pittsburgh really had no choice. . . . It was diversify or die." The inaccurate way to read that statement is to infer that Pittsburgh somehow decided to diversify its economy in the wake of the collapse of steel, and the results are on display today, particularly the region's "eds and meds" industries. But the implied statement that Pittsburgh somehow planned for the end of steel is historically inaccurate. Important investments in "eds and meds" were made in the 1950s, but those investments bore meaningful fruit only much later. When the steel industry collapsed in the early 1980s, the University of Pittsburgh, Carnegie Mellon University, and the University of Pittsburgh Medical Center (now UPMC), today Pittsburgh's three leading institutions and each of them global in its reach, were competent regional enterprises. The collapse of steel was not expected or desired.

The better and more accurate way to read the statement above is that Pittsburgh had economic diversity thrust upon it. When steel died, for many years Pittsburgh wished and waited for another large-scale industry to arrive and restore the region, for a substitute to be found to replace US Steel as an oligopolistic but reliable and stable anchor. Over a very long period of time, Pittsburghers threw off the psychological shackles that kept the population hoping and waiting for the big thing that would save the city. That includes both the business community and the population at large. The people of Pittsburgh have at long last accepted a lesser role for steel (which survives in the Pittsburgh region, primarily through small specialty steel producers and suppliers). That is, eventually, Pittsburghers learned to stop worrying and love economic diversification. (More on the economy as such appears below.) They really had no choice. Fortunately for the region, some key "eds and meds" investments had been made way back when, and those investments were waiting for more attention.

Having gradually accepted the reality of a "new-ish," more diverse economy, Pittsburghers have concluded that they were not sad sack losers for letting steel slip away. Pittsburghers have decided they were gritty after all. The city is still here; therefore it has grit. Pittsburgh's character today is its reward for not having melted away, like the Wicked Witch of the West, when Pittsburgh steel had the cold water of new competition poured on it.

Hipness

History and culture have many dimensions. The flip side of grit is hip. Is Pittsburgh hip? The short answer is that it never was and it never will be, at least so long as anyone thinks that "hip" is defined by a New York or Los Angeles aesthetic. But in the last few years Pittsburgh seems to have attracted and supported a younger, more progressive social, cultural, and political "scene" than anyone might have thought possible as recently as ten years ago. It is wrong to put too much emphasis on surface phenomena like a single Whole Foods grocery store, which has been thriving for several years in Pittsburgh's East Liberty neighborhood and which, with adjacent stores and restaurants and a nearby regional outpost of Google, gives a patina of cool to part of a single neighborhood. But below the surface, there is definitely something happening.

Ten years ago, the region was gripped with public fear of "brain drain," anxiety that the area's adolescents and recent college graduates would leave Pittsburgh and take the brightest ideas and most passionate energy with them. "Brain drain" as a slogan reflects anxiety grounded in a localized economic and cultural model, the worry that it will no longer have local resources to support and reproduce itself. By the time that concern arose in Pittsburgh, the anxiety was almost entirely misplaced. Particularly in the latter part of the 20th century and continuing today, young people in the United States are fated to move around. Leaving home and leaving their native region seems to be a modern American birthright. Pittsburgh is a more rooted (some would say, "European") city than many of its peers, but it never had any realistic hope that its experience over the long run would be different.

Pittsburgh's legitimate anxiety was and to some extent remains that no one from other parts of the country and the world wants to move to the region. That anxiety has its cousin in the celebration, noted above, of the city's "livability" ratings. More dynamic cities, places where "hip" really means something, are places where population churn is a fact of life. People go, people come. This includes immigrant populations willing to work at dangerous jobs for low wages; immigrant groups often take root, accumulate wealth, and build middle class institutions in their adopted communities. New ideas are constantly being imported as well as exported.

Is that happening in Pittsburgh? Population trends overall have not changed dramatically in Pittsburgh. The 2010 census shows that the city's population continues to decline slowly, to just over 300,000 people, and the regional population, at roughly 2 million people, is staying mostly flat. Age distributions, however, are changing. After enduring decades of being labeled one of the (demographically) oldest cities in the United States, Pittsburgh is now getting younger.[37] To be sure, much of the shift can be attributed to the demise of older Pittsburghers. The birth rate in Pittsburgh is quite low; Pittsburgh deaths are higher. But at the margins and in some particularly visible parts of the region, there seems to be movement around Pittsburgh. In arts, culture, entrepreneurship, neighborhood advocacy and development, and politics, there is an emerging tier of 20-something leaders who embrace and are building enthusiastically on what I call the "best of Pittsburgh's past"—the neighborhoods, the older racial and ethnic communities, even the steel industry and its associated blue-collar sensibility. Residential and retail revival in Pittsburgh neighborhoods like Lawrenceville, East Liberty, the Mexican War Streets, and parts of the South Side, the Strip, and even Downtown are emblematic of the new younger tone of Pittsburgh. The start-up economy in Pittsburgh (more on that below) is slowly but surely leveraging this younger talent. A leading young computer science researcher at Carnegie Mellon University, Luis von Ahn, sold his company to Google, which is developing a growing research facility in Pittsburgh and is keeping von Ahn and his

---

[37] Economists predicted the shift a decade ago. *See* Christopher Briem, *We're getting younger every year,* PITTSBURGH POST-GAZETTE, Jan. 2, 2000, *available at* http://www.post-gazette.com/forum/20000102edbriem8.asp. Recent census figures bear it out. *See* Gary Rotstein, *Census finds Pittsburgh is growing younger,* PITTSBURGH POST-GAZETTE, May 19, 2011, *available at* http://www.post-gazette.com/pg/11139/1147664-53.stm.

team in place. The Warhol Museum, a Pittsburgh institution that houses the largest permanent collection of Andy Warhol's works (Warhol was born and raised in Pittsburgh), has become a focal point for cutting-edge arts and culture in the region and is widely respected beyond Western Pennsylvania.

Sports

No account of Pittsburgh's history and culture is complete without a review of the topic that binds more Pittsburghers together than any other: sports and professional sports in particular. Few cities anywhere in the world derive their identities so directly from their sporting successes and failures as Pittsburgh does. The city is known for three teams in particular: the Steelers, of the National Football League; the Pirates, of Major League Baseball; and the Penguins, of the National Hockey League. When any of those teams wins a championship, Pittsburgh residents and former Pittsburghers everywhere (a "diaspora" with its genesis in the out-migration from Pittsburgh spurred by the collapse of steel in the 1980s and now often referred to as Steelers Nation) share an intangible collective sense of pride in the city itself, as if they had something directly to do with what happened on the field or on the ice.

In other words, today's aura of Pittsburgh success owes no small debt to the recent successes of its professional athletes, particularly in football and in ice hockey. It also owes no small debt to long-ago athletic successes. The Pirates won the World Series over the favored New York Yankees in 1960 under circumstances so miraculous that fans still gather on the anniversary of the final game to relive the deciding moment: a home run in the ninth inning by Pirates second baseman Bill Mazeroski. The Steelers won four Super Bowl championships during the 1970s, and the Pirates won the World Series again in 1971 and 1979, at a time when steel still ruled the region. Pittsburgh called itself the "City of Champions" then (the city was also home to an extraordinarily successful college football team at the University of Pittsburgh). Without the Steelers and Pirates of the 1970s, one may wonder legitimately whether there would have been much to revive in Pittsburgh in the late 1990s. The collapse of the steel industry in the early 1980s imposed a collective psychic trauma on the region that has faded ever so slowly over time. That trauma was mitigated in part by psychic spillover benefits from the championship years,[38] and

---

[38] It helped considerably that the Steelers and Pirates of the 1970s were characterized by coaches and star players who aligned themselves with the city's image

those championships have been given new life by more recent victories—two more Super Bowl titles for the Steelers and Stanley Cup (ice hockey) championships for the Penguins. It is not too much to declare that fan support for Pittsburgh sports teams is ecstatically tribal; it spans gender and generation. Moreover, the force of Pittsburgh fandom is essentially unifying. In contrast to tribal support for football (soccer) clubs in many major European cities—consider Glasgow, or Manchester, or Istanbul—Pittsburghers' loyalties are undivided.[39] And for reasons noted earlier in connection with Pittsburghers' arguable grit, the passion and loyalty associated with Pittsburgh sports teams, while strong to begin with, may have intensified in recent years, initially as compensation for the loss of the region's dominant industry, and more recently in proportion to the region's recent renewal. Where Pittsburghers all once had the steel industry in common, now they all share football. Pittsburgh fans are expressing and bonding communally over their intense pride in their great city, first despite its overall economic condition and now to celebrate it.

Does the aura translate into economic good fortune? The reputational benefits of Pittsburgh fandom do not necessarily translate into income or wealth for the region. To the extent that professional sports have a direct bearing on the economic fortunes of a city, the balance of payments decidedly favors team ownership and the athletes themselves. All three teams now play their home games in recently-constructed modern facilities that are among the most lavish (for players) and fan-friendly in their respective leagues; all three were built on a newer "urbanist" model that wove them into the fabric neighborhoods close by to Downtown Pittsburgh. But the teams do not create wealth; they redistribute wealth. To a team owner or player, or a broadcaster or other rights-owner, the obsessive loyalty of fans is highly lucrative. For fans, being fantastically and obsessively loyal is expensive. Being a supporter takes up time and, between tickets and fan gear, a lot of money. Fans receive psychic income, which is real enough if it motivates engagement with the community at large but which does

---

of itself: down-to-earth, hard-working, no-nonsense, family-oriented men. All of Pittsburgh's professional sports teams feature black and yellow or black and gold—the official colors of the City of Pittsburgh—as their official team colors. At the Pittsburgh International Airport a handful of years ago, I rode a tram standing next to Lynn Swann, one of the superstar players from the Steelers of the 1970s and still a Pittsburgh-area resident. Another tram rider turned to him and said, modestly, "Thanks for the good years, Lynn," and then walked away. Swann nodded an acknowledgement. No autograph or even a handshake was expected.

[39]   A Pittsburgh Steelers game against the Baltimore Ravens, perhaps the team's biggest rival, engenders passions on both sides that might approximate the passions unleashed by a *Clásico* between Real Madrid and FC Barcelona.

not pay for food or housing. (Pittsburgh's baseball fans do not earn even that, however. The Pirates have not had a winning season since the early 1990s, though the team is profitable.) In its disparate economic impacts, Pittsburgh's sporting tribalism bears more than a passing resemblance to the steel industry.

Government

Having set out a broad range of cultural dimensions of Pittsburgh's current status, in this and the following sections I turn to some institutional and economic considerations. What roles have Pittsburgh politicians and politics and local government played in the region's evolution over the last three decades? I begin this quick review with a nod to a recent essay at a respected online Pittsburgh magazine, Pop City: *Five Things that Allowed Pittsburgh to Turn the Corner.*[40]

The author, who works for the Hillman Company, a Pittsburgh investment firm, identified five things that allowed Pittsburgh to turn its corner, toward renewal: RAD (the "Regional Asset District" that collects and distributes local sales and uses taxes to fund certain cultural services in the region); home rule for Allegheny County, where the city of Pittsburgh is located; Pittsburgh's Life Sciences and Digital Greenhouses; river and trail restoration and access; and creation of the County's Department of Human Services. This is a decidedly traditional Pittsburgh list in its focus on government and top-down organization as drivers of change. That is no surprise. The Hillman Company and the Hillman name are two of the most respected institutions in the entire region and icons of the Pittsburgh establishment. In a sense the list is representative of the perspective that is sometimes called "Renaissance III," a modern public–private partnership leading Pittsburgh toward future success, continuing the traditions and successes of Renaissance I and Renaissance II.

Each of these items either came into being or came to prominence during a five-year period—1995 to 2000—that preceded the current sense of Pittsburgh renewal and therefore could be said to have set the stage for later success. Three of them, home rule for Pittsburgh's home county, the Regional Asset District, and consolidation of disparate health and family services into a single county-wide Department of Human Services, followed public acknowledgement that the county (with well

---

[40]   *See* John Denny, *Five Things that Allowed Pittsburgh to Turn the Corner*, Pop City, Sept. 9, 2009, *available at* http://www.popcitymedia.com/features/5things090909.aspx.

over a million residents) had weak government institutions relative to
the city of Pittsburgh (with roughly 350,000 residents, at that time). The
two Greenhouses, which are incubators of and investors in early stage
technology companies located in Pittsburgh, are local implementations
of a statewide, government-directed-and-funded economic-development
strategy. Particularly in their early years of operation, both relied heavily
on state funding.

While there is no doubt that each of the items on that list has played
an important role in Pittsburgh over the last ten years, it also true that
as with any government programs, the story in each case is full of misses
as well as hits. The recession that began in 2008 exposed the flaw in the
RAD formula. RAD support displaced direct appropriations from state
and local budgets, and recipients of RAD funds now fight over a smaller
pool of RAD-specific tax revenue. Home rule gave Pittsburgh a strong
county executive, which is an elected political position, but in practice
that office has run into frequent conflict with the Mayor of Pittsburgh
over control of a vision for the region's future. Beyond some streamlining
of county bureaucracies that were long considered bastions of patronage
for lesser-elected officials, the executive's role in regional renewal and
growth has been poorly defined. (In this chapter I have tried to emphasize
the importance of Pittsburgh as a region as well as a city, but for decades
the city proper has been the conceptual driver of Pittsburgh success—and
failure.) The Department of Human Services is a success story, but it may
be the exception that proves the rule. Beyond ensuring effective delivery
of services to populations who have neither access nor money to obtain
resources otherwise, the county government is relatively toothless. In
addition, that department, for all of its good work, is not in a position to
address deeper structural problems that divide wealthier Pittsburgh communities from their poorer neighbors. (More on structural challenges,
below.) As for the Greenhouses, despite some successes in supporting
innovation regionally, state-directed investment via the Greenhouses has
stood in the way of authentic entrepreneurship and economic development as much as they have facilitated it, by crowding out private sector
investment and initiative. There is more on this topic, too, below.

More broadly, the story of Pittsburgh government has many more
chapters than these five. In general, it is as easy to see Pittsburgh's governments as obstacles to revival as it to see them as facilitators. For example,
revival and renewal in Pittsburgh has taken place almost entirely in the
private and not-for-profit sectors. Pittsburgh's public sector groans under
the weight of an accumulated unfunded pension liability of hundreds of
millions of dollars, owed primarily to public safety employees (police and
firefighters) and to public school teachers, that is so severe that in late

2003 the city was labeled officially "distressed" under Act 47, a state law in Pennsylvania. Since then, the city's finances have been supervised both by a state-appointed Act 47 team of advisors and by a state-appointed Intergovernmental Cooperation Authority. Pittsburgh is neither insolvent nor bankrupt under federal law. But the city does not have enough revenue to pay all of its debts, and despite the continuing decline in the city's population, the city's deep-rooted neighborhood culture has made it extraordinarily difficult to consider reducing the levels of public services supplied by the city.

Moreover, the Mayor and City Council of the city of Pittsburgh, which govern the city, are frequently at loggerheads and even then are only parts of the vast mosaic of regional and local government institutions in the Pittsburgh area, some of them public, some of them partly public and partly private. "Fragmentation" is the local watchword. The city of Pittsburgh has ninety neighborhoods that are officially recognized by the city. Many of those are supported by Community Development Corporations, which have flourished over the last decade and which are responsible for freshening up many a neighborhood economy. Allegheny County as a whole, with just over 1 million inhabitants, has 130 municipalities, each of which has varying levels of authority over local taxes, public schools, and land use policy. In many cases, the Pittsburgh region, like Pittsburgh neighborhoods, thrives on this continuation of historic patterns of very close local control of local matters. But spillovers are increasingly frequent; no town, like no neighborhood and no man, is an economic or policy island. Despite the investment of Allegheny County itself with certain political authority in the mid-1990s, the redistribution of regional population over the last several decades from the city of Pittsburgh to the broader region has not been matched by a reallocation of public authority and resources. That population shift is complicated by the fact that many regional residents commute to jobs in the city of Pittsburgh, yet pay only nominal taxes to the city. Many policymakers in the Pittsburgh region promote a broad consolidation of city and county governments. If suburban income were taxed as part of a regional solution, the city's unfunded pension liabilities might be reduced significantly, for example. Consolidation itself may or may not be a panacea with respect to aligning regional costs and benefits. The point is that the demographic shape of the city of Pittsburgh and the surrounding region has changed fundamentally; how governments deal with those things largely has not. Real, productive, disciplined broad-based inter-governmental cooperation is necessary to get things done in Pittsburgh, but it is rare. Renaissance I was possible in part because political and economic resources aligned in concentrated fashion in the city of Pittsburgh fifty years ago, together with enlightened leadership in both public and private sectors. That alignment no longer exists.

Sharing the Wealth

A big part of Pittsburgh's revitalization story focuses on the diversification of the region's economy. Pittsburgh's historic focus on steel production and other manufacturing, supported by a strong regional banking, has been supplanted by a broad range of economic drivers. Educational services dominate the stage, via the region's many colleges and universities; a medical services provider, the UPMC Health System, is the region's single largest employer. Financial services remain strong, along with energy production, chemicals, and engineering and specialty manufacturing (including steel, as well as medical devices). Several of Pittsburgh's legacy industrial firms retain significant presences in the region, including Alcoa, PPG Industries, and the H.J. Heinz Company. Westinghouse, a legendary Pittsburgh name originally associated with the Westinghouse Electric Corporation, survives in the Pittsburgh region via a descendant devoted to nuclear engineering. All of these enterprises, including UPMC and the region's leading universities, have adopted outward-looking global business strategies.

Alongside what might be called Pittsburgh's large-firm economy is an increasingly diverse and successful range of industries grounded in emerging firms and technologies, many of them built around research spun off from research at the University of Pittsburgh, Carnegie Mellon University, and UPMC. Pittsburgh is known for high-quality development in robotics, information technology, computer science, life sciences (particularly tissue regeneration), and what is now known as "entertainment technology," including videogames. A variety of incubator and accelerator firms in the region, many of them seeded with state-supplied funding, have nurtured a growing number of these enterprises to viability. Pittsburgh is increasingly known nationwide as a place where technology-oriented innovation will receive strong community support, from entities such as the Digital Greenhouse, the Life Sciences Greenhouse, and Innovation Works.[41] Those firms and the neighborhoods where many of them and their employees are located, such as Pittsburgh's South Side,

---

[41]   A newer entity, the Energy Alliance of Greater Pittsburgh, does not fund new enterprises itself but serves as a clearinghouse of information about funding opportunities and advocates on behalf of technology developers and other firms who are exploiting Western Pennsylvania's energy resources.

the Strip District, Lawrenceville, the Oakland neighborhood, and East Liberty and Larimer, have experienced a decade-long upsurge in related residential and commercial development: rehabbed warehouses, renovated homes, and new stores and restaurants. The arts community has rebounded in tandem with technology-oriented development, both at the higher end (such as commercial film production) and at the smaller end (a growing number of visual artists and musicians, relying on living and working costs that compare quite favorably with alternatives in New York). Suburban communities on all sides of the city of Pittsburgh have benefited from re-located and expanded offices associated with small- and mid-sized company innovation. There is no single "technology corridor" or valley in Pittsburgh.

Enthusiasm for all of that development should be tempered by recognition of just how much of Pittsburgh, both city and region, remains essentially untouched by it. There is a structural problem at work. Pittsburgh's prosperity was driven by the fact that Pittsburgh possessed a nearly unique combination of access to raw materials, transportation, and financial resources, which came together in the 20th century in the steel industry, and in the 19th century in iron production and glassmaking. Because the location of those things was distributed broadly across the region, with mills and factories located up Pittsburgh's rivers and valleys, Pittsburgh's economic might, and the blue collar population that supported it, was distributed across the region rather than being concentrated in one place, such as Downtown.

When the steel economy crashed and the mills closed, those valley communities were the hardest hit. As the region's economy has slowly re-emerged and parts of it have been redeveloped, there has been little reason, in purely economic terms, to focus on them. Pittsburgh's new economy, and particularly its "eds and meds" and technology communities, can be located anywhere and generally are located where the population is clustered, and particularly the better educated, white-collar population. In a manner of speaking, steel money was sucked out of one part of the Pittsburgh region; new money is largely being injected elsewhere.

That proposition should be understood in tandem with a history of racial and ethnic diversity that has left Pittsburgh composed almost exclusively of white majority and black minority populations. There are, in fact, at least three Pittsburghs today. There is the city and region that is the object of some guarded optimism, courtesy of emerging economic development in "eds and meds" and technology sectors. I call that "First World Pittsburgh." Alongside First World Pittsburgh there is the fading steel-producing region, much of which lays outside of the city itself and much of which is home to abandoned manufacturing sites. (Many of the steel-producing sites in Pittsburgh were located up the Monongahela River, leading to its informal moniker: the Steel Valley.) I call that Second World Pittsburgh, characterized mostly by pure pessimism. (Some mills continue to operate profitably, but with a fraction of their former work-forces.) Finally, there is Pittsburgh's African-American population, which is modest in size and, to the extent that it is concentrated in a handful of city neighborhoods (notably, Homewood and the Hill District), quite poor.[42] A recent local news story captured the problem in a headline: "Pittsburgh's 'Livable' label called lie for blacks."[43] I call this Third World Pittsburgh, burdened by poverty and crime and no obvious way out. Pittsburgh's black population swelled during the middle part of the 20th century during precisely the era when growth in manufacturing in Pittsburgh was slowing and reducing the number of available jobs.

Some details might be added to that rough sketch, particularly within First World Pittsburgh. That cluster includes "Suburban Pittsburgh" and "City of Pittsburgh" subdivisions. The two groups share positions of power but do not identify with each other. First World Pittsburgh also includes other distinct sub-groups: "Traditional Pittsburgh," Pittsburghers, especially older Pittsburghers, who long primarily for a res-toration of the prestige that the city enjoyed in its golden age; "Corporate Pittsburgh," often but not exclusively Pittsburghers in positions of govern-ment and business authority, who associate Pittsburgh with the benevo-lent governing style that characterized the city during Renaissance I; and "New Pittsburgh," the younger Pittsburghers and newer arrivals who are often at the forefront of new efforts in arts, technology, and real estate development, who often bring global perspectives to bear on local issues and who are sometimes impatient for "Traditional Pittsburgh" and "Corporate Pittsburgh" to get out of the way. Second World Pittsburgh, the Pittsburgh of fading mill towns and neighborhoods, has its own divi-sions, as does Third World Pittsburgh. Some "New Pittsburgh" energy spills over into efforts to revive and renew these places, for example. And none of the boundaries among these broad groups is impermeable, and people within each group are more, and sometimes less, capable of change.

---

[42]   Pittsburgh's African-American community is economically diverse, but its middle and upper classes are scattered across the region.

[43]   *See* Moustafa Ayad, *Pittsburgh's 'Livable' label called lie for blacks*, PITTSBURGH POST-GAZETTE, July 20, 2007, *available at* http://www.post-gazette. com/pg/07201/803126-53.stm. That story reported on a report prepared by faculty members at the University of Pittsburgh's School of Social Work, titled *Pittsburgh's Racial Demographics: Differences and Disparities*. The report is online at http:// www.cmh.pitt.edu/pdf/Demographics_Complete.pdf (last visited June 2, 2011).

No matter how you divide up the community, however, it is clear that "Pittsburgh," like many cities and regions, is an amalgam of cultural and economic interests that are in conflict as often as they are aligned. It is tempting and even sometimes right to see Pittsburgh's revitalization as the product of the convergence of these interests, and to see flaws in the revitalization project as the products of a failed infrastructure of cooperation. If First World Pittsburgh supports and protects only First World Pittsburgh, then Pittsburgh's renewal is not taking root across the broader community. Even the struggling Steel Valley is sometimes characterized by micro-versions of these same conflicts. In Braddock, Pennsylvania, a mill town near Pittsburgh that is home to the region's first and largest integrated steel mill, the Edgar Thomson Works, the force and face of "new," Braddock Mayor John Fetterman, has struggled both against what is left of the town's old guard and against claims that Fetterman himself has favored friends and family in promoting arts- and culture-based renewal.[44]

Land Use and Redevelopment

A post-industrial city such as Pittsburgh has to account for its land, because no other resource was so dedicated specifically to supporting the structure of its former economy. Perceptions of Pittsburgh's renewal owe much of their resonance to productive reuse of several prominently located former steel mill sites, along with other redevelopment of prominent parcels in Downtown Pittsburgh and along its rivers.

This visible transformation of Pittsburgh over the last fifteen years is marked by a quick review of the banks of the Monongahela River, which arrives in Downtown Pittsburgh from the south. In Homestead, just outside Pittsburgh's city limits, the site of the former Homestead Works steel mill is now occupied by an enormous outdoor mall and office complex, called the Waterfront. Heading downriver into Pittsburgh, the site of the former LTV steel works in the South Side neighborhood is now occupied by the Southside Works office and retail complex. The former Jones & Laughlin mill site, facing the Southside Works, is occupied by a series of modestly scaled, light office buildings that house Pittsburgh's technology incubators and accelerators and research facilities. Modern office buildings dot the Downtown Pittsburgh skyline, many of them

---

[44] *See* Sue Halpern, *Mayor of Rust*, N.Y. TIMES MAGAZINE, Feb. 11, 2011, at MM30, *available at* http://www.nytimes.com/2011/02/13/magazine/13Fetterman-t.html.

products of Renaissance I and Renaissance II. The tallest of them, built in 1970 as the headquarters of US Steel, now boasts the letters "UPMC" on the sides of its top-most floors, both signaling the presence of the corporate offices of that organization and embodying in a single image the metaphorical shift underway in Pittsburgh.[45] On the other side of the Point, on the Allegheny River, an older and unloved concrete product of Renaissance I, the multi-sport Three Rivers Stadium, was torn down in 2001 after thirty years of use to make way for modern, separate facilities for football (Heinz Field) and baseball (PNC Park) and an expanding array of office buildings, hotels, and concert venues. The new David Lawrence Convention Center sits just upriver, also replacing an outmoded Renaissance I predecessor. Where Pittsburghers once poured steel into molds, and where land once stood abandoned and vacant, today they watch, play, convene, office, and shop. Contemporary culture is quick to recognize this as progress.

Virtually none of this real estate development happened without substantial input and investment from Pittsburgh's city government, principally from a Renaissance I-era municipal agency, the Urban Redevelopment Authority (URA), which is one of the oldest and most prominent examples of its type anywhere in the United States. The Waterfront development in Homestead was executed outside the city limits; public investment in that project consisted of a major rebate of expected property tax revenues, via a state "Tax Increment Financing" program that encourages redevelopment of "blighted" property. The other projects identified above, however, all involved substantial coordination and investment either from the URA or from its municipal cousin, the Sports & Exhibition Authority (SEA). The agencies offer planning support, and importantly, both some public financing and the ability by law to coordinate public financing (at tax-subsidized rates) with private investment (which earns market returns). The URA previously played a key role during the 1950s in the successful redevelopment of the Point, in Downtown Pittsburgh, and in the 1960s in the unsuccessful redevelopment of Pittsburgh's East Liberty neighborhood, what was then Pittsburgh's second-largest business zone. Today, it is most prominently

---

[45]   *See* Dan Fitzpatrick, *Top of the triangle: UPMC getting ready to put its name on U.S. Steel Tower*, Pittsburgh Post-Gazette, Apr. 25, 2008, *available at* http://www.post-gazette.com/pg/08116/876329-28.stm. The "Top of the triangle" in that headline is a local inside joke; "Top of the Triangle" was the name of an elite restaurant that operated for years at the top of the building and that catered to U.S. Steel executives. The restaurant space has been renovated and is now occupied by UPMC's leadership team.

associated with riverfront development, although it manages residential redevelopment throughout the city.

In part because the URA has long played such a large role in Pittsburgh real estate, developers of almost all types of projects have gotten accustomed to a significant public role in their efforts. The advantage of this approach has been a city today that is somewhat more coordinated in its appearance and function than cities where development policy is channeled largely via zoning regulation. Pittsburgh has a larger residential community in its Downtown neighborhood today, and in renovated warehouses and factories in the adjacent Strip District neighborhood, compared to a decade ago. Both are products of URA interest and investment. The drawback to this approach is that certain development opportunities go unexplored, either because they do not fit the government's vision—note above, for example, the relative absence of light office and light industrial facilities suitable for start-up technology firms—or because political considerations spill over from the Mayor's administration, which has a strong formal role in the URA, to the adjacent planning agencies. The URA is responsible for many of Pittsburgh's current amenities, but the URA's vision is derivative of an older Pittsburgh, both in the sense that the vision is planned from above, and in the sense that it is planned by elites. For both reasons, it may have crowded out other private investment.

If land use policy has been exercised in such an unorthodox way, related tax policy has been equally unorthodox. There are at least three tax notes worth mentioning in connection with Pittsburgh's revitalization.

The real estate tax assessment system in Allegheny County was overhauled a little over a decade ago in an effort to assess each parcel at its actual market value. Given dramatic changes in property values over decades during which new assessments had not been conducted, and the difficulties associated with re-assessing every parcel in the county virtually overnight, the overhaul led to allegations, ultimately sustained by the Pennsylvania Supreme Court, that inequities in the new system were so profound that the entire system was declared unconstitutional. Under Pennsylvania law, however, the bulk of property taxes are paid to municipal school districts, but assessments are conducted primarily by county authorities. A successor system has yet to be devised and fully implemented.

Disruption in the tax system has not in itself impaired Pittsburgh's renewal, but the reforms of a decade ago may yet have deeper consequences. As Pittsburgh moved to a new assessment system in 2001, it also abandoned its land tax, sometimes called a land value tax, or a split-rate property tax system. Under such a system, related to the single-rate land tax proposed by Henry George,[46] real property is taxed at two rates, one (lower) rate for improvements, and a second (higher) rate for the land itself. The goal of a split-rate land tax is to discourage land speculation and holding under-developed property, and to encourage development of raw land. (In theory, a pure land tax is a means of equalizing wealth across society, on the premise that land itself is a form of wealth equivalent to improvements, chattel property, and money. Conceptually, taxes on the land would be paid by landowners; taxes on improvements would be paid by improvers or tenants.[47]) For decades during the 20th century, Pittsburgh taxed undeveloped land at a much higher rate than it taxed developed land. There is some evidence that the split-rate system encouraged construction in Pittsburgh, especially the commercial construction associated with Renaissance II during the 1980s and early 1990s. It has been suggested that this change adversely affected private incentives to engage in real estate development.

Finally, there are two other aspects of Pittsburgh's residential taxation system to consider. One is its tax lien system. The city of Pittsburgh has had a large number of vacant and abandoned properties in its neighborhoods, and liens for unpaid taxes on those properties have stood in the way of selling them and getting development moving. Pittsburgh recently started to buy back the liens, in effect getting taxes out of the way of improving the neighborhoods with private capital. The huge number of affected properties means that this project has a long way to run, but the fact that it got started at all is a positive sign. Two is Pittsburgh's high deed transfer tax, which punishes those who buy and sell homes, discouraging turnover and returning the story thematically to one of its starting point. The note brings me full circle: Pittsburgh is particularly "livable," and affordable, for those who have little interest in moving elsewhere.

Summary

The narrative is long, full of color and some detail. What does it add up to? My goal in this contemporary account of Pittsburgh has been both to illustrate those features of the city and region that justify the claim that it has

---

[46] *See* John A. Swain. *The Taxation of Private Interests in Public Property: Toward a Unified Theory of Property Taxation,* 2000 UTAH L. REV. 421, 478–80 (describing the Georgist approach).

[47] Not only does the land tax idea have the virtue of progressivism, it has also been shown to be economically efficient in urban contexts. *See* Joseph E. Stiglitz, *The Theory of Local Public Goods,* in Martin S. Feldstein & Robert P. Inman eds., ECONOMICS OF PUBLIC SERVICES (London, UK: Macmillan, 1977).

been revitalized in the wake of the collapse of the steel industry, and also to point out those features that justify skepticism regarding the extent and depth of that revitalization. The following statistics capture the yin and yang of Pittsburgh today. On the one hand, despite all of the new investment, new and expanded institutions, and diversification of Pittsburgh's economic base described above, the rate of new business formation in Pittsburgh remains remarkably low, particularly in comparison to rates in peer Rust Belt cities (Baltimore, Cleveland, Cincinnati, Milwaukee). A report in 2008 concluded, "The Pittsburgh region has the third lowest rate of startup businesses in manufacturing of any of the top forty regions, and the lowest startup rate in every other sector, from retail to finance."[48] On the other hand, in 2004 for the first time there were equal numbers of women and men in Pittsburgh's workforce; since then, women have outnumbered men.[49] Pittsburgh's Asian-Indian population nearly doubled between 2000 and 2010. The numbers seem small in absolute terms— from roughly 8,500 people to roughly 14,500 people—but the trend and the impact are unmistakable. This is a community that is generally well

---

[48] A leading local economic development consultant and scholar wrote recently: "In regions like Charlotte, Denver, Kansas City, and Minneapolis, more than 1 out of every 6 workers (17–18%) is employed by a locally-owned firm 10 years old or younger. In Silicon Valley, more than 1 out of every 5 workers (22.3%) is employed in a firm that is young. But in the Pittsburgh region, only about 1 in every 7 workers (14.3%) is employed by a locally-owned firm 10 years old or younger." Harold D. Miller, *Want More Jobs? Attract More Entrepreneurs*, PITTSBURGH'S FUTURE, Jan. 13, 2008, *available at* http://pittsburghfuture.blogspot.com/2008/01/want-more-jobs-attract-more.html (last visited June 2, 2011). A complete set of comparative statistics is available through the Pittsburgh TODAY project, a research resource maintained at the University of Pittsburgh. Employment in new businesses is described in data collected at http://www.pittsburghtoday.org/view_NewBusinessFormation2.html (last visited June 2, 2011).

[49] In December 2007, researchers at the University of Pittsburgh's Center for Social and Urban Research published a comprehensive report titled *Gender Wage Disparity in the Pittsburgh Region: Analyzing Causes and Differences in the Gender Wage Gap*. It included this statement:

Women are singularly responsible for the region regaining its employment and labor-force levels above their peaks prior to the massive job losses of the 1980s . . . in fact, total employment and total labor force would reach their all-time peaks in the Pittsburgh region in the late 1990s. This expansion in the local labor force, despite the large structural job loss of the 1980s, was only possible because of the dramatic increase in female labor force participation.

SABINA DEITRICK, GENDER WAGE DISPARITY IN THE PITTSBURGH REGION: ANALYZING CAUSES AND DIFFERENCES IN THE GENDER WAGE GAP 8 (2007) *available at* http://www.ucsur.pitt.edu/files/frp/DeitrickGenderWageDisparity12-07.pdf.

educated and entrepreneurial. Pittsburgh cannot escape its industrial history and the spillover economic, cultural, and demographic effects of that history. Pittsburghers as a whole would say that they have no desire to escape that history. But there are modest signs that the region may be headed towards an era of stability and perhaps even prosperity.

IV CONCLUSION

This chapter has attempted to assess the challenges of revitalizing a depressed post-industrial economy by examining the modern state of a primary example of such a city—Pittsburgh, Pennsylvania—both by contrasting that city with its earlier self and by framing that examination in terms offered by a leading urban economist, Benjamin Chinitz. Chinitz's work, published in 1961 and based in part on a review of Pittsburgh then, emphasized the role of supply considerations in regional growth, and particularly the supply of a diverse field of firms and sources of labor and capital.

In view of Chinitz's framing, the state of Pittsburgh now is not surprising, as an economy part of the way to restoration of its good health with a diverse, innovation-based economy built on the rubble of a collapsed industrial monoculture. That is so despite the fact that it is essentially impossible to diagnose a cause-and-effect relationship between any particular step that Pittsburgh took (or had thrust upon it) either as a matter of public policy or as a matter of economics, history, or culture. Pittsburgh has not reinvented itself in the wake of the collapse of the steel industry. Reinvention has happened, in part. The difference between those two statements is important. "Pittsburgh," if that name means "the government, business, and educational leaders of the city and region," was forced by circumstance to try to execute a strategy of economic diversification and real estate development. Much of the region's subsequent success should be attributed not to top-down policy or legal changes but instead to payoffs of institutional investments made decades ago or to changes in investment and employment patterns made possible by the elimination of dominant firms, or both.

Pittsburgh's relative success today bears the hallmarks both of the long struggle to recapture regional prosperity that Chinitz predicted in the wake of troubles in concentrated Pittsburgh economy, and also of emerging Chinitz-style agglomeration. In both senses, Pittsburgh's evolution toward a new economy remains a work in progress. Via lots of individual and local efforts, project by project and neighborhood by neighborhood, change has accumulated over time to the point where Pittsburgh is able to stand back and point with justifiable pride to a more or less crazy quilt of relative prosperity, rather than a single pattern of progress. The people of Pittsburgh, over a long period of time and in fits and starts involving some who were already here, some who moved in, and some who have since moved on, invested time and money in things that they were and are passionate about. Some of that is scientific and technological research; some of it is the arts; some of it is starting and growing businesses; some of it is building institutions; some of it is building buildings; some of it is nurturing communities and families. Some of it is an intense desire to get rich; some of it is an intense desire to give back. That collective energy was once tethered to the fact and the mythos of the steel industry. The literal tethers largely disappeared by the mid-1980s. The metaphorical and emotional tethers have been fraying for some time. That collective energy is now tethered instead to the idea of a new Pittsburgh, built on the foundations of the old Pittsburgh. Revitalization is bottom up, not top down, and the pattern of revitalization reveals some significant gaps. Much of Pittsburgh remains poor, however, and the revitalization narrative has a long way to go before Pittsburgh may justifiably declare itself restored. If, as Chinitz hypothesized and as more recent economists argue, economic growth is most pronounced in regions characterized by high rates of new business formation, then Pittsburgh, with a low rate on that metric, has a long way to go.

The lesson here for law reformers and policymakers may not be that Pittsburgh would have been better off leaving redevelopment to the private market, rather than trying to direct it as Pittsburgh had directed both industry and public policy for many decades. Despite the suggestion above that Chinitz's research, and more recent work by Edward Glaeser, point to minimizing government participation in economic development strategies, Pittsburgh's experience shows that a government role in economic development can be useful, particularly given the absence of underlying agglomeration effects in the region. Even stronger government intervention than what Pittsburgh experienced might have been helpful, in certain respects. Formation of new firms might have been encouraged by more aggressive federal policies directed to commercialization of federally funded university research, or by changes in Pennsylvania's employment law to facilitate employee mobility.[50] But Pittsburgh made a great deal of progress without either of those steps being taken, and even accounting for

---

[50] Unlike California, Pennsylvania enforces "reasonable" noncompetition agreements.

the risk that government processes, like market processes, have been and are subject to abuse and exploitation for a variety of well-known reasons.

Instead, it is better to say that government (and its products, law and policy) have been most effective and productive when they have supported access and community engagement by a broad spectrum of firms, organizations, and individuals and have been least effective or productive when they have limited engagement or discouraged or slowed down forms of community participation, whether related to business opportunity or to some other form of culture. Public-private partnerships, such as the original Allegheny Conference on Community Development, thrived and helped Pittsburgh considerably when the region's economy was most concentrated in steel. As that economy broke down and has slowly been replaced in recent years by a more diversified model, the Pittsburgh region has prospered most in recent years when the cost of participation—neighborhood engagement, redevelopment of older and empty building sites, entrepreneurship, individual well-being and happiness—has been the lowest. The example of the ACCD suggests that the appropriate role of the public sector in a concentrated economy was to consolidate resources, including new entrants and opportunities for community participation, so that the consolidated resources could work to offset the harmful spillovers of that economy. In an agglomerated economy, the role of the public sector may be the reverse, that is, to protect and enable a broadly distributed range of equivalent resources, such as entrepreneurship, so that they can leverage and extend the positive spillovers from that economy. In Pittsburgh's experience, industrial and cultural histories are sources of great community pride and power in the former context, but are also great sources of drag and delay in the latter. As Chinitz might have said, sentiment is, in part, a price paid by entrepreneurs.

The challenge for contemporary policymakers is that history and culture change slowly, if at all, and rarely in response to policy changes. Government sponsorship of real estate development and entrepreneurship, evidenced in Pittsburgh by contemporary institutions like the URA and Innovation Works, are sources of growth but are also costs of participation. Government's role in renewal and growth is susceptible to continued policy adjustment, at least in principle. We do not know what Pittsburgh might look like if and when government sponsorship were withdrawn, if for no other reason than that public funds might be directed to other things. Pittsburgh might crash again, for it would turn out that Pittsburgh's post-industrial economy is as dependent on central state support as its industrial economy was dependent on a steel oligopoly. Or, the most optimistic vision implicit in the work of Ben Chinitz might prevail, and Pittsburgh might then discover that in the absence of a central government role in development, the region has supplies of time, energy, initiative, passion, vision, and capital that are large and diverse enough not only to keep Pittsburgh on its current positive path but also to propel it forward sustainably, and on a more broadly prosperous trajectory well into the 21st century.

8. IP and entrepreneurship in an evolving economy: a case study

Michael Risch*

INTRODUCTION

That intellectual assets—whether protected or not—are of growing importance in evolving economies is practically unassailable.[1] Unfortunately,
getting that message across to members of those economies might prove
difficult. This chapter takes a ground-level look at one law school's
attempt to aid an evolving economy through entrepreneurial legal assistance. The West Virginia University Entrepreneurship Law Clinic (hereinafter "ELC") was formed to help entrepreneurs and small businesses
throughout the state to start and run businesses. The goal was to help
those businesses leverage their intellectual property to drive economic
development in the state.

The results, however, were unexpected. To be sure, the ELC helped
many entrepreneurs, but little of that aid involved intellectual property
(IP), with the notable exception of trademark protection. The problem

*   ©2011 The author thanks participants at the Evolving Economies Conference
at Texas Wesleyan Law School for their helpful comments and the West Virginia
University College of Law for permission to tell this story and share the data.
Research assistance was provided by Cailyn Reilly, Gabriele Wohl, and Jenny Maxey.

[1]   *See, e.g.,* Megan M. Carpenter, *'Will Work': The Role of Intellectual Property
in Transitional Economies – from Coal to Content,* in Shubha Ghosh & Robin Paul
Malloy, (eds), CREATIVITY LAW AND ENTREPRENEURSHIP 49 (Cheltenham, UK,
Northampton, MA, U.S.A.: Edward Elgar Publishing, 2011); Elias G. Carayannis,
*et al., Technological learning for entrepreneurial development (TL4ED) in the
Knowledge Economy (KE): Case Studies and Lessons Learned,* 26 TECHNOVATION
419, (2006); Lubomira Ivanova & Anne Layne-Farrar, *The Role of Intellectual
Property Rights in Transition Economies: Lessons from Bulgaria* (September 30,
2008), available at http://ssrn.com/abstract=1275988; Josh Lerner, *Patent Protection
Over 150 Years,* NBER Working Paper No. 8977 (2002), *available at* http://
www.epip.eu/papers/20030424/epip/papers/cd/papers_speakers/Lerner_Paper_
EPIP_210403.pdf; Sunil Kanwar and Robert Evenson, *Does Intellectual Property
Protection Spur Technological Change?,* 55 OXFORD ECONOMIC PAPERS 235 (2003).

Table 8.1   GDP for West Virginia in 1997, 2002 and 2009

Industry (in millions)	1997	% Total	2002	% Total	2009	% Total
Mining	$2,848	8.94	$2,927	7.94	$5,985	11.99
Manufacturing	$5,908	18.55	$5,243	14.22	$5,577	11.17
Information	$987	3.10	$1,254	3.40	$1,415	2.84
Finance and insurance	$1,347	4.23	$1,937	5.25	$3,005	6.02
Professional and technical services	$1,170	3.67	$1,724	4.68	$2,503	5.02
Health care and social assistance	$3,026	9.50	$4,083	11.07	$5,950	11.92
Private industries Total	$31,853		$36,874		$49,907	

was not so much a lack of desire by entrepreneurs, but rather a lack of business plans, ideas, and training to create and build IP-based businesses.

This experience can be generalized. While IP is the new trick that will help an evolving economy grow, one must first teach the old dogs—and their young offspring. In this sense, the ELC's best clients may be the least expected: university professors and students. They are great clients not because of the business they bring to the clinic, but because of the symbiotic relationships innovative faculty and new college graduates and lawyers might forge early in their careers that will lead to a new IP-based business culture.

WEST VIRGINIA AS AN EVOLVING ECONOMY

West Virginia is an evolving economy, even if its residents are unaware of it. Indeed, a few of my former colleagues in West Virginia expressed surprise that I was discussing West Virginia in a "evolving economy" book. West Virginia has traditionally been a mining and manufacturing state, but that is changing—at least in part. The U.S. Bureau of Economic Analysis tracks the industry transformation: Table 8.1 shows West Virginia's GDP in three select years for a few industries.

The drop in manufacturing, both in absolute terms and as a percentage of GDP is significant, and perhaps surprising to some. This shift alone shows that West Virginia's economy is evolving.[2] Two other industries are

---

[2]   *See* Carpenter, *supra* note 1, for an account of the decrease in manufacturing and historical importance of mining.

also worth discussion. First, the conventional wisdom is that employment in mining is decreasing as mechanization increases, but the data does not necessarily bear that out.

Mining appears to be a larger percentage of GDP now than in 1997. Employment wage data also shows that wages in mining have at least held steady in traditional mining, and have risen in oil and gas extraction. An increase in oil and gas represents a large portion of the increase in overall mining industry wages and GDP.

While these levels are perhaps lower than in the 1950s or even 1980s, this chapter is focused on the current evolution rather than the drop from the more distant past. To be sure, extraction is significantly down from historical peaks. Now, however, despite mechanization and modernization, West Virginia's evolution is not currently trending away from natural resource extraction as much as some might think. It may be that the transition in mining was mostly complete by the mid-1990s; this may be why some were surprised to hear that the economy is evolving.

The second industry worth consideration is information. While absolute GDP in information industries has grown somewhat, its percentage of total GDP has remained steady, which is a bit surprising given the technological boom of the last fifteen years. In fact, gross wages in this industry have actually decreased, possibly because of automation and outsourcing. In other words, fewer people are employed in West Virginia generating the same percentage of GDP in information industries.

Based on these trends, it appears that the political and business leaders of West Virginia are keenly aware of the need for economic development generally and of entrepreneurship and innovation specifically. When I joined the West Virginia University (WVU) faculty in 2007, there were many economic development programs and agencies throughout the state. None of these programs, however, addressed the legal issues relating to entrepreneurship and innovation.

There is little doubt of West Virginia's need for a broad-based entrepreneurship and innovation law program. In 2007, LexisNexis (lawyers. com) listed a total of twenty-three lawyers practicing intellectual property in West Virginia, and the IP committee of the state bar was approximately the same size. While there may be more than this associated with corporations, fewer than twenty-five IP attorneys statewide is too few, even for a state the size of West Virginia. The number is certainly too few to meet the needs of a state that wants to foster entrepreneurship and innovation.

Similarly, Richard Gruner, a law professor at John Marshall School of Law, studied the number of patent attorneys in given states and locales in an effort to find a link between the number of IP attorneys and the amount of innovation. West Virginia ranks toward the bottom of per capita patent attorneys. In 2007, there were fewer than fifteen patent lawyers living in the state, and most of them worked for Mylan, a pharmaceutical company. Whether IP attorneys fuel industry or the technology industry creates demands for IP attorneys, a link between the two suggests that having more trained IP attorneys in West Virginia would be desirable.[3]

FOUNDING THE WVU ENTREPRENEURSHIP LAW CLINIC

The West Virginia University College of Law's Entrepreneurship Law Clinic was a long time coming. In the late 1990s, Joyce McConnell, WVU's associate dean of academic affairs,[4] envisioned an economic development center at the College of Law. By 2005, she and Dean John Fisher had convinced the provost to create a new faculty position for a professor with entrepreneurial experience to work with WVU's research commercialization group.[5]

Academia moves slowly, and it was not until 2007 that I joined the faculty as that professor. My charge was deceptively simple: to start a program of my choosing to advance economic development in the area.

I spent my first year doing due diligence. I met with lawyers in the area, WVU's economic development team, the director of the business school's Entrepreneurship Center, and others to learn about entrepreneurship in the area. I researched the entrepreneurship programs at other law schools[6] and identified all of the entrepreneur and small business support organizations I could find. Finally, I taught an Intellectual Property Practicum that accepted real assignments from law firms that

---

[3] *See, e.g.*, Anne Kelly, *Practicing in the Patent Marketplace*, 78 U. CHI. L. REV. 115, 115 (2011) (discussing growth in patent licensing).

[4] Joyce McConnell is now Dean of the College of Law.

[5] Many schools, especially public schools, have such research arms to separate research grant and patent exploitation from public funds. At WVU, this was called the "Research Corp."

[6] *See* Patricia H. Lee, *The Role and Impact of Clinical Programs on Entrepreneurship and Economic Growth*, *in* ENTREPRENEURSHIP AND INNOVATION IN EVOLVING ECONOMIES (*infra*, Chapter 9) for a discussion of programs at law schools.

were supervised by area attorneys; this provided me with information about IP needs in the state.

Toward the end of that first year, I developed a proposal for an ambitious Entrepreneurship, Innovation, and Law Program. The proposal described five subject areas: 1) Clinical Education/Public Service—the Entrepreneurship Law Clinic; 2) Outreach—informal programs for the public and lawyers, beginning with a Law Review Symposium on digital entrepreneurship; 3) Curriculum—development of a cohesive set of classes that support and teach entrepreneurship; 4) Scholarship—support for scholarship in entrepreneurship; and 5) Internship/Externship development—connecting students with firms, companies, and agencies that could provide an educational benefit.

Most of these prongs were implemented in the ordinary course of school business. For example, we obtained grant funding for the Digital Entrepreneurship symposium, which was well attended and hosted scholars and practitioners from all over the country.[7] Furthermore, the law school implemented an extensive externship program with its own director, and entrepreneurial externships were incorporated into that program.

The clinic, however, ran into some hiccups. Despite work during the first year, the grant proposal was considered too uncertain, but we were not deterred. Taking the advice of the Benedum Foundation's program coordinator, we spent the summer of 2008 meeting with law firms, small business advisors, and other constituents to introduce the clinic and generate interest and, more importantly, referrals.

The meetings were time well spent. I learned much more about entrepreneurial support within the state, met many of the lawyers working in the area, made contacts with business professors, and even found my first adjunct professor.

However, one group of lawyers I *did not* meet was IP lawyers. I met a couple of lawyers working in IP, but they worked for big firms for big clients. The lack of IP lawyers in the state was quite apparent.

This shortage, I theorized, must have meant that there was a large population of burgeoning companies that would be unable to find representation. I believed that the ELC would fill that void, providing IP services to entrepreneurs, among the other services provided. At the end of the summer, Benedum granted us sufficient funds to launch a pilot clinic, and we were able to test that theory beginning in the fall of 2008.

---

[7]   *See* Michael Risch, *Virtual Rule of Law*, 112 W. VA. L. REV. 1 (2009).

Table 8.2   Type and amounts of services provided by the ELC in its first two years

Type of Service	Clients Served Year 1	Clients Served Year 2
Amendments to Organizational Documents	2	4
Articles & Operating Agreements/Bylaws	14	17
Business Plan Counseling (competition)	10	10
Contracts Drafting/Reviewing	8	25
Copyright Counseling	3	5
Dissolution/Buy-Outs	4	2
Employee Handbooks/Policy Manuals	2	1
LLC Formation	6	12
Nonprofit Filings	7	3
Patent Searches	2	6
Website Terms of Use	N/A	5
Trademarks	10	24
Informational Memorandums	N/A	17
Cease-and-Desist Letters	N/A	3
Tax Recommendations	N/A	11
Annual Report Filings	N/A	2

CLIENTELE IN AN EVOLVING ECONOMY

As expected, there was no shortage of clients during the first two years at the clinic. The ELC served forty-six and sixty clients respectively. However, surprisingly few of the clients required intellectual property services, despite our best efforts to find IP issues among client needs. Table 8.2 lists the type and amounts of services provided by the clinic during those two years.

While the amount of IP work grew during the second year, it was still much less than I had hoped for or expected. For example, there were only eight total patent searches, resulting in a single provisional patent application referred out to a patent attorney (located nearly three hours away in Charleston, WV). Similarly there was some copyright assistance, but this was less than 7.5% of the work, and only for two or three clients. One bright spot was trademark work; students either cleared marks, filed applications, or both, 34 times.

The lack of IP work was not due to company type. Figure 8.1 details the types of clients served by the ELC in its second year.

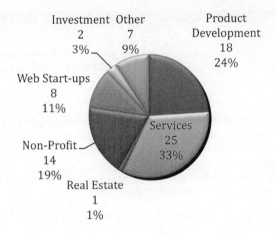

Figure 8.1   Types of clients served by the ELC in its second year

As the figure shows, there were plenty of clients that might have needed IP services including more than fifty product, service, or internet companies. The question, then, is what to make of the relatively light IP needs of ELC clients, as well as potential clients that never even visited the ELC.

IP IN AN EVOLVING ECONOMY

ELC students were tasked to find IP needs of their clients, and they answered identified needs. This implies that the clients simply did not need such services. Each type of IP tells a different story.

Trademarks. Trademarks were a bright spot. Many of the clients needed trademark services. This, however, says little about the underlying entrepreneurial endeavors, nor does it speak to West Virginia's evolving economy. One would expect that any business with a name might need trademark services. Indeed, trademark filings may have been over-represented because the ELC obtained grant money that paid for filing fees. If the clients had been asked to pay the filing fees, it is probable that there would have been fewer filings. In any event, to the extent that protecting marks is important for entrepreneurs in evolving economies, the ELC succeeded.

Copyright. The copyright work was split between advice about the use of content created by others and protecting the clients' own creative work. The shortage of such work implies, quite simply, that there was little of either, and the entrepreneurs visiting the clinic were not involved in copyrightable creative expression.

Patent. Because the clinic was not supervised by registered patent attorneys, the work was limited to prior art searches that the client could then examine or deliver to a patent attorney to determine whether the expense of a patent filing was justified. The clinic did not provide such advice. The patent work was especially disconcerting for two reasons. First, the lack of clients needing searches implied limited inventive activity. Second, the searches almost always yielded existing patents that were identical to the idea our client brought. This led to the unfortunate takeaway that the client would not only be barred from patenting, but also faced risk of lawsuit if it went forward with the business plan.

Trade Secret. There was almost no trade secret work, although many of the employment agreements included confidentiality provisions. This implies that the types of products and services being offered were self-revealing. If so, then protection by copyright and patent would have been more important—and the lack of such work implies that business ideas of ELC clients might have been easily duplicated if successful. This result, of course, might be better for growth in an evolving economy.[8]

The type of IP work performed for ELC clients is a telling piece of the puzzle. The clients surely *wanted* IP services; the problem is that they did not *need* IP services. And they did not need IP services because they were not ready for them.

Instead, the typical entrepreneur had created simple mechanical products, performed services similar to many competitors, or otherwise did not create a new or unique business model or intellectual asset. This is not to fault our clients: they had great ideas, worked hard, and delivered better results than their competitors, all without heavy use of IP.

Of course, it is possible that West Virginia is teeming with startups receiving paid IP services from lawyers both within and outside the state.

---

[8] DORON S. BEN-ATAR, TRADE SECRETS (New Haven, U.S.A.: Yale University Press, 2004) 99-101 (arguing that America's early economic development was founded on the emigration of skilled labor from Europe to the United States and the ensuing knowledge transfer); Yochai Benkler, *Growth-Oriented Law for the Networked Information Economy: Emphasizing Freedom to Operate Over Power to Appropriate*, RULES FOR GROWTH: PROMOTING INNOVATION AND GROWTH THROUGH LEGAL REFORM 314 (The Kauffman Task Force on Law, Innovation, and Growth, Kansas City, MO, U.S.A.: Ewing Marion Kauffman Foundation, 2011) ("The benefits of crisply defined and enforced appropriation models are outweighed by the fact that in order to secure that appropriability, the law has set up a set of rules that, in protecting yesterday's actors, limits to too great an extent the freedom of new innovators to operate today.").

Given my discussions with other lawyers and referral agencies, there were a few startups with technology, but not too many. WVU ran a business incubator that had very few technology clients compared to incubators in other states.

There were, however, many people with ideas but little knowledge about business plans, little resources for development, and little training about how to best create new intellectual assets.

In short, the ELC may have been ahead of the curve with respect to IP. To be sure, the clinic was necessary and helpful with respect to many other legal needs facing West Virginia entrepreneurs, but its role in aiding IP development was trailing. With both time and help—partly from the ELC, but mostly from elsewhere—West Virginia entrepreneurs will eventually find their IP legs and start running.

IMPLICATIONS

The WVU ELC experience reveals a central conceit of those who believe law can create economic development in an evolving economy. With the possible exception of legal structure allowing for enforceable transactions,[9] the law does not create economic development. Instead, it must follow and support that development. There can be no IP protection without IP, and there can be no IP without knowledge, investment,[10] and infrastructure.[11] One study categorizes priorities for growth:

> The priorities of new venture formation in the knowledge economy are: [computers] and Internet access; linkages to investors and lenders; formation of lean management and advisory boards comprised of experienced individuals . . .; and planning and securing facilities. The priorities of e-development and sustained growth are: the ability to evaluate and react to risk well; protection of product; stimulation of existing market; and the available population of skilled knowledge workers. . . .[12]

---

[9]   *See generally* Michael Risch, *Virtual Rule of Law*, 112 W. Va. L. Rev. 1 (2009), for a discussion of the role of law in a new economy, albeit a "virtual" one.

[10]   *See* Brian Krumm, *State Legislative Efforts to Improve Access to Venture Capital, in* Entrepreneurship and Innovation in Evolving Economies (*infra*, Chapter 2) for discussion about state run venture capital.

[11]   *See, e.g.*, Ivanova & Layne-Farrar, *supra* note 1, at 20 (describing slow growth in Bulgaria despite intellectual property rights due to lack of supporting infrastructure).

[12]   Carayannis, *supra* note 1, at 435.

Protection of products is low on the list and comes only after successful formation. This does not mean that IP clinics and other IP lawyers should abandon the effort.[13] Rather, efforts should be retargeted to better meet the needs of entrepreneurs in the evolving economy.

Provide generalized services – not just IP. Even if entrepreneurs in some evolving economies are slow to develop IP, they still need other legal services.[14] This means that clinics should provide not only IP services, but also other entrepreneurial services such as incorporation, contract, employment, and real estate. A generalized entrepreneurship clinic—as opposed to a specialized IP clinic—would serve at least three purposes in an evolving economy. First, it would support entrepreneurs while they transition to IP-based businesses. Second, it would provide another means for encouraging entrepreneurs to develop IP while pursuing non-IP businesses. Third, it would ensure that IP services were in place when necessary.

Seek out university professors and students. Law school clinics are in a good position to both encourage and serve university professors and students. Professors and students starting businesses are more likely than most to develop intellectual assets.[15] This is especially true where the school provides a concentration in engineering and sciences. Furthermore, some universities grant the right to exploit intellectual property back to professors. These professors and their companies can be the leading edge of technology growth in an area. Finally, academic relationships can be helpful even without startups. Most students find employment at companies, many professors consult with business, and some professors even transition out of academia. Their experience with IP and IP-based legal services provided by clinics can help encourage

---

[13]   Alizabeth Newman, *Bridging the Justice Gap: Building Community by Responding to Individual Need*, 17 CLINICAL L. REV. 615, 621–30 (2011) (discussing need for clinical services in underserved economies).

[14]   Oliver R. Goodenough, *Digital Firm Formation*, RULES FOR GROWTH: PROMOTING INNOVATION AND GROWTH THROUGH LEGAL REFORM 343 (The Kauffman Task Force on Law, Innovation, and Growth Kansas City, Missouri, U.S.A.: Ewing Marion Kauffman Foundation, 2011) (discussing importance of company formation to growth).

[15]   Robert E. Litan and Robert Cook-Deegan, *Universities and Economic Growth: The Importance of Academic Entrepreneurship*, RULES FOR GROWTH: PROMOTING INNOVATION AND GROWTH THROUGH LEGAL REFORM 56–59 (The Kauffman Task Force on Law, Innovation, and Growth, Kansas City, MO, U.S.A.: Ewing Marion Kauffman Foundation, 2011) (discussing importance of university faculty innovation).

the development of intellectual assets long after the clinic has stopped representation.

Partner with business schools and other strategic coaches. Clinics should partner with students at affiliated business schools to provide joint advice to startups. The ELC students did their best to provide general business advice where necessary, with varying results based on the students' own education and experience. Such efforts would be bolstered by others who are actively pursuing degrees in business planning and management. One of the biggest hurdles facing the ELC clients was the development of a business plan that would differentiate the business from competitors both locally and nationally.[16] Other groups in the area provided small business assistance, but in my experience that assistance was more basic, even if more necessary. Community development organizations were focused on business plans for survival—how to get bank loans, how to track money, how to advertise, etc. These are critically important skills in any economy, let alone an evolving one. The goal of a joint business/law clinic is to work with other development organizations to aid entrepreneurs in taking the next step toward IP differentiation.[17] Furthermore, the experience would provide law students with exposure to new skills to aid their own strategic advice while in practice.[18]

Provide training on the importance of IP. Not all IP encouragement need be provided directly to legal clients. Entrepreneurial clinics should also offer generalized outreach, through websites, brochures, and live seminars. These materials and classes would teach about the different types of intellectual property, why each type is important for different kinds of businesses, and how each type can be protected. The overriding goal is the same: encouraging the development of IP while waiting for the area's entrepreneurs to catch up.[19]

---

[16]   Kevin Rivette and David Kline, *Discovering New Value in Intellectual Property*, Jan–Feb. 2000 HARVARD BUSINESS REV. 54, 54 (Xerox CEO: "I'm convinced that the management of IP is how value added is going to be created . . . . Increasingly, companies that are good at managing IP will win.").

[17]   Newman, *supra* note 13 at 635 (discussing importance of focus on the individual, even in economic growth clinics).

[18]   *See*, Sean M. O'Connor, *Transforming Professional Services to Build Regional Innovation Ecosystems,* in ENTREPRENEURSHIP AND INNOVATION IN EVOLVING ECONOMIES (*infra*, Chapter 4) for further discussion about lawyers as strategic consultants.

[19]   *See*, Michael J. Madison, *Contrasts in Innovation: Pittsburgh Then and Now*, *in* ENTREPRENEURSHIP AND INNOVATION IN EVOLVING ECONOMIES (*infra*, Chapter 7) for a case study of one region's experience with changing entrepreneurship.

CONCLUSION

Intellectual property will surely be important to some, if not all, growth areas in evolving economies. The West Virginia experience indicates that the law may not drive IP growth as much as lawyers would like to think. Instead, IP protection will likely trail the development of intellectual assets to protect. As a result, IP lawyers should focus not only on protection, but also on development: development of IP-producing founders, development of IP-based business plans, and development of businesses that survive long enough for their founders to execute the business plans.

In this "chicken and egg" problem, the technical must come first. Once the effort begins, however, momentum and symbiosis should help entrepreneurs and their IP lawyers jointly to increase the pace of evolution.

9. The role and impact of clinical programs on entrepreneurship and economic growth

Patricia H. Lee*

I. INTRODUCTION

The interplay of entrepreneurship law clinical programs and economic growth first interested me when I directed the first entrepreneurship law clinical program designed to represent entrepreneurs with their private sector business transactions in 1998.[1] The idea of dedicated law students advocating on behalf of emerging entrepreneurs in a law school clinical

* ©2011 Professor Lee thanks Megan Carpenter, Professor of Texas Wesleyan Law School for convening the Evolving Economies conference and book project and all of the authors in this upcoming book; WVU College of Law Professors William Rhee, Gregory Bowman, Jena Martin-Amerson, Atiba Ellis, and Megan Annitto for their thoughtful comments about the scholarship; Brian Corcoran, who as a third-year WVU law student and member of the Entrepreneurship, Innovation and Law Program assisted with numerous hours of legal research and data collection; Dallas F. Kratzer III, a second-year WVU law student, who assisted with citations; Marcus Lee, from Northwestern University Medill School of Journalism who provided helpful editorial and journalistic comments; Brandon Lee, a volunteer with the National Institute for Urban Entrepreneurship who spent many hours assisting with data entry and appendices; Professor Michael Risch for his vision in founding the program at WVU College of Law and Dean Joyce McConnell of WVU College of Law for her constant support of WVU law faculty, staff and students.

[1] William Mellor & Patricia H. Lee, *Institute for Justice Clinic on Entrepreneurship: A Real World Model in Stimulating Private Enterprise in the Inner City*, 5 J. SMALL & EMERGING BUS. L. 71 (2001) (providing a brief overview of the watershed decisions and building blocks necessary to open a clinical legal program at the University of Chicago School of Law, which was designed to educate law students, assist entry-level entrepreneurs with start-up transactions, and help entrepreneurs navigate the regulatory arena; and illustrating the transformative potential of entrepreneurship in economically depressed communities).

setting[2] was, on the one hand, a means to provide real skills training to law and business students and, on the other, a means to advance the cause of economic growth. As dot.com companies grew, the idea of advocating on behalf of entrepreneurs from divergent walks of life so that they too could contribute to economic growth and participate in the American dream of starting their own business, seemed just and plausible. The time never seemed better, considering a convergence of technology, entrepreneurial enthusiasm and law and business students eager to assist clients. However, unbeknownst to most market participants, including myself, the dot.com era, or as some would call it, the information technology bubble, would end by early 2000.[3]

Despite the demise of venture funding for dot.com businesses and the unique exuberance of the era, in the next decade, law clinical programs continued to play a vibrant role of representing and advocating on behalf of entrepreneurs, small businesses, and nonprofits. First, the economy continued to evolve in several ways. Communities across America experienced a downturn in the economy. People lost jobs due to global job outsourcing by giant multinational corporations; and other individuals forfeited home and business assets at rates unseen since the depression. Second, since giant corporations were no longer the predominant job creators as they once were,[4] small and microenterprise innovators stepped into a new role of creating a majority of the U.S. jobs and a greater share of economic growth. Thus, it should be no surprise that as small and microenterprises grew there would be an increasing

---

[2]   Thomas Morsh & Patricia H. Lee, Entrepreneurship and Law, Address at the United States Association of Business and Entrepreneurship Conference (Feb. 17, 2000); *see also* THE ASSOCIATION FOR LEGAL CAREER PROFESSIONALS, 2010 SURVEY OF LAW SCHOOL EXPERIENTIAL LEARNING OPPORTUNITIES AND BENEFITS (2011), http://www.nalp.org/uploads/2010ExperientialLearningStudy.pdf (last visited Aug. 5, 2011) (reporting that, of associates who had participated in at least one legal clinic during law school, 63.1% rated their clinic experience as very useful, the highest ranking possible in the survey; this percentage of satisfaction with clinical programs and externships was higher than groups reported for classroom skills courses and pro bono offerings).
[3]   James K. Galbraith & Travis Hale, *Income Distribution and the Information Technology Bubble* (Univ. of Texas Inequality Project, Working Paper No. 27, 2004), *available at* http://utip.gov.utexas.edu/papers/utip_27.pdf (last visited Aug. 5, 2011).
[4]   R.M. HODGETTS & DONALD F. KURATKO, ENTREPRENEURSHIP: THEORY, PROCESS, AND PRACTICE 4–5 (Mason, Ohio, U.S.A.: South-Western et al., 6th ed. 2004) (explaining that, since 1980, Fortune 500 companies have lost more than five million jobs, but more than thirty-four million new jobs have been created).

role on the part of law clinical programs there to support this growth and innovation.

The seedling idea that start-up firms are engines of economic growth,[5] and create jobs, is now a consensus idea with data to support it. A recent Kauffman Foundation study noted that while existing firms are net job destroyers, they are losing one million jobs net combined per year. In contrast, in their first year, new firms add an average of three million jobs.[6] Existing law clinical programs that serve entrepreneurs, small business and nonprofits have been in a position to assist individuals and enterprises in contributing their respective goods and services, living out their dreams, and creating economic and job growth for their communities.

This chapter provides an overview of the historical foundation and educational milestones of law clinical education and programs. The chapter further illustrates what clinical scholars describe as the third wave of clinical legal education,[7] as a time frame that includes the evolution and growth of entrepreneurship/transactional law clinical programs. This evolution starts with traditional clinical programs in the early 1900s, expands to community economic development programs in the 1980s and then evolves into a variety of entrepreneurship/transactional programs.[8] The empirical data retrieved from law school websites, brochures, newsletters, list-serves and personal contacts for the period ending June 2011, details law school capacity, numbers of programs, state geographic distribution,

---

[5]   Tim Kane, *The Importance of Startups in Job Creation and Job Destruction*, KAUFFMAN FOUNDATION (Kansas City, Missouri, U.S.A.: Ewing Marion Kauffman Foundation, July 2010), http://www.kauffman.org/uploadedFiles/firm_formation_importance_of_Startups.pdf (last visited Aug. 8, 2011) (revealing that, both on average and for all but seven years between 1977 and 2005, existing firms are net job destroyers, losing one million jobs net combined per year, and that, in contrast, new firms, within their first year, add an average of three million jobs per year); *see also Embracing Innovation: Entrepreneurship and American Economic Growth*, KAUFFMAN FOUNDATION (Nov. 4, 2008), http://ssrn.com/abstract=1260355.
[6]   *Id.*
[7]   Margaret Martin Barry, Jon C. Dubin & Peter A. Joy, *Clinical Education for This Millennium: The Third Wave*, 7 CLINICAL L. REV. 1, 4 (2000).
[8]   Entrepreneurship/transactional clinical programs are defined as law clinical programs that include the following types of live client clinics in law school settings: entrepreneurship, small business, intellectual property, housing and tax representation (transactional and not litigation focused) and the more traditional community economic development programs. Not included in the definition are law clinical programs that focus principally on civil and criminal litigation, arbitration, mediation or administrative matters, although these particular clinics offer extremely valuable services to clients and advance student learning.

and states that lead with these types of programs. In the next section, we discuss our insights and our findings.

II. INSIGHTS

Insight 1: Law School Capacity

Most law schools have a law clinical program. Among all of the law schools in the country, there were a total of 1,258 clinical programs. Of those programs, 110 of the 200 ABA-approved law schools are hosting 138 entrepreneurship/transactional law clinical programs. (See Appendices 9A.1, 9A.2 and 9A.3.) What we found was that some schools had more than one program. Generally, the higher the law school ranking, the more of these types of clinical programs that we found were offered by the school. This aspect of the data presented at least one unexpected finding. Schools that we found in the top tier that had multiple entrepre-neurship/transactional clinical programs were: Yale, Harvard, Stanford, Loyola Marymount University (Los Angeles), Arizona State University, American University (Washington, DC), Illinois Institute of Technology (Chicago-Kent), University of Virginia, William Mitchell College of Law, Columbia University, Fordham University, Northwestern Lewis & Clark College, Pennsylvania State University, University of Pennsylvania, Vanderbilt University, University of Utah (Quinney), University of Washington, Brooklyn Law School, and Seattle University.

One might not expect that the more prestigious universities would be at the forefront of advancing entrepreneurship/transactional clinical programs. Rather, our expectation was that law schools designed to educate law students to provide practical legal training might host the vast majority of these law clinical programs. Therefore, to the extent that there is a correlation between law school rankings and the number of entrepreneurship/ transactional law clinical programs offered, calls for more research to assess the goals and objectives of these programs and to gain an appreciation of the reasons multiple programs may provide added value to the school, law students and the community.[9] One might conjecture that higher-ranked universities have a greater ability to broaden their capacity

---

[9] The rationale for the creation of entrepreneurship/transactional clinical programs may vary: societal concerns, student demand, foundation and other philanthropic support, market and academic competitive forces, job-creation initiatives, faculty and alumni interest, and faculty clinical and experiential tenure track incentives.

of offerings, in light of endowments and the interests and demands of their admitted student population, alumni pool and their local community.

Insight 2: Number of Entrepreneurship/Transactional Clinical Programs

Of the 110 law schools with 138 entrepreneurship/transactional clinical programs, the average number of programs per law school was greater than one largely because of the top-tier law schools. Seventy-nine top-tier law schools hosted 104 such programs. In third- and fourth-tier law schools, the average number of their entrepreneurship/transactional clinical programs was equal to one such program per law school. (See Appendices 9A.1, 9A.2 and 9A.3.) We found twenty-five third-tier law schools are hosting twenty-five programs and nine fourth-tier law schools are hosting nine programs.

Insight 3: State Geographic Distribution

As of June 2011, there were thirty-eight states and the District of Columbia with at least one entrepreneurship/transactional program in a law-school setting.[10] At the same time, a dozen states currently do not offer such a program in their state.[11] Alaska, Delaware, Iowa, Louisiana, Mississippi,[12] Montana, Nevada, North Dakota, Rhode Island, South Dakota, Vermont, and Wyoming are the states currently without such a clinical program as of June 2011, although Mississippi is developing a new program.

As we discuss in the next section, law schools and states that do have

---

[10]   California and New York have the most entrepreneurship/transactional clinics with ten such clinics in each state; Illinois has seven clinics; Ohio and Pennsylvania each have six clinics; Massachusetts, Minnesota, Washington, North Carolina, Florida and the District of Columbia each have four clinics; Michigan, Oregon, Texas, and Virginia each have three clinics; Maine, New Jersey, South Carolina, Missouri, Tennessee, Connecticut, Arizona, Kansas, Colorado, Maryland, Indiana and West Virginia each have two clinics in state; and with only one such clinic in the state are Idaho, Alabama, Georgia, Nebraska, Kentucky, Arkansas, New Mexico, New Hampshire, Utah, Hawaii, and Wisconsin.

[11]   Additional research is needed to determine what additional roles law schools and states provide that do not host such a clinical program.

[12]   *News from the Clinical World*, AALS CLINICAL SECTION NEWSLETTER (Ass'n Am. L. Sch., Washington, D.C., U.S.A.), Spring 2011, at 18–19 (noting that the University of Mississippi Law School is developing a new transactional law clinic with the assistance of Brian Price, director of Harvard's Transactional Law Clinics). Since this program is in development for the upcoming year, it has been counted in the aggregate figure.

entrepreneurship/transactional clinical programs are fostering entrepreneurship and contributing to the economic growth in their state and local area. The impact of not having such a program at a contributing institution (i.e. a law school) is likely to be profound. We contend that there are ramifications relating to business start-ups, job creation, investment in new private or public enterprises, academic and educational legal skills training and interdisciplinary collaborations. Each of these categories would be opportunities that clinical entrepreneurship/transactional programs create in their respective sponsoring institution and community.

In the next section, we look closer at the role and impact of these law clinical programs. Measurements and benchmarks are useful and provide a means to determine whether, what manner and to what extent clinical programs play a role in fostering entrepreneurship and impacting economic growth.

III. ROLE AND IMPACT ON ECONOMIC GROWTH AND ENTREPRENEURSHIP

[T]he entrepreneurial team is a key ingredient in the . . . venture.[13] – Jeffrey Timmons

The World Bank defines *economic growth* as the quantitative change or expansion in a country's economy as measured by a country's gross domestic product (GDP) or gross national product (GNP).[14] These indicators provide benchmarks on how well the country is doing financially. On a macroeconomic level, economic growth is measured by several factors, including: investments, both nonresidential and residential fixed investment, private investment, personal consumption, exports, imports (which would subtract from the increases), and federal government spending. From the first quarter to the second quarter of 2010, the Bureau of Economic Analysis reported increases in real GDP that primarily reflected positive contributions from nonresidential fixed investment, personal consumption expenditures, exports, federal government spending, private

---

[13] JEFFREY A. TIMMONS & STEPHEN SPINELLI, NEW VENTURE CREATION: ENTREPRENEURSHIP FOR THE 21ST CENTURY (U.S.A.: McGraw-Hill/Irwin, et al. (eds), 7th ed. 2007).

[14] Glossary of Terms, THE WORLD BANK GROUP, http://www.worldbank.org/depweb/english/beyond/global/glossary.html (last visited Aug. 4, 2011).

inventory investment, and residential fixed investment. Imports, which are a subtraction in the calculation of GDP, increased.[15]

What we do know is that in the last twelve years, gross domestic product has grown over 30%, from $41 billion in 1998 to over $53 billion in 2010.[16] However, there is a growing consensus that points out that it is new business starts of small business and entrepreneurs that has been and continues to be essential to enhance GDP. What has been learned is that a significant portion of this growth was and still is attributable to start-up enterprises.[17] Much has changed in America, when two-thirds of jobs created are derived from start-up enterprises.[18]

Additional figures have come to light that reflect positive economic growth, but a jobless recovery, necessitating a call for the need for a jobs bill.[19] Acknowledging the important contribution of small businesses to economic growth, the ADP Small Business Report states the economic indicators for the month of August relating to this contribution.[20] They reported that the only small business economic growth came from the service sector. Total small business employment lost 6,000 jobs and the goods producing sector lost 21,000 jobs. However, the service-providing sector increased the supply by 15,000 jobs.[21] Partly due to business concerns about regulations, taxes, future health care costs, plus job mismatch,

---

[15]   Press Release, U.S. Dep't of Commerce, Bureau of Econ. Analysis, National Income and Product Accounts (July 29, 2011, 8:30 a.m.), http://www.bea.gov/newsreleases/national/gdp/gdpnewsrelease.htm.

[16]   *See Real Gross Domestic Product Data from U.S. Dep't of Commerce*, FED. RESERVE BANK OF ST. LOUIS (July 29, 2011, 10:46 a.m.), http://research.stlouisfed.org/fred2/data/GDPC1.txt.

[17]   John C. Haltiwanger, Ron S. Jarmin & Javier Miranda, *Who Creates Jobs? Small vs. Large vs. Young* (Nat'l Bureau of Econ. Research, Working Paper No. 16300, 2010), *available at* http://www.nber.org/papers/w16300.

[18]   Steve Lohr, *To Create Jobs, Nurture Startups*, N.Y. TIMES (Sept. 11, 2010), http://www.nytimes.com/2010/09/12/business/12unboxed.html; *see also* Haltiwanger et al., *supra* note 18; Whitehouse, *Open for Questions: Startup America*, YOUTUBE (March 23, 2011), http://www.youtube.com/watch?v=tlm6PMmZxuQ (with Karen Mills, administrator with the U.S. Small Bus. Admin., discussing the Startup America Initiative and noting that "we know that two out of three jobs are created by small business in this country, but the fast-growing entrepreneurial companies actually create most of the net new jobs").

[19]   Neil Irwin, Lori Montgomery & Alec MacGillis, *White House Crafts Jobs Bill, A Year into Stimulus Effort*, WASH. POST , Feb. 18, 2010, http://www.washingtonpost.com/wp-dyn/content/article/2010/02/17/AR2010021701958.html.

[20]   *July 2011 ADP National Employment Report*, AUTOMATIC DATA PROCESSING, INC. (Aug. 3, 2011), http://www.adpemploymentreport.com/pdf/FINAL_Report_July_11.pdf.

[21]   *Id.*

the job force continues to decline.[22] Although it is a great measurement of the impact of start-up enterprises, a closer look suggests that there are two trends to be mindful of and, if not addressed, is a troubling sign for the future. First, the private sector continues to cut thousands of jobs.[23] Second, small start-ups are still too small to contribute to increases in employment figures. Thus, while economic growth statistics may appear encouraging, unemployment and joblessness may occur nevertheless.

This paradox is a result of two trends: giant companies contributing to growth but not to jobs[24] and smaller enterprises satisfying self-employment in early stage development, but at sizes not large enough to employ more people in the start-up years. These trends have jobs and self-employment hanging at the precipice. It is entrepreneurship/transactional clinical programs that offer one solution to the possibility of long-term job creation.

Entrepreneurship/transactional law programs do and can play an instrumental role as a resource and a member of the entrepreneurial team to help early stage companies grow and ultimately, create jobs, revenues and economic growth. The Annie Casey Foundation completed two reports of the entrepreneurship law program at The University of Chicago School of Law, which is located in an urban community of Chicago. What this foundation found was the following:

> Since its creation in 1998, the Clinic has provided intensive assistance that has resulted in creation or expansion of a business to 156 entrepreneurs, including current clients. Several hundred more have attended Clinic-sponsored workshops and networking opportunities, or have been able to turn to the Clinic for answers to questions or brief consultations. Most businesses helped by the Clinic are minority-owned, and a significant portion are headed by women. . . . [A]n informal survey conducted in 2005 found that half of the Clinic's former clients were still in business and that over half had employees in addition to the owner. When compared with national data that are available, this suggests that Clinic-assisted businesses are doing at least as well as the average, if not better—a result that is especially notable given that inner city entrepreneurs are at a particular disadvantage, because they rarely have financial flexibility to handle unexpected expenses or problems.[25]

---

[22] Jonathan Cheng & Justin Lahart, *Economic Outlook Darkens*, WALL ST. J., June 1, 2011, http://online.wsj.com/article/SB10001424052702302657404576359122470523138.html.

[23] *Id.*

[24] Roya Wolverson, *Why Don't Jobs and Corporate Profits Match Up*, TIME, June 3, 2011, http://curiouscapitalist.blogs.time.com/2011/06/03/why-dont-jobs-and-corporate-profits-match-up.

[25] *Institute for Justice: Building Wealth through Entrepreneurship*, THE ANNIE E. CASEY FOUNDATION (Baltimore, Maryland, U.S.A.: The Annie E. Casey

To the extent that there are 138 clinical law programs nationwide, we can begin to consider projections of what the likely impact is on economic growth. Using two examples of two clinical programs, the University of Chicago Law School and the West Virginia University College of Law, one can begin to evaluate the impact of these Entrepreneurship/transactional clinical programs.[26] On average, the University of Chicago program assisted approximately thirty to forty entrepreneurs and small businesses per year. On average, the West Virginia University program assisted well over forty start-ups per year. If we assume a conservative estimate of 138 law school clinical programs helping thirty enterprises per year, this would translate into 4,140 enterprises per year nationally. If 4,140 enterprises generate a minimum of $30,000 per year, this translates into $124,200,000. If all 200 ABA-approved law schools hosted one such program that helped fifty start-ups to generate $ 30,000 per year, the contribution to GDP would be an astounding $300,000,000! It is unlikely that a small law school clinical program realizes this potential.

Another way of looking at growth would be to consider job growth. As a projection, if the 4,140 enterprises hired two full-time employees or contractors, at a minimum wage per year for fifty weeks (nationally set at $7.25 in 2011)[27] this would translate into $120,060,000 added to GDP.[28] Additionally, we note the fact that any additional income generated by a start-up enterprise and its respective employees and contractors has a multiplier effect in the local community. Every revenue dollar raised is either

---

Foundation, Jan. 2008), http://www.aecf.org/~/media/Pubs/Topics/Economic%20Security/Other/InstituteforJusticeProgramProfile/INSTJ.pdf (last visited Aug. 5, 2011).

[26] Since July 1, 2010, I have served as the Director of the WVU College of Law Entrepreneurship, Innovation and Law Program, which is currently a pilot project of the U.S. Patent and Trademark Office. The program will host fourteen law students in the 2011–12 academic year. Previously, during the fall 2009 to spring 2011 period, law students assisted over 119 entrepreneurs, small businesses, and non-profits, of which approximately 100 were start-up enterprises. Just in the past year, the clinical program helped entrepreneurs, small businesses, and nonprofits with sixteen trademarks. About 75% of the clients are from West Virginia. The other 25% come from the bordering states of Pennsylvania and Maryland and from Washington, D.C., principally, although some are from other locations, including California and other countries.

[27] *Wages – Minimum Wage*, U.S. DEP'T OF LABOR, http://www.dol.gov/dol/topic/wages/minimumwage.htm (last visited Aug. 5, 2011).

[28] Additional research is needed to determine the number of start-ups assisted by all of the entrepreneurship/transactional clinical programs and other data points, such as jobs created by the start-up business, their growth in revenues, as well as their sustainability over time.

saved or consumed on items such as food, gas, clothing, transportation, and other goods and services.

Law clinical programs, entrepreneurship,[29] and economic growth, are interconnected, partly because of the nature of the clinical program's role in representing entrepreneurs and small businesses and partly due to the clients' success in accomplishing their objectives after receiving legal and technical services. Generally, the role of an entrepreneurship/transactional clinical program is to[30] advance:

- *Experiential learning* for law students interested in the area of focus of the clinical program;
- *Educational legal skills training* of law students so that they can use these skills in their lives and careers;
- *Legal and technical assistance* on legal matters critical to the success of a start-up enterprise (i.e. intellectual property, contacts, choice of entity, organization structure, licensing and permitting, basic tax, employment and business counseling, organizational governance, and regulatory compliance), and as in accordance with the canons of professional ethics of the state; and
- *A clinical setting or forum* in a law school that provides an outlet for law students to experience and learn skills and for clients to obtain legal help.

By advancing economic activities in communities with multiple constituencies (students, alumni, entrepreneurs, the university, faculty, and greater community), the role of such clinical programs could be seen as transformational to an enterprise or community's ability to advance entrepreneurship and economic growth.

Historically, traditional scholarship did not study small enterprise

---

[29] Several national organizations produce journals that provide updates on the theory and practice of entrepreneurship, including Baylor University and The Ewing Marion Kauffman Foundation in Missouri, which provides funding for scholarship and conferences of university professors and clinicians. The list-serves on entrepreneurship have proliferated and include such list-serves as E-Law List-serve of Clinical Entrepreneurship Practitioners, United States Association for Small Business and Entrepreneurship, and a list-serve at The Academy of Management.

[30] Although related, and perhaps very important to the pedagogy of many clinical programs, this chapter does not directly address in great depth the literature or programs whose sole or primary purpose relates to social justice, environmental justice, economic liberty, economic justice, or academic skills training on transactional documentation (without representation of a live client).

economic growth and productivity, but rather large firm growth and productivity.[31] Economic historian Daniel Bell explains the motivations for
this particular type of scholarship, noting that it was only after World War
II with the rebuilding of the shattered economies of Germany and Japan
and the concern with economic development of the post-colonial nations
that systematic attention turned to growth theory in economics.[32] Studies
focused their concerns on large firms' rate of capital investment, worker
output, technology and economic growth. Secondly, the perspective of the
research derived either from the firm's self-interest or sociological studies
about workers' rights and productivity.

As the U.S. economy continues to evolve, there is a need for a new paradigm and that is the study of smaller enterprises, their impact on economic
growth, job creation and economic development as is currently being done
by the Kauffman Foundation researchers and scholars.[33] Also, there is a
need to better understand and to study the role that law schools have in
GDP, in addition to the study of entrepreneurship/transactional clinical
programs.

In the next section we look at the historical evolution of the clinical law
programs and how they have grown and changed over the years.

IV.   HISTORICAL FOUNDATION (FIRST 100 YEARS OF CLINICAL LEGAL EDUCATION)

[T]o be leaders in the legal profession, Wigmore reasoned, his students needed
to be sensitive to the needs of all segments of society.[34] – Thomas Geraghty,
Associate Dean of Clinical Legal Education, Northwestern University School
of Law

---

[31]   Robert M. Solow, *A Contribution to the Theory of Economic Growth*, 70
THE QUARTERLY JOURNAL OF ECON. 65, 65–74 (1956); *see also* Robert M. Solow,
Technical Change and the Aggregate Production Function, 39 REV. OF ECON. AND
STATISTICS 312, 312–320 (1957).

[32]   DANIEL BELL, THE COMING OF POST-INDUSTRIAL SOCIETY: A VENTURE IN
SOCIAL FORECASTING ix-xvii (New York, U.S.A.: Basic Books, 1976).

[33]   U.S. DEP'T OF HOUSING AND URBAN DEV., BUILDING THE ORGANIZATIONS
THAT BUILD COMMUNITIES: STRENGTHENING THE CAPACITY OF FAITH- AND
COMMUNITY-BASED ORGANIZATIONS, Roland V. Anglin (ed.), (Washington D.C.: U.S.
Department of Housing and Urban Development, Office of Policy Development
and Research, 2004).

[34]   Thomas F. Geraghty, *Legal Clinics and the Better Trained Lawyer (Redux)+:
A History of Clinical Education at Northwestern*, 100 NW. U.L. REV. 231, 232
(2006).

To better understand the context of the current law clinical programs, we have set forth a brief historical timeline of milestones in the early development of legal service clinical education.[35] The original nonprofit philanthropic efforts to help families through the hardships of poverty evolved into law school collaborations at the beginning of the twentieth century. Margaret Martin Barry, Jon C. Dubin, and Peter A. Joy characterize this collaborative period as the first wave of clinical legal education[36] in the United States. These scholars explain that during the first wave, the early programs were to provide hands-on opportunities to learn and practice lawyering skills and legal analysis and also to serve a social justice mission by providing legal assistance to those unable to hire attorneys.

The historical timeline of legal services for underserved populations dates back to as early as 1857 in the Midwestern city of Chicago, Illinois. At that time, the Chicago Relief and Aid Society, was an organization that helped families get through the devastating hardships of poverty, world wars, epidemics and natural disasters.[37] Another organized provider of legal aid started in Chicago in 1886, called the Protective Agency for Women and Children, which was founded to protect young, working women.[38] By 1888, The Bureau of Justice formed in Chicago. It was the first unrestricted legal aid organization[39] and in the next year, the New York Legal Aid Society provided unrestricted legal aid, in New York City.[40]

At the turn of the twentieth century, in 1905, the Bureau of Justice combined with the Protective Agency for Women and Children to form

---

[35]   This chapter by no means is intended to provide a comprehensive background on the development of clinical education in the U.S. For more information on this topic, *see* JOHN M. MAGUIRE, THE LANCE OF JUSTICE: A SEMI-CENTENNIAL HISTORY OF THE LEGAL AID SOCIETY, 1876–1926 ((Littleton, Colorado, U.S.A.: Fred B. Rothman & Co. 1982) (1928); JOHN SAEGER BRADWAY, THE DUKE UNIVERSITY LEGAL AID CLINIC Handbook (Durham, North Carolina, U.S.A.: Duke Univ. Press 1954); Geraghty, *supra* note 35; William V. Rowe, *Legal Clinics and Better Trained Lawyers: A Necessity*, 11 U. ILL. L. REV. 591 (1917).

[36]   Barry et al., *supra* note 8, at 6 ("[L]aw students at several law schools in the late 1800's [sic] and early 1900's [sic] established volunteer, non-credit 'legal dispensaries' or legal aid bureaus to provide hands-on opportunities to learn and practice lawyering skills and legal analysis, and also to serve a social justice mission by providing legal assistance to those unable to hire attorneys.")

[37]   *About Us – History*, METROPOLITAN FAMILY SERVICES, http://www.metrofamily.org/about-us/history.aspx (last visited Aug. 5, 2011).

[38]   Christopher Thale, *Legal Aid*, ENCYCLOPEDIA OF CHICAGO, http://encyclopedia.chicagohistory.org/pages/734.html (last visited Aug. 5, 2011).

[39]   McGUIRE, *supra* note 36, at 238.

[40]   *Id.*

the Chicago Legal Aid Society (later renamed the Legal Aid Bureau of United Charities of Chicago).[41] Chicago continued to play a significant role, as a location where a university would first collaborate to provide critical legal services to the poor. In 1910, the future dean of Northwestern University, John Henry Wigmore, developed a program with the Chicago Legal Aid Society.[42] But it would take another decade when a foundation would advocate for practical skills training opportunities, as had occurred between Northwestern University and the Chicago Legal Aid Society. Practical skills training in legal education and community initiatives were advocated in a Carnegie Foundation for the Advancement of Teaching study published in 1921,[43] authored by Alfred Z. Reed. This study "identified three components necessary to prepare students for the practice of law: general education, theoretical knowledge of the law, and practical skills training."[44] Soon thereafter, John S. Bradway started an experimental, six-week, faculty-supervised clinic at the University of Southern California in 1928. By 1931, Bradway had established the first full-fledged, faculty-supervised clinic at Duke University.[45] In 1947, Professor Charles Miller opened the University of Tennessee's Legal Clinic. [46] The University of Chicago Law School's Mandel Legal Aid Clinic, "opened with two attorneys and one secretary . . . its creators firmly believed that the Clinic would help people well into the twenty-first century."[47] Dean Edward H. Levi wrote in a 1951 memo:

> Such a legal clinic would be a major step in American legal education. It would put the law schools in a position where they would be dealing with the facts of actual cases. . . . It would be an experiment in the training of lawyers using techniques analogous to those employed in medical schools.[48]

During this early era of legal services, traditional legal services were provided in a few communities across the country, and not in law school

---

[41]   Thale, *supra* note 39.

[42]   Geraghty, *supra* note 35, at 231.

[43]   ALBERT ZANTZINGER REED, TRAINING FOR THE PUBLIC PROFESSION OF THE LAW (New York, NY, U.S.A.: Arno Press, Inc. 1976) (1921).

[44]   *Legal Clinic*, WIKIPEDIA, http://en.wikipedia.org/wiki/Legal_clinic (last modified June 25, 2011, 4:06 p.m.).

[45]   J.P. Ogilvy & Karen Czapanskiy, *Clinical Legal Education: An Annotated Bibliography*, 12 CLINICAL L. REV. 101 (2005).

[46]   Frank S. Bloch, *Framing the Clinical Experience: Lessons on Turning Points and the Dynamics of Lawyering*, 64 TENN. L. REV. 989, 989 (1997).

[47]   Robin I. Mordfin, *History of the Mandel Clinic and Kane Center*, U. CHI. L. SCH., http://www.law.uchicago.edu/node/735 (last visited Aug. 5, 2011).

[48]   *Id.*

settings, at least not until around 1910. These legal services were focused principally on civil litigation matters of the urgent needs of underprivileged and underserved individuals. These university-based collaborations began to provide solutions to address gaps in legal services and that movement grew and changed during the last fifty years. In the next section we discuss the last fifty years and its relationship to the current growth of entrepreneurship/transactional clinical programs.

V. LAW SCHOOL CLINICAL PROGRAM GROWTH—LAST FIFTY YEARS

After the 1921 Carnegie Mellon study, universities began to adopt clinical programs and by 1951, there existed six university-based programs in six states (Illinois, New York, Pennsylvania, North Carolina, Tennessee, and California) and with only a handful of law schools providing these services. It wasn't until the 1960s that there was a greater understanding of the need for (and a role for the provision of) nationwide legal services for underserved populations.

The second wave of clinical legal education was a period of marked growth and expansion from the 1960s through the late 1990s.[49] During this period, while legal clinical programs were adopted by law schools across the country, a network of legal service offices supported from federal funding grew at the same time. Below, we detail some of the milestones during this important time in clinical legal education.

In 1965, President Lyndon Johnson's Great Society program expanded and transformed legal aid. In 1965, a network of neighborhood legal service offices opened with federal funding, under the umbrella of United Charities and the City of Chicago. Differences in philosophy and willingness to challenge government agencies in court divided the more activist, federally funded programs from older programs and, in 1973, they were reorganized as the independent Legal Assistance Foundation of Chicago, funded, since 1974, mainly by the federal Legal Services Corporation.[50] The city of Chicago continued to play a major role, when Northwestern University's Bluhm Legal Clinic opened its doors in 1969 with two staff attorneys and twelve students. Today, just to illustrate the level of growth in clinical programs, Northwestern has more than twenty clinical professors who mentor over 120 students taking clinical courses each year. Each

---

[49] Barry et al., *supra* note 8, at 25–26.
[50] Thale, *supra* note 39.

clinic operates as a quasi-law firm, wherein students assist clients with practical legal matters under the tutelage of full-time faculty from the school.[51]

During the 1970s, the Legal Assistance Foundation grew to about ninety lawyers, though subsequent funding cuts led to fluctuations in its size, and it turned to private sources to supplement its income. Despite efforts by some conservatives to eliminate these agencies, the Legal Assistance Foundation pursued a reformist agenda. In addition to representing some 30,000 to 40,000 clients in their dealings with landlords, creditors, and government agencies, the organization pursued cases with broad impact on the rights of welfare recipients, the disabled, immigrants, prisoners, tenants, and victims of discrimination.[52]

Later, in the 1980s, there was the growth of community and economic development clinical programs. It has been noted that

[c]ommunity economic development is a strategy that includes a wide range of economic activities and programs. The concept of "economic development" emerged in response to tenacious poverty and the need for jobs, affordable housing, and other essentials for human existence. Central to the notion of "community development" is the ability of people living in the same community to work together to solve common problems. Community development is described as being broader than economic development because it includes community building and highlights improvement of community life beyond that which is purely economic.[53]

A further evolution of the community and economic development clinical programs of the 1980s was the idea that clinical programs could also provide individualized representation to entrepreneurs, small business and nonprofits. Community based approaches to economic growth were more centralized and collaborative, whereas entrepreneurship and other transactional clinical programs were individualized and client centered, with law students at the helm of the representation. The complexities of larger-scale community economic development projects, as well as law schools seeking to find solutions to legal issues of the underprivileged,

---

[51] *About Us*, N.W. UNIV. SCH. L., http://www.law.northwestern.edu/legalclinic/geninfo.html (last visited Aug. 5, 2011).

[52] Thale, *supra* note 39.

[53] Susan R. Jones, *Promoting Social and Economic Justice through Interdisciplinary Work in Transactional Law*, 14 WASH. U. J.L. & POL'Y 249, 250 n.3 (2004); *see also* DAVID COLEMAN ET AL., A LAWYER'S MANUAL ON COMMUNITY-BASED ECONOMIC DEVELOPMENT 1-3 (Oakland, California, U.S.A.: Nat'l Econ. Dev. & Law Ctr. 1999).

created a momentum for specialized entrepreneurship/transactional programs. What emerges is a clinical program with a ready constituency of students, entrepreneurs, alumni, staff and donors seeking to solve a puzzle in a community, as we further discuss in Section VI.

Maybe this is fortuitous, but clinical law professors have a unique opportunity and role to apply and test the rule of law and legal doctrine. Yet, that role may be limited in its ability to change or expand upon the rule of law/doctrine.[54] As clinical professors focus on and practice in a specific area of the law, their guidance provides a supervised outlet for law students to work with clients who are in need of legal services in that specific legal area. This is true whether the clinician is working with disadvantaged populations on their family, criminal, housing law matters, or on their client's entrepreneurial, nonprofit, or small business matters. Clinical professors teach students skills to access the relevant law for the matter at hand and through legal representation, students will have the opportunity to test that the rule of law is operable to their representative clients. To the extent that the law school, the governing policies and state regulations allow clinical professors the ability to challenge unconstitutional, unreasonable or illegal laws the role is unfettered. Generally, the opportunity to change or expand the law is more limited, for reasons that are beyond the scope of this chapter.

However, to illustrate the distinctions in a clinical professor's role in applying, testing, challenging, and expanding, an example is set forth. If a clinical professor assists entrepreneurs with their occupational licensing legal needs, the clinical professor would work with law students in understanding licensing laws. Students would apply the laws and assist entrepreneurs in obtaining a license. However, if an entrepreneur is denied the license for a reason that the clinical professor or student might consider to be unconstitutional, they might seek to challenge the law, but that would require a litigation strategy. Typically, this is not a role contemplated by

---

[54]   *See, e.g,* Sussex Common Assoc. v. Rutgers, 6 A.3d 983 (N.J. 2011); *News from the Clinical World,* AALS CLINICAL SECTION NEWSLETTER (Ass'n Am. L. Sch., Washington, D.C.), Spring 2011, at 13 ("An amicus brief filed on behalf of the clinical programs at the Newark and Camden law schools [in New Jersey] was prepared by the Constitutional Litigation Clinic on the Newark campus. That brief argues that the Appellate Division opinion was contrary to a 1989 opinion of the Supreme Court involving the status of law school clinicians under the State Conflict of Interest Law. That decision, *In the Matter of the Appearance of Rutgers Attorneys* [116 N.J. 216 (1989)], held that the law school's clinical lawyers were *not* state actors when they represented clients before state administrative agencies. The Conflict on Interest Law forbade state employees from representing clients before such agencies.").

entrepreneurship/transactional clinical programs, for a variety of reasons, part of which may stem from limitations of law school governance and protocols, state regulation, or other administrative body that regulates the law school or the practitioner. Although this situation may be challenging for clinical entrepreneurship/transactional professionals, it has not impeded the growth of these types of law school clinical programs.

VI. ENTREPRENEURSHIP/TRANSACTIONAL CLINICAL PROGRAMS—GROWTH

The rationale for the momentum of the growth in entrepreneurship/ transactional clinical programs in the late 1990s is partly explained in the Introduction and in Section V, but also has been characterized by clinicians as a third wave of clinical legal education where law school clinics continue to play an important role in making access to justice a reality for many low-income people[55] and by legal scholars as a period requiring a response from the legal academy to address the special role for transactional attorneys, distinct from the role of the litigator that has received most of the attention in legal education since the Harvard appellate case method was adopted.[56] We begin to see a convergence of two themes: access to justice and the role of entrepreneurial/transactional practitioners in law school settings.

Not so surprisingly, entrepreneurship/transactional clinical programs in law school settings have grown over the past dozen years. Along with that growth is new support by the ABA advocating for the expansion of clinical programs;[57] a new Transactional Law section within the Association of American Law Schools and a new Transactional Law subsection with the Association of American Law Schools Clinical Law Section.[58] In the new millennium, these types of programs grew significantly in law schools

---

[55] Barry et al., *supra* note 8, at 26.

[56] Celeste M. Hammond, *Borrowing from the B Schools: The Legal Case Study as Course Materials for Transaction Oriented Elective Courses: A Response to the Challenges of the MacCrate Report and the Carnegie Foundation for Advancement of Teaching Report on Legal Education*, 11 TRANSACTIONS 9, 47 (2009).

[57] *ABA Adopts Policy to Improve Legal Profession, Advance Justice*, ABA, http://www.abanow.org/2011/08/aba-adopts-policy-to-improve-legal-profession-advance-justice (last visited Aug. 9, 2011).

[58] Gordon Smith, *AALS Section on Transactional Law and Skills*, THE CONGLOMERATE (June 13, 2011), http://www.theconglomerate.org/2011/06/aals-section-on-transactional-law-and-skills.html (noting the approval of a new transactional law and skills committee of the Association of American Law Schools).

around the country,[59] but as illustrated by the appendices (9.1A, 9.2A and 9.3A) the 138 programs represent less than 11% of all clinical programs. In light of their interaction with economic transactions of their client populations, the entrepreneurship/transactional clinical programs in law school settings are defined to include:

- Entrepreneurship Law
- Community Economic Development[60]
- Intellectual Property Law
- Small Business Law
- Tax and Housing (Transactional)

Clinical programs driving entrepreneurship and economic growth and in transformative ways was inferred by clinicians as early as 2001. Once these transformative opportunities are unleashed for entrepreneurs of modest means, we believe that America can experience the full potential of the promise of an entrepreneurial renaissance.[61] But it wasn't until economists framed the scope of the era that the interconnectedness of these programs and assistance to start-ups shed light on the magnitude of the possibilities for growth. Economists recognized the late 1990s as a remarkable nationwide insurgence of productivity growth and innovation in the United States, made possible largely by new, innovative companies, and not by the established giants that had previously dominated the U.S. economic landscape.[62] One might query whether entrepreneurship/transactional

---

[59] Barry et al., *supra* note 8, at 71–72.

[60] Community and economic development clinical programs were included in the categorization, partly because of their original economic and transactional focus, but also due to constraints on time to distinguish between the characteristics of the specific economic oriented program from other entrepreneurship/transactional clinical programs. Those further distinctions would be the subject of another research project.

[61] Mellor & Lee, *supra* note 2, at 90 (illustrating the transformative potential of entrepreneurship in economically depressed communities and describing the methodology and pedagogy of newly developing programs and the rationale for their advancement within the law school setting). *See also* Anthony J. Luppino, *Minding More than Our Own Business: Educating Entrepreneurial Lawyers through Law School-Business School Collaborations*, 30 W. NEW ENG. L. REV. 151 (2007); Eric J. Gouvin, *Teaching Business Lawyering in Law Schools: A Candid Assessment of the Challenges and Some Suggestions for Moving Ahead*, 78 UMKC L. REV. 429 (2009); Susan R. Jones, *Small Business and Community Economic Development: Transactional Lawyering for Social Change and Economic Justice*, 4 CLINICAL L. REV. 195 (1997).

[62] WILLIAM J. BAUMOL, ROBERT E. LITAL & CARL J. SCHRAMM, GOOD CAPITALISM,

clinical programs were the chicken or the egg in this insurgence of innovation and productivity growth. Were law clinical programs driven by the
increased demand of entrepreneurs and other organizations, or was the
existence of these clinical law programs a value added in the development
of these new, innovative companies? More empirical research is needed to
assess these correlations.

What we found in our data compilation illustrates a strong involvement
by the ABA-approved law schools in the U.S.[63] in the nationwide insurgence of innovation and economic growth. Although entrepreneurship/
transactional programs developed at law schools across the country[64] and
are only 11% of the mix of clinical programs, their potential is huge
and the impact can be measured by start-ups, revenues, jobs, transactions,
and other meaningful measures of activity.

VII. EXPANDING THE ROLE AND IMPACT OF ENTREPRENEURSHIP/TRANSACTIONAL CLINICAL PROGRAMS

Entrepreneurship and innovation are imperative today. On the one
hand, our country is challenged to provide an adequate supply of jobs
for everyone who would like to have a job. On the other, states are challenged to provide a safe infrastructure, whether that is roads, bridges, and
transportation or a healthy economic engine for its residents. In light of
the nation's evolving economy, clinical law programs that serve entrepreneurs, small business and nonprofits are serving and will continue to serve
a necessary leadership role in helping grow start-ups, create jobs, educate
law students, inform entrepreneurs, and educate the community.

With the rise of small enterprises' contribution to economic growth,
coupled with large-firm global outsourcing of jobs, it behooves law school

---

BAD CAPITALISM, AND THE ECONOMICS OF GROWN AND PROSPERITY (New Haven,
Connecticut, U.S.A.: Yale Univ. Press 2007).

[63]   *ABA-Approved Law Schools*, ABA, http://www.americanbar.org/groups/
legal_education/resources/aba_approved_law_schools.html (last visited Aug. 9,
2011).

[64]   The information concerning the number of law school clinics and the presence of entrepreneurial/transactional clinics was gathered by the author from law
schools' websites, the E-law database maintained by The Kauffman Foundation
and Prof. Anthony Luppino of University of Missouri-Kansas City School of
Law, and surveys, e-mail conversations, and telephone interviews conducted by
the author. For more information concerning clinics at law schools, consult the
appendices to this chapter.

and clinical leadership and policy makers to rethink the ideal roles of these programs in fostering entrepreneurship, economic growth, and innovation. With a better understanding of their role in the community, deans, directors, law students, and the clients they serve can begin to leverage their resources and become more effective. Collaborations, whether it is research related, transactional, planning, advisory, or academic will likely enhance the local, regional, and national economy. As we have illustrated in this chapter, law schools that host entrepreneurship/transactional law clinical programs are directly involved in fostering entrepreneurship and economic growth. The manner in which these clinical programs are involved in entrepreneurship and economic growth, is by and through their assistance in representing entrepreneurs, small business and nonprofits in business start-ups, job creation and innovation. However, there still remain many opportunities for more law schools and for all of the states to participate further by adopting and developing such programs.

VIII. CONCLUSION

As our economy continues to evolve, it is predictable that the role of clinical law programs will change to adapt to the needs of entrepreneurs, small businesses and nonprofits. Scholars, deans, clinical directors, policymakers, and interested parties, should continue to actively participate in the evolving economy of the U.S. The very essence of America as a prosperous nation depends on our involvement. Once we begin to assess and measure the role that law clinical programs have in creating jobs, assisting with businesses' start-ups and helping to generate revenue and growth, we can then begin to scale their positive economic impacts and generate fully operational law clinical programs helping innovators nationwide. The solution to enhancing entrepreneurship, economic growth and innovation may be within the reach of each state and may be located in a local law school clinical program.

Table 9A.1 Schools ranked in the top 100 (by alphabetical order by state) and the number of clinical and E-transactional clinical programs*

2011	2010	2009	Law School	City	State	# Clinics	# Transactional
35	38	30	University of Alabama	Tuscaloosa	AL	7	1
85	86	94	University of Arkansas-FayeBeville	Fayetteville	AR	10	1
40	38	55	Arizona State Univ. (O'Connor)	Tempe	AZ	11	3
42	42	43	University of Arizona (Rogers)	Tucson	AZ	5	1
3	3	3	Stanford University	Stanford	CA	11	2
9	7	6	Univ. of California-Berkeley	Berkeley	CA	4	1
6	15	15	Univ. of California (Los Angeles)	Los Angeles	CA	18	1
18	18	18	Univ. of southern California (Gould)	Los Angeles	CA	5	1
23	28	35	Univ. of California-Davis	Davis	CA	4	0
42	42	39	Univ. of California (Hastings)	San Francisco	CA	5	1
54	52	55	Pepperdine University	Malibu	CA	4	0
54	56	71	Loyola Marymount University	Los Angeles	CA	4	2
67	56	61	University of San Diego	San Diego	CA	14	1
101	93	101	Chapman University	Orange	CA	8	1
84	93	85	Santa Clara University	Santa Clara	CA	3	0
100	98	98	University of San Francisco	San Francisco	CA	8	1
100	98	101	Univ. of the Pacific (McGeorge)	Sacramento	CA	9	0
47	38	45	Univ. of Colorado-Boulder	Boulder	CO	9	2
77	80	77	Univ. of Denver (Sturm)	Denver	CO	6	1
1	1	1	Yale University	New Haven	CT	6	2
56	54	52	University of Connecticut	Hartford	CT	5	1

			University	City	State		
14	14	14	Georgetown University	Washington	DC	14	0
20	20	28	George Washington University	Washington	DC	14	1
50	48	45	American Univ. (Washington)	Washington	DC	11	2
79	98	94	Catholic Univ.of America (Columbus)	Washington	DC	2	0
47	47	51	Univ. of Florida (Levin)	Gainesville	FL	6	0
50	54	51	Florida State University	Tallahassee	FL	0	0
77	60	71	University of Miami Coral	Gables	FL	11	0
30	22	20	Emory University	Atlanta	GA	10	1
35	28	35	University of Georgia	Athens	GA	3	0
61	60	65	Georgia State University	Atlanta	GA	6	0
95	72	101	Univ. of Hawii-Manoa (Richardson)	Honolulu	HI	10	1
27	26	26	University of Iowa	Iowa city	IA	6	0
5	5	6	University of Chicago	Chicago	IL	4	1
12	11	10	Northwestern University	Chicago	IL	5	1
23	21	23	Univ. of Illinois-Urbana-Champaign	Champaign	IL	10	1
71	78	87	Loyola Univ. Chicago	Chicago	IL	5	1
61	80	77	Illinois Institute of Tech. (Chgo-Kent)	Chicago	IL	10	2
84	98	87	DePaul University	Chicago	IL	9	1
23	22	23	Univ. of Notre Dame	Notre Dame	IN	6	1
23	27	23	Indiana Univ.-Bloomington	Bloomington	IN	6	1
79	86	87	Indiana University-Indianapolis	Indianapolis	IN	5	0
79	67	65	University Of Kansas	Lawrence	KS	11	1
71	64	55	University of Kentucky	Lexington	KY	2	0
100	101	98	Univ.of Louisville School of Law(Brandeis)	Louisville	KY	1	0
47	48	45	Tulane University	New Orleans	LA	6	0
84	80	75	Louisiana State Univ.-Baton Rouge	Baton Rouge	LA	8	0
2	2	2	Harvard University	Cambridge	MA	30	2
22	22	20	Boston University	Boston	MA	5	0

Table 9A.1 (continued)

2011	2010	2009	Law School	City	State	# Clinics	# Transactional
27	28	26	Boston College of Law	Newton	MA	7	1
71	86	94	Northeastern University	Boston	MA	5	0
42	48	43	University of Maryland	Baltimore	MD	19	1
101	101	100	University of Maine School of Law	Portland	ME	5	1
7	9	9	Univ. of Michigan-Ann Arbor	Ann Arbor	MI	12	1
95	101	101	Michigan State Univ. College of Law	East Lansing	MI	5	1
20	22	20	Univ. of Minnesota-Twin Cities	Minneapolis	MN	21	1
101	98	101	William Mitchell College of Law	St.Paul	MN	12	2
18	19	19	Washington Univ.in St.Louis	St.Louis	MO	14	1
101	93	65	University of Missouri	Columbia	MO	5	0
101	101	94	Saint Louis University School of Law	St.Louis	MO	3	1
11	11	10	Duke University	Durham	NC	8	1
30	28	30	Univ.of North Carolina-Chapel Hill	Chapel Hill	NC	4	1
39	38	40	Wake Forest University	Winston-Salem	NC	6	1
84	93	101	University of Nebraska-Lincoln	Lincoln	NE	3	0
61	72	77	Seton Hall University	Newark	NJ	7	0
84	80	77	Rutgers the State Univ.of NJ-Camden	Camden	NJ	4	1
84	80	87	Rutgers the State Univ.of NJ-Newark	Newark	NJ	7	1
79	67	77	Univ.of New Mexico	Albuquerque	NM	5	1
71	78	75	Univ. of Nevada-Las Vegas (Boyd)	Las Vegas	NV	7	0
4	4	4	Columbia University	New York	NY	9	2
6	6	5	New York University	New York	NY	31	1

			University	City	State		
13	13	13	Cornell University	Ithaca	NY	11	1
30	34	30	Fordham University	New York	NY	15	2
50	52	49	Yeshiva University (Cardozo)	New York	NY	13	1
67	67	61	Brooklyn Law School	Brooklyn	NY	18	2
95	72	87	St. John's University	Jamaica	NY	7	0
84	86	100	Hofstra University	Hempstead	NY	7	1
100	86	101	Syracuse University	Syracuse	NY	7	1
84	101	85	Univ. at Buffalo Law School	Buffalo	NY	8	1
35	34	35	Ohio State Univ.(Moritz)	Columbus	OH	7	1
61	56	55	Case Western Reserve University	Cleveland	OH	4	1
61	56	52	University of Cincinnati	Cincinnati	OH	7	1
71	72	71	University of Oklahoma	Norman	OK	4	0
67	64	61	Lewis&Clark College(Northwestern)	Portland	OR	8	2
79	80	77	University of Oregon	Eugene	OR	7	1
7	7	8	University of Pennsylvania	Philadelphia	PA	10	2
71	67	71	University of Pittsburgh	Pittsburgh	PA	6	1
84	67	61	Villanova University	Villanova	PA	5	1
60	72	65	Pennsylvania State Univ.(Dickerson)	U.Park	PA	6	2
61	72	65	Temple University(Beasley)	Philadelphia	PA	2	0
101	101	87	U. of South Carolina School of Law	Columbia	SC	5	1
16	17	17	Vanderbilt University	Nashville	TN	7	2
56	60	59	Univ.of Tennessee-Knoxville	Knoxville	TN	6	1
14	15	15	Univ.of Texas-Austin	Austin	TX	17	1
50	48	49	Southern Methodist Univ. (Dedman)	Dallas	TX	6	1
56	60	59	University of Houston	Houston	TX	6	1
56	64	65	Baylor University (Umphrey)	Waco	TX	0	0
42	42	41	Brigham Young University (Clark)	Provo	UT	0	0
42	42	45	University of Utah (Quinney)	Salt Lake City	UT	19	2

Table 9A.1 (continued)

2011	2010	2009	Law School	City	State	# Clinics	# Transactional
9	10	10	University of Virginia	Charlottesville	VA	20	3
7	28	28	College of William and Mary(M-W)	Williamsburg	VA	5	0
30	34	30	Washington and Lee University	Lexington	VA	6	0
40	42	41	George Mason University	Arlington	VA	3	1
67	86	77	Univ. of Richmond (Williams)	Richmond	VA	7	1
30	34	30	University of Washington	Seattle	WA	14	2
84	86	77	Seattle University	Seattle	WA	14	3
101	101	100	Gonzaga University School of Law	Spokane	WA	7	1
35	28	35	Univ. of Wisconsin-Madison	Madison	WI	9	1
95	101	87	Marquette University College of Law	Milwaukee	WI	4	0
95	93	101	West Virgina University	Morgantown	WV	7	2
NEW			University Of Massachusetts School of Law	North Dartmouth	MA		1

* Law school rankings are based on the rankings assembled by U.S. World & News Report over the last three years. The current rankings may be accessed at http://grad-schools.usnews.rankingsandreviews.com/best-graduate-schools/top-law-schools/law-rankings (last visited Aug. 7, 2011). All other information provided in the appendix was retrieved via law schools' websites, the E-law database maintained by Jared Konczal of The Kauffman Foundation, Prof. Anthony Luppino of University of Missouri-Kansas City School of Law, and surveys, e-mail conversations, and telephone interviews conducted by the author and research assistants. For more information, *see Law School Entrepreneurship Clinics*, ENTREPRENEURSHIP.ORG, http://www.entrepreneurship.org/en/entrepreneurship-law/law-school-entrepreneurship-clinics.aspx (last visited Aug. 11, 2011).

APPENDIX 9A.2

Table 9A.2   Third tier law schools (by alphabetical order by school) and clinical and E-transactional programs*

School	City	State	#Clinics	#E/Transactional
Albany University	Albany	NY	7	0
Campbell University	Raleigh	NC	2	0
Chapman University	Orange	CA	7	1
Cleveland State University	Cleveland	OH	6	1
Creighton University	Omaha	NE	2	1
CUNY-Queens College	Flushing	NY	7	1
Drake University	Des Moines	IA	1	0
Florida International University	Miami	FL	5	1
Gonzaga University	Spokane	WA	7	1
Howard University	Washington	DC	6	1
John Marshall Law School	Chicago	IL	2	1
Loyola University New Orleans	New Orleans	LA	2	0
Mercer University	Macon	GA	1	0
New York Law School	New York	NY	7	0
Ohio Northern University	Ada	OH	2	1
Pace University	White Plains	NY	6	0
Quinnipiac University	Hamden	CT	6	0
Samford University	Birmingham	AL	1	0
Southwestern Law school	Los Angeles	CA	3	0
St. Louis University School of Law	St.Louis	MO	4	1
Stetson University	Tampa Bay	FL	7	0
Texas Tech University	Lubbock	TX	8	0
Franklin Pierce Law Center (U. of NH)	Concord	NH	10	2
University of Akron	Akron	OH	3	1

Table 9A.2 (continued)

School	City	State	#Clinics	#E/Transactional
University of Arkansas-Little Rock	Little Rock	AR	3	0
University of Baltimore	Baltimore	MD	9	1
University of Idaho	Moscow	ID	9	1
University of Memphis	Memphis	TN	1	0
University of Mississippi	Oxford	MS	2	1
University of Missouri	Columbia	MO	5	0
University of Missouri-Kansas City	Kansas City	MO	5	1
University of Montana	Missoula	MT	4	0
University of South Carolina	Columbia	SC	5	1
University of St. Thomas	Minneapolis	MN	0	0
University of Tulsa	Tulsa	OK	1	0
University of Wyoming	Laramie	WY	4	0
Vermont Law School	South Royalton	VT	5	0
Washburn University	Topeka	KS	6	1
Wayne State University	Detroit	MI	7	1
Willamette University	Salem	OR	6	1
William Mitchell College of Law	Saint Paul	MN	1	4

* Law school rankings are based on the rankings assembled by U.S. World & News Report over the last three years. The current rankings may be accessed at http://grad-schools.usnews.rankingsandreviews.com/best-graduate-schools/top-law-schools/law-rankings (last visited Aug. 7, 2011). All other information provided in the appendix was retrieved via law schools' websites, the E-law database maintained by Jared Konczal of The Kauffman Foundation, Prof. Anthony Luppino of University of Missouri-Kansas City School of Law, and surveys, e-mail conversations, and telephone interviews conducted by the author and research assistants. For more information, *see Law School Entrepreneurship Clinics*, ENTREPRENEURSHIP.ORG, http://www.entrepreneurship.org/en/entrepreneurship-law/law-school-entrepreneurship-clinics.aspx (last visited Aug. 11, 2011).

APPENDIX 9A.3

*Table 9A.3   Fourth-tier law school clinical (alphabetical order by school) and E-transactional clinical programs**

School	City	State	#Clinics	#E/Transactional
Appalachian School of Law	Grundy	VA	0	0
Atlanta's John Marshall Law School	Atlanta	GA	0	0
Ave Maria School of Law	Naples	FL	4	1
Barry University	Orlando	FL	3	0
California Western School of Law	San Diego	CA	0	0
Capital University	Columbus	OH	2	0
Duquesne University	Pittsburgh	PA	6	1
Faulkner University (Jones)	Montgomery	AL	3	0
Florida A&M University	Tallahassee	FL	7	1
Florida Coastal School of Law	Jacksonville	FL	5	0
Golden Gate University	San Francisco	CA	3	1
Hamline University	Saint Paul	MN	3	0
Liberty University	Lynchburg	VA	0	0
Mississippi College	Jacksonville	MS	0	0
New England School of Law	Boston	MA	2	1
North Carolina Central University	Durham	NC	11	0
Northern Illinois University	DeKalb	IL	3	1
Northern Kentucky Univ. (Chase)	Highland Heights	KY	7	1
Nova Southeastern Univ. (Broad)	Ft. Lauderdale-Davie	FL	5	0
Oklahoma City University	Oklahoma City	OK	3	0
Phoenix School of Law	Phoenix	AZ	3	0
Regent University	Virginia Beach	VA	1	0

APPENDIX 9A.3

Table 9A.3 Fourth-tier law school clinical and E-transactional clinical programs*

School	City	State	#Clinics	#E/Transactional
Roger Williams University	Bristol	RI	3	0
South Texas College of Law	Houston	TX	6	0
Southern Illinois Univ.-Carbondale	Carbondale	IL	2	0
Southern University	Baton Rouge	LA	7	0
St. Mary's University	San Antonio	TX	3	0
St. Thomas University	Miami Gardens	FL	6	0
Suffolk University	Boston	MA	9	0
Texas Southern Univ. Marshall	Houston	TX	3	0
Texas Wesleyan University	Fort Worth	TX	1	0
Thomas Jefferson School law	San Diego	CA	4	0
Thomas M. Cooley Law School	Lansing	MI	7	0
Touro College (Fuchsberg)	Central Ship	NY	0	0
University Of Dayton	Dayton	OH	1	0
University Of Detroit	Detroit	MI	9	0
University Of North Dakota	Grand Forks	ND	1	0
University Of South Dakota	Vermillion	SD	0	0
University Of DC (Clarke)	Washington	DC	8	1
University of Toledo	Toledo	OH	4	0
Valparaiso University	St. Valparaiso	IN	8	0
Western New England College of Law	Springfield	MA	6	1
Western State University	Fullerton	CA	1	0

Whittier Law School	Costa Mesa	CA	4	0
Widener University	Wilmington	DE	6	0

* Law school rankings are based on the rankings assembled by U.S. World & News Report over the last three years. The current rankings may be accessed at http://grad-schools.usnews.rankingsandreviews.com/best-graduate-schools/top-law-schools/law-rankings (last visited Aug. 7, 2011). All other information provided in the appendix was retrieved via law schools' websites, the E-law database maintained by Jared Konczal of The Kauffman Foundation, Prof. Anthony Luppino of University of Missouri-Kansas City School of Law, and surveys, e-mail conversations, and telephone interviews conducted by the author and research assistants. For more information, *see Law School Entrepreneurship Clinics*, ENTREPRENEURSHIP.ORG, http://www.entrepreneurship.org/en/entrepreneurship-law/law-school-entrepreneurship-clinics.aspx (last visited Aug. 11, 2011).

10. The rule of law, privatization, and the promise of transborder licensing

Andrea L. Johnson*

Rules don't ensure sustainable economic development; people do.

I. INTRODUCTION

The rule of law in the international context is defined using different terminology, but has the same basic components: a set of rules by which persons have equal access to a legal system that is transparent, has an independent decision-making body, and where the rules are applied in a nondiscriminatory fashion.[1] Historically, a government's failure to adhere to the rule of law leads to a lack of trust and predictability necessary to attract foreign investment. In the 1990s, privatization of state-owned assets and enterprises in developing countries became a plausible way to stabilize financial markets, spur foreign investment, retire debt, and improve local economies.[2] The theory was that foreign investment in sectors such as telecommunications stimulated economic development in new and existing

---

* The author would like to acknowledge Tara Pelan, Esq. for her valuable contributions to this chapter.

[1] *See* Simon Chesterman, *An International Rule of Law?*, 56 Am. J. Comp. L. 331 (2008) (hereinafter "Chesterman"). The World Justice Project (WJP) identifies four universal principals for the rule of law: 1) government and its officials are accountable under the law; 2) the laws are clear, publicized, stable and fair, and protect fundamental rights, including the security of persons and property; 3) process by which the laws are enacted, administered, and enforced is accessible, fair, and efficient; and 4) access to justice is provided by competent, independent, ethical adjudicators, attorneys, and judicial officers. M. Agrast, J. Botero, & A. Ponce, Measuring the Rule of Law, *in* World Justice Project Working Paper No. 1, (WJP Rule of Law Index 2010), *available at* http: http://www.worldjusticeproject.org/

[2] Andrea L. Johnson, *Privatization of Telecommunications Networks to Spur Foreign Investment*, 32 Law/Technology 1, 2 (1999), published by World Jurist Association.

industries by financing upgrades to a developing country's infrastructure. Such actions led to competition, which drove innovation and new service offerings, and ultimately led to job creation.

The U.S. legal system is based upon the rule of law, and many argue that it is a vital component to increase U.S. exports of goods and services to other countries. According to the U.S. International Trade Commission (USITC), U.S. small- and medium-sized enterprises (SMEs) accounted for about 30% of known U.S. merchandise exports between 1997 and 2007. However, only 1% of all U.S. SMEs export to another country, and of those, 58% export to only one country.[3] As a result, President Obama has pledged to double exports by 2015 as a way to create high-paying jobs for U.S. citizens.[4]

The law plays an important role in fostering entrepreneurship and innovation by prioritizing areas for entrepreneurial growth, and identifying key sectors that the government will support. However, the law can only provide the framework for growth. The law is also important in helping entrepreneurs understand the transaction costs of doing business. With the growth of technology, "old" economies, such as manufacturing of goods and privatization of telecommunication sectors, are being replaced with "new" economies, such as intellectual capital and the exchange of intellectual property. New economies hold great promise for job creation because the government's role is minimized and the relationship of the parties elevated. Lessons learned from privatization of telecommunications can provide insights into areas in new, emerging economies where sustainable development has the best chance of thriving.

While the rule of law is considered fundamental to establishing an international order, in reality it is more aspirational, focusing on the means to desired goals such as increasing trade or foreign investment, as opposed to an end in itself. The rule of law is important in defining the rights and entitlements for parties in international business transactions. However, it has proven to be inadequate to stimulate sustainable economic development. Reasons for this include lack of understanding of the legal and regulatory processes in place to facilitate economic development, conflict of laws between member countries, ineffective enforcement, and some inherent limitations of government-imposed measures to reallocate resources to stimulate market access.

---

[3] Tim Truman, *Export Promotion Linked to Job Creation*, INTERNATIONAL TRADE ADMINISTRATION, Dec. 9, 2009, http://www.trade.gov/press/press_releases/2009/exports_120909.

[4] *See* Exec. Order No. 13,534, 75 Fed. Reg. 12,433 (Mar. 11, 2010).

Under the traditional theory, the transactional costs or "pain points" derived from compliance with government regulation in many countries, including the United States, caused many entrepreneurs to perceive the rule of law as a stick rather than a carrot; and that it was intended to impede, rather than to encourage, foreign investment. This view may well be true, as well as justified, if the national interests of the country, however they are defined, are threatened or undermined by foreign parties. Moreover, even when laws are used as a carrot to stimulate foreign investment or as a shield to protect local markets, many entrepreneurs and governments, including the United States, are quick to condemn such practices as discriminatory, without acknowledging the legitimacy of the government's right to prioritize nationalist goals. Consider the following examples.

China has a program to award grants to makers of windpower equipment from a special government fund. The United States has charged that it violates World Trade Organization (WTO) rules because it provides an import substitution subsidy[5] that is harmful to foreign U.S. investors and inherently distorting, which is prohibited by U.S. law.[6] U.S. steel workers have also complained about a range of practices in the clean-energy sector, including "prohibiting subsidies, export restraints, discrimination against foreign companies, and requirements that foreign companies transfer technology to their domestic counterparts."[7]

---

[5]   Import substitution subsidy is a "government subsidy whose payment is contingent on its recipients using or purchasing domestically made goods over imported goods." RICHARD SCHAFFER, FILIBERTO AGUSTI, & BEVERLEY EARLE, INTERNATIONAL BUSINESS LAW AND ITS ENVIRONMENT 375 (Cincinnati, Ohio, U.S.A.: South Western Educational Publishing, 7th edn. 2009). Import substitution subsidies are used to neutralize foreign competition over domestic suppliers by providing financial assistance to certain industries to help them compete. FOLSOM, GORDON, & SPANOGLE, INTERNATIONAL BUSINESS TRANSACTIONS 428 (Eagan, Minnesota, U.S.A.: West, 10th edn. 2009). China had a practice between 1979 and 2001, when it became a member of the WTO, of using import substitution subsidies and export-oriented subsidies, that made export subsidies contingent upon export performance. *Id* (citing WTO Trade Policy Review, *People's Republic of China*, WT/TPRS/S/161 (June 26, 2006). Both are prohibited under WTO rules. Under WTO rules, a subsidy is illegal and actionable if the country can show that the subsidy has an adverse effect. There are three types of harm from an import subsidy: 1) to domestic country of import; 2) rival exporters competing in a subsidized market of a third country; and 3) exporters competing in subsidizing country's domestic market. The United States subsidizes agribusiness, beef, and pharmaceuticals.
[6]   Sewell Chan, *U.S. challenges Chinese aid for makers of wind power equipment*, N.Y. Times Dec 23, 2010.
[7]   *Id.*

By contrast, consider the U.S. government-sponsored 8(a) programs administered by the Small Business Administration (SBA) that provide set-asides or low-cost loans for small business,[8] or grants from U.S. AID, which are limited to U.S. citizens; or the use of tax credits[9] to encourage economic development, which are limited to resident aliens and U.S. citizens. Depending upon your perspective, such programs can be viewed as discriminatory and a failure of the rule of law to protect foreign investors, or, alternatively, as justifiable to protect U.S. companies and markets from foreign competition. In either case, most scholars would agree that such programs are legitimized by a set of rules that establish the priorities for economic development within the country.

The preferred view is that the rule of law serves a function, i.e., to promote development, rather than defining a "status," such as "developed" or "developing."[10] This paradigm shift views the rule of law, not to define the economic success or failure of a country, but merely to provide a gauge for evaluating the relative risks and costs associated with doing business. This view differs from traditional notions of the rule of law, which tend to focus on the vertical relationship between the government and a party, rather than the horizontal relationship between sovereign countries, or domestic and foreign parties, which is more meaningful in the international context.[11]

This chapter examines the role of the rule of law to stimulate or impede economic development in the telecommunications sector of developing countries like Argentina and Cuba, and how transborder licensing, or exporting intellectual property, such as know-how, patents, and copyrights, requires a paradigm shift that deemphasizes the rule of law and the

---

[8]   Under the SBA guidelines, applicants for 8(a) certification must be U.S. citizens. The specific requirements are that the business must be unconditionally owned and controlled by one or more disadvantaged individuals who are U.S. citizens and who are of good character. SBA 8(a) Business Development, http:// www.sba.gov/content/8a-business-development-0 (last visited on Mar. 25, 2011). The 8(a) program provides set asides million of federal contract dollars for certified small businesses. *See* 13 C.F.R. § 124.

[9]   Earned income tax credits, for example, which reduce the amount of income tax owed by low-to moderate-income workers, apply only to U.S. citizens or legal residents. Nonresident aliens must be married to a U.S. citizen. Disability Benefits 101—Working with disability in California, http://www.disabilitybenefits101.org/ ca/programs/work_benefits/eitc/faqs.htm#_q1434 (last visited on Mar. 25, 2011). Resident and nonresident aliens are taxed differently under IRS rules. IRS Topic 851: Resident and Nonresident Aliens, http://www.irs.gov/taxtopics/tc851.html (last visited on Mar. 25, 2011).

[10]   Chesterman, *supra* note 2 at 361.

[11]   *Id.* at 333, 357.

role of the government in favor of building social trust between private parties. Argentina was selected because it was a model for privatization during the early 1990s, and enjoyed moderate success attracting foreign investment to open new markets, such as Internet and E-commerce, but has been challenged at privatizing more established markets, such as basic telephony and wire line services.[12] Today, Argentina's trade policy is primarily driven by its domestic agenda and more nationalist priorities, as opposed to encouraging foreign investment. Cuba was selected because while the government began efforts to privatize its markets at the same time, market access has been limited to other Latin American countries, Mexico, and Canada. However, since 2009, Cuba and U.S. trade relations are improving and telecommunication markets have started to open up for U.S. SMEs.

The next section defines the rule of law and identifies key distinctions in applying the rule of law domestically and internationally. The third section examines how the rule of law serves as the foundation for privatization of telecommunications, but has limited utility for sustainability because it focuses on the vertical relationship between the government, its citizens, and foreign investors, and usually only comes into play when there is a dispute and the relationship is over. The fourth section examines how countries like the United States and Argentina compare in adhering to the rule of law through different indicators. The last section recommends a paradigm shift, acknowledging the role of the rule of the law, but elevating the horizontal relationship between the contracting parties to achieve sustainable economic growth. This chapter concludes that the greatest potential for success by U.S. companies in developing countries like Cuba, is to focus on licensing U.S. intellectual capital, know-how, and property.

II.   DEFINING THE RULE OF LAW IN ECONOMIC DEVELOPMENT

There are three elements or core values to the rule of law. First, the power of the state should not be exercised in an arbitrary fashion, but

---

[12]   *See* I-policy.org, Argentinian Progress in Telecommunications and E-Commerce—Information Policy, http://www.i-policy.org/2010/11/argentinian-progress-in-telecommunications-and-e-commerce.html (last visited March 30, 2011); Roberto Bouzas & Hernan Soltz, *Argentina and GATS: A Study on the Domestic Determinants of GATS Commitment,* in WTO MANAGING THE CHALLENGES OF WTO PARTICIPATION: CASE STUDY 2, *available at* http://www.wto.org/english/res_e/booksp_e/casestudies_e/case2_e.htm.

characterized by laws or rules that are prospective in nature, accessible, and clear.[13] Second, the law must be applied to the sovereign and instrumentalities of it; such as agencies within the government, or with an independent decision maker, such as a judiciary, which applies and interprets that law.[14] Finally, the law must apply equally to all persons without prejudice or discrimination.[15] Some scholars add a fourth element that requires government officials to be held accountable for their actions as it relates to enforcement of the law.[16]

There is much debate about what adherence to the rule of law means. In developing a legal framework for international trade, historically, many developed countries perceived that adherence to the rule of law was only achieved when a country adopts certain aspects of the U.S. legal system, such as "strategic litigation and activist judges." While this view is the foundation for the U. S. legal system, it has been found to be incompatible with existing legal systems of many developing countries. As a vehicle to stimulate economic development, this view has inherent limitations because parties tend to resort to the courts and seek redress under the rule of law only when there is a dispute, or when the relationship has soured. At this point, the relationship is over, which offers few benefits toward fostering sustainable economic development.

There is another school that perceives the rule of law on a continuum, which has relative importance in relationship to other countries, regions, and economic factors. Here, much of the focus is on the effectiveness of the interaction between different segments of the government.

> The rule of law is fundamental to achieving communities of opportunity and equity—communities that offer sustainable economic development, accountable government and respect for fundamental rights.[17]

Under this view, the rule of law is often examined when focusing on the vertical and hierarchical relationship between the government and its citizens, such as in human rights and criminal violations. Governments play a critical role in economic development as regulators, stakeholders,

---

[13] Chesterman, *supra* note 2 at 342.
[14] *Id.*
[15] *Id.*
[16] WJP Rule of Law Index 2010, *supra* note 2 at 8.
[17] *Id.* The WJP's work is based upon the premise that the rule of law is critical in creating opportunities for sustainable economic development and that the most effective way to advance the rule of law is through multidisciplinary collaboration. *Id* at 3.

and facilitators. Governments' primary role is as regulator in legislating the legal framework within which privatization will occur and ensuring that the rules are transparent and nondiscriminatory. Governments are also critical stakeholders in economic development, because much of the infrastructure in the country was once state-owned and controlled, which means the governments had to divest their interest in order to stimulate foreign investment. Finally, governments are facilitators in that they can allocate resources, determine the order and timing by which markets are made accessible to competition, and provide incentives to assist underrepresented players in the market.

At issue is whether government initiatives, alone, are adequate to create and sustain new markets and to promote sustainable economic development and growth in developing countries. This author believes that while the role of the government and the rule of law are essential initially, to foster economic development, they are ineffective alone to sustain economic growth. Let's first distinguish the application of the rule of law domestically and in the international context.

A. Applying the Rule of Law Domestically and Internationally

To provide a context for understanding international business transactions, it is important to highlight key distinctions between the exercise of the rule of law in domestic transactions, and its application in international business transactions. Governments tend to have greater power to create and enforce domestic rules because they have authority to exercise jurisdiction over activities within their borders. National laws standardize certain business norms and practices, despite differences between regional and local laws. Foreign persons seeking to do business within the country must, therefore, submit to the jurisdiction and the laws of the host country. However, in international law involving parties from multiple jurisdictions, there is no central governing authority or rule of law to define the rights and duties of parties.

Intellectual property rights are limited geographically to the territory of the country, and can be enforced within the jurisdiction of the country or countries under whose laws they are granted.[18] However, when parties are involved in a transborder licensing transaction involving know-how and intellectual capital, the nature and scope of the services rendered can easily traverse geographical boundaries. This is particularly true in

---

[18] INTELLECTUAL PROPERTY HANDBOOK: POLICY, LAW, AND USE 7, *available at* http://www.wipo.int/about-ip/en/iprm/.

collaborations among interdependent nations or technology transfers of intellectual property from government R&D centers to educational institutions and private companies.

Countries have formed international organizations and entered into treaties and international agreements in an attempt to standardize the rule of law and to develop a mutual recognition of rights and duties among nations. Transactions involving intellectual property, such as patents, trademarks, and copyrights, are subject to international treaties, arising out of unions[19] created by sovereign countries, such as the Berne Convention, the Agreement on Trade Related Aspects of Intellectual Property Rights (TRIPS), and the Patent Cooperation Treaty (PCT). These treaties provide legal protection between countries,[20] facilitate international protection and cooperation,[21] or establish minimum standards, procedures, and classification systems for trading in goods and services.[22]

Theoretically, the rule of law should function as it would in a domestic transaction. The practical reality, however, is different. Unlike international protection of copyright, IP owners of patents and trademarks must still register with the governing body of each country where protection is sought and not every country may recognize or protect the IP in the same way. This lack of uniformity and standardization highlights the inherent limitations of an international system based upon the rule of law.

---

[19] "The Unions administered by WIPO are founded on the treaties. A Union consists of all the States that are party to a particular treaty. The name of the Union is, in most cases, taken from the place where the text of the treaty was first adopted (thus the Paris Union, the Berne Union, etc.). The treaties fall into three groups." *Id.*

[20] Such treaties include the Paris Convention, the Madrid Agreement for the Repression of False and Deceptive Indications of Source on Goods, and the Lisbon Agreement for the Protection of Appellations of Origin and their International Registration. *Id.* at 8.

[21] These treaties include the Patent Cooperation Treaty, which provides for the filing of international applications for patents; the Madrid Agreement Concerning the International Registration of Marks; the Lisbon Agreement, which has already been mentioned because it belongs to both the first and second groups; the Budapest Treaty on the International Recognition of the Deposit of Microorganisms for the Purposes of Patent Procedure; and the Hague Agreement Concerning the International Deposit of Industrial Designs. *Id.*

[22] These agreements include the International Patent Classification Agreement (IPC); the Nice Agreement Concerning the International Classification of Goods and Services for the Purposes of the Registration of Marks; the Vienna Agreement Establishing an International Classification of the Figurative Elements of Marks; and the Locarno Agreement Establishing an International Classification for Industrial Designs. *Id.*

Another distinction in applying the rule of law domestically and in international business transactions is that courts in international law do not tend to be "independent" and do not apply or enforce the law with the same consistency. At the domestic level, there is an ultimate authority or arbiter of disputes, such as the U.S. Supreme Court for the United States that ensures consistency in decision making. There is no ultimate arbiter at the international level. Moreover, there is no concept of "separation of powers," a legislature or executive, although bodies have been voluntarily established for the benefit of its members, who exercise quasi-legislative and quasi-judicial functions. The absence of these doctrine or legal structures makes any attempt to fairly assess a state's achievement of the rule of law misleading and inaccurate.

Sovereign countries must consent to the jurisdiction of and voluntarily be subject to the sanctions imposed by so-called "independent" judicial bodies, created by treaties and international organizations. International bodies, such as the World Trade Organization, International Center for the Settlement of International Disputes (ICSID), United Nations, and International Court of Justice do not exist as "autonomous and complete jurisdictions" as is present in the national legal system.[23] Moreover, such bodies often have a narrow focus, i.e., the WTO's focus on trade relations between sovereign countries, or ICSID's focus on disputes involving a private party and a sovereign state, or among sovereign states.

Due to the high cost of litigation and the uncertainty with conflict of laws, entrepreneurs are increasingly more likely to opt for Alternative Dispute Resolution (ADR) over the local civil justice system to resolve disputes, because it provides a greater chance to preserve the business relationship. In ADR, the rule of law becomes less central to resolving the dispute than trying to achieve a mutually acceptable agreement between the parties.

It is also not uncommon for domestic courts to tend to favor the interests of local or national parties. This is particularly true in employment law or labor issues involving local nationals employed for foreign parties, regardless of the country.[24] In this context, the rule of law can reveal shortcomings in enforcement but does not provide any insight as to how to do business successfully in that country. Moreover, even where there is an independent judicial body, a court may be reluctant to impose criminal penalties for certain types of nonviolent or commercial crimes, such as piracy, counterfeiting, or gray goods.

---

[23]   Chesterman, *supra* note 2 at 355.
[24]   Folsom, et al., *supra* note 6 at 265.

A gray market involves the trade of goods through distribution channels that, while legal, are unofficial, unauthorized, or unintended by the original manufacturer.[25] The gray market's informal economy can account for a large part of a developing nation's income.[26] Gray markets exist to reflect the operational codes and social norms of the nation. They also exist because the local entrepreneur cannot afford the transactional costs associated with the "formal" economy and compliance with regulatory framework, processes, and bureaucracy.

Enforcement of trademark infringement in gray goods is inconsistent at best, and nonexistent in many developing countries, due to cultural differences and views about whether piracy is really a crime. Argentina is a member of the WTO and the WIPO, and has signed several international agreements protecting intellectual property, including TRIPS. Argentina also has a number of laws recognizing IP rights, and criminalizes IP infringements, where violators can draw prison terms of two months to four years, and double that for repeat offences.

Despite the presence of these laws on the books, Argentina has one of the largest markets for pirated goods in the world, in an area known as La Feria la Salada, which is 20 hectares on the outskirts of Buenos Aires, employing 40,000 people and generating $40 million per year.[27] Providers of gray goods are so bold as to have their own website, despite the fact that their activities are illegal.[28] According to the International Property Rights Index, which compares IP protection in 125 countries, Argentina ranks 85 out of 125 developing countries, including other countries in South and Latin Americas.[29] Many attribute the lack of enforcement to a judiciary that appears reluctant to impose criminal penalties for trademark infringement.[30]

This inconsistency makes it difficult to reconcile the rule of law when it is not inspired by preexisting operational codes. An operational code is an unwritten set of rules that develop out of custom and practice. If the

---

[25] Weicher, *Kmart Corp. v. Cartier, Inc: A Black Decision for the Gray Market*, 38 AMER. U. L. REV. 463 (1989) (cited in Folsom, et. al., *supra* note 6 at 976).

[26] The Economist Intelligence Unit, *Argentina: Licensing and Intellectual Property* (Aug. 13, 2010), *available at* http://www.eiu.com/index.asp?layout=VWArticleVW3&article_id=347349819&country_id=1470000147&page_title=Latest+analysis&rf=0.

[27] *Id.*

[28] *Id.*

[29] *Id.* Argentina ranks below Chile (34), Uruguay (50), Brazil (64), Colombia (67), and Mexico (72), but above Peru (88), Paraguay (118), Bolivia (119), and Venezuela (121).

[30] *Id.*

protocol for developing the rule of law does not embrace and reflect to some extent the operational codes, then a government can legislate certain behavior, but it will unlikely be enforced. Enforcement, in turn, depends upon another set of evolving operational codes that may not accommodate the changing economics of doing business. Therefore, the rule of law is inadequate and cannot effectively exist without catering to operational codes.

A final distinction between the rule of law in the domestic context and internationally is the presence of external influences that impact on the politics of international law that is not apparent in U.S. domestic law. Consider, for example, the role of the World Bank and International Monetary Fund (IMF) in impacting economic growth in a country. Even though the World Bank and IMF are technically constrained from interfering in the "politics" of the country, their influence necessarily impacts on policies and the criteria and conditions imposed upon developing countries seeking aid.

For example, the IMF defines the rule of law as "the extent to which agents have confidence in and abide by the rules of society, and in particular the quality of contract enforcement, the police, and the courts, as well as the likelihood of crime and violence."[31] To the extent that IMF conditions or concessions for aid tend to favor foreign investors, some developing countries like Argentina, have elected to default on repayment of IMF loans to protect national and local interests,[32] or more significantly to avoid what are perceived as discriminatory policies against the country seeking the aid. The distinctions in applying the rule of law domestically and internationally suggest that considering the rule of law may be illustrative, but not determinative of whether trading with a country is attractive, or how to ensure that investment will sustain economic development.

B. Privatization and the Rule of Law

Privatization is a three-step process initiated by a government to open local markets to foreign investment. In privatizing the telecommunications sector, the goals were to expand coverage, provide more efficient services and affordable pricing through competition. The absence of competition results in lack of economic incentives toward innovation.

---

[31]   Chesterman, *supra* note 2 at 347 (citing footnote 85).
[32]   Andrea L. Johnson, *Evaluating Privatization of Telecommunications to Foster Economic Growth: Argentina Revisited*, 36 Law/Technology Journal 1, World Jurist Association 1 (2003).

Historically, it did not matter whether the country was a market economy, where market forces are relied upon to foster and sustain growth, or a non-market economy, where the supply of goods and services, as well as market access, is controlled by the government. Similarly, the effects of privatization tend to be the same in developed as well as developing countries. The distinction is in matters of degree only.

Under WTO mandates, the first step requires the government to pass laws transferring stock ownership from the government to privately owned companies that can attract foreign investment.[33] This is the foundation for developing a system of rules or a regulatory framework that promotes transparency and predictability. Transparency, or more accurately, the lack thereof, typically affects the transaction costs imposed by government requirements on foreign investors. These requirements include registration, permitting, imposition of tariffs, duties, or other import controls designed to limit or restrict access to markets or protect local markets. The focus is not only on whether these rules exist, but also on how they are applied and whether they are applied uniformly and in a nondiscriminatory manner. Local laws can promote transparency, but depend upon legislative support and buy-in from agencies that must enforce these rules.

The second step requires the government to introduce limited competition from foreign companies.[34] While encouraging direct foreign investment, many governments impose restrictions or limitations on foreign ownership to guarantee minimum local participation.[35] This is to ensure that the benefits of foreign investment reach the local economy and players. The third and final step requires governments to pledge to open other markets to full competition.

Privatization is a top-down approach that was followed by most developing countries, like Argentina, as a condition for getting IMF aid. However, there has always been a tension between the need to promote foreign investment while protecting local markets. When the rule of law favors or elevates one party's interest over the other, or has unintended consequences to harm local markets by destabilizing the local economy, the response by the government generally is to ignore the law, or to nullify the effect by failing to enforce the law. This has been apparent in how countries respond to IMF and U.S. AID conditions for getting aid. The IMF has been criticized as using a "one size fits all approach" to giving

---

33 *Id.* at 6–7.
34 *Id.*
35 *Id.*

aid.[36] This approach does not consider economic indicators that reveal the long-term viability of existing markets and the ability of the political and regulatory structure to withstand the adjustments in markets when there is a large infusion of capital.[37]

Argentina followed the IMF approach by embracing pro-market principles when privatizing its public telecommunication services during the early 1990s. It opened up its capital and financial markets to foreign competition, eliminating hyperinflation by pegging the peso to the dollar, a condition imposed by the IMF. In addition, it accepted other IMF controls without question and debate, such as reduction in spending, stabilizing the currency and increasing taxes. Tens of billons of dollars in loans and investment poured into the country, resulting in a recession that caused tax revenues to fall and the fiscal deficit to widen. Additional reforms failed, causing the banks to close in 2002, which led to riots and violence.

Over the next year, growth in basic telecommunications services and infrastructure development stopped and then declined, small companies went bankrupt, and political turmoil followed. In response, Argentina adopted a more nationalistic approach, focusing on infrastructure development, restoring the trust of its people by investing money back into the economy rather than paying off IMF debt.[38]

Argentina is a good example where legislative mandates to promote competition in established markets led to regulated company monopolies that engaged in anti-competitive practices to preserve market dominance.[39] The process began with the privatization of the state-owned operator, ENTEL. Basic telephone markets were opened up and operators from Italy, Spain, and France entered and dominated the market. [40] In 2000, then-Argentinian President de la Rua passed legislation that deregulated all aspects of the industry.[41] However, in response to efforts by the government to promote further competition in other telecom markets, such as international long distance, incumbents Telecom Argentina and

---

[36]   *Id*. at 19.
[37]   *Id*.
[38]   *Id* at 11.
[39]   *Telecom Nationalization Could be More than a Threat, Analyst Says – Argentina*, BUSINESS NEWS AMERICAS, (Jan. 22, 2010), *available at* http://www.bnamericas.com/news/privatization/Telecom_nationalization_could_be_more_than_a_threat,_analyst_says.
[40]   Telecom Argentina was jointly owned by Italy and France. Telefonica de Argentina was owned by Spain.
[41]   This includes local, national, and international long distance, cable, wireless, satellite, IP telephony, and Internet.

Telefonica combined to form a Telintar SA, which allowed them to maintain their monopoly.

In 2010, the government urged Telecom Argentina to sell its 50% stake. The company has consistently refused and the government has set a timeline for compliance. In response to court action to suspend the timeline, the government intends to seize control of the telecommunications sector to force divestiture of these companies,[42] claiming that market growth has been thwarted by anticompetitive practices[43] by the incumbents. Argentina's planning minister has said that full nationalization is possible if the judicial system continues to block the government's resolve to kick out Telecom Italia.[44]

Over the last ten years, while Argentina has privatized portions of its telecommunications sector, full competition has yet to be realized.[45] The failure of privatization is attributed to three factors: 1) the widespread corruption and extraction of foreign earnings out of the country; 2) the lack of enforcement of the rule of law; and 3) unilateral fiscal policies imposed by the IMF.[46]

The failure of the rule of law was not just that laws were not enforced, but there was a lack of consensus on the proper approach. The regulatory infrastructure was relatively new at the time and was not firmly established. Moreover, the persons setting the policy and making WTO and IMF policies were finance and trade ministers making agreements under political pressure asserted by international trade organizations. Unfortunately, they were not the persons who were actually charged with implementing the regulations.

This is where the operational codes trumped the law. To truly understand the realities of doing business abroad, one must realize that the local government self-interest will likely prevail, when confronted with a perceived threat from foreign parties. From a policy standpoint, pursuit of the national interest tends to lead to a politics of exclusion.

Despite privatization and deregulation, the rule of law was seen as

---

[42] BUSINESS NEWS AMERICAS, *supra* note 40.

[43] The Argentina government has claimed that the Telefonica's indirect stake in Telecom Italia, which owns a 50% stake in Sofora, a holding that controls Telecom Argentina, violates Argentina's antitrust laws, because Telefonica controls its rival. *Id.*

[44] *Id.*

[45] I-policy.org, Argentinian Progress in Telecommunications and E-Commerce—Information Policy, http://www.i-policy.org/2010/11/argentinian-progress-in-telecommunications-and-e-commerce.html (last visited Aug. 27, 2011);

[46] *Id.* at 15.

an impediment to economic growth and ultimately proved ineffective to sustain growth. Newer markets in Argentina, such as the Internet over cable, have leapfrogged over basic telephony in terms of market penetration, access to services, and affordable pricing, precisely because the industry developed with minimal government intervention. As of 2010, Argentina is the third largest Internet market in Latin America, with an estimated 13 million Internet users and 1.45 million broadband subscribers.[47]

The lessons learned show that privatizing existing markets will never be sustainable because regulation creates artificial boundaries that when deregulated, cannot be recreated under a market approach. The effect is either government nationalization or a restructuring of the market by new industries that bypass the existing infrastructure and thereby necessitate a fundamental change in the business model, such as going from per-minute usage pricing to flat rate; or negotiated, differential pricing to compulsory flat-rate pricing.

While privatization does provide economic growth potential and benefits to countries that pursue it, "the process must be more carefully managed to account for the particular goals and needs of each developing country . . . one prescription does not cure all."[48] As a result, history has shown that the rule of law can promote economic development through privatization of telecommunications, but such growth may not be sustainable.

III. ASSESSMENT OF THE RULE OF LAW IN THE UNITED STATES AND ARGENTINA

Traditionally, adherence to the rule of law was the minimal requirement before investment in a developing country was recommended. However, that view was shortsighted. Instead, the rule of law should be judged on a continuum as an ideal as opposed to a normative reality.[49] This is particularly true in an international business transaction where there is a lack of consensus on objective criteria to measure the rule of law, which will vary in different context; for example, human rights, criminal violations, and economic development.[50] Traditional notions of the rule of law determine

---

[47]   *Id.*
[48]   Andrea L. Johnson, *supra* note 33 at 21.
[49]   Simon Chesterman, *supra* note 2 at 342, 360.
[50]   *Id.* at 347.

the level of economic development of the country that justify labels of being "developed," "developing," or "less developed."[51]

It is important to note that such labels tend to project a certain paternalism by more-developed countries about the way countries should be, even though these same countries have been criticized as not adhering to the same standards projected on developing countries.[52] Nations may be labeled differently and appear on multiple lists, depending upon who is making the designation. For example, the World Trade Organization does not classify member countries, nor does it define what is a developed or developing country. Instead, members self-identify as "developed" or "developing" to take advantage of some benefits, such as longer transition periods to privatize markets.[53] However, entitlement to benefits as a developing country is not automatic. As a practical matter, the country providing the preference tends to decide who is on the list of developing countries and, therefore, entitled to receive the preference.[54] For purposes of this discussion, the designations "developed" and "developing" will be used for statistical convenience and do not express a judgment about the development stage reached by a particular country.

Many scholars believe that any sovereign country, including the United States, regardless of the label attached to it, will disregard, fail to comply, or ignore the rule of law in pursuit of or to preserve their national interests.[55] In fact, there is strong evidence that concessions offered under WTO obligations can often be driven more by a need to "lock in" domestic policy reforms rather than to appeal to notions of reciprocity, prescribed under WTO mandates.[56]

The author acknowledges the inherent limitations in any attempt to

---

[51]   The United Nations states "There is no established convention for the designation of 'developed' and 'developing' countries or areas in the United Nations system. In common practice, Japan in Asia, Canada and the United States in northern America, Australia and New Zealand in Oceania, and Europe are considered 'developed' regions or areas." United Nations Statistics Division, http://unstats.un.org/unsd/methods/m49/m49regin.htm (last visited Mar. 27, 2011). South and Latin America countries generally are considered "developing." Factors that impact the classification include Gross Domestic Power (GDP); per capita income; economic vulnerability or wealth; literacy; currency devaluation; political conflict; population; and quality, depth, and breadth of markets versus non-market economies.

[52]   Chesterman, *supra* note 2 at 346–47.

[53]   World Trade Organization, Development Definitions, http://www.wto.org/english/tratop_e/devel_e/d1who_e.htm (last visited on Mar. 27, 2011).

[54]   *Id.*

[55]   Roberto Bouzas, *supra* note 13.

[56]   *Id.*

determine whether an investor or entrepreneur should invest in that country based upon adherence to the rule of law. Nevertheless, such studies can be useful to frame the issues that need to be addressed and the factors to be considered in evaluating potential export markets. According to the World Jurist Project, Rule of Law Index (2010),[57] 35 countries, including the United States and Argentina, have been ranked based upon a quantitative assessment of their adherence to the rule of law in 10 different factors.[58] Countries are scored and ranked globally, by regions and income groups.[59] Generally, correlating the income designations in this study to UN designations, high-income countries are generally considered "developed;" and upper-middle, middle, and low-income countries are considered "developing."[60] The WJP's work is based upon the premise that the rule of law is critical in creating opportunities for sustainable economic development and that the most effective way to advance the rule of law is through multidisciplinary collaboration.[61]

A. United States

According to the Rule of Law Index, the United States is ranked 11th out of 35 countries on any of the 9 principles identified to assess adherence to the rule of law.[62] That is the good news. The bad news is that when judged

---

[57]   WJP Rule of Law Index 2010, *supra* note 2 at 1.

[58]   *Id.* at 1. The factors that were evaluated were: 1) limited government power; 2) absence of corruption; 3) clear, publicized and stable laws; 4) order and security; 5) fundamental rights; 6) open government; 7) regulatory enforcement; 8) access to civil justice; 9) effective criminal justice; and 10) informal justice. Each of these factors was broken down into 49 subcategories. These factors and subcategories are grouped based upon the 4 principles discussed above: accountable government (factors 1 and 2); security and fundamental rights (factors 3, 4, and 5); open government and regulatory enforcement (factors 6 and 7); and access to justice (factors 8, 9, and 10).

[59]   *Id.* at 14. Countries are grouped according to per capita income level of its citizens as high, upper middle, lower middle, and low. Of the 35 countries evaluated, 11 countries were categorized as high income, including the United States; 7 countries, including Argentina were categorized as upper middle income; 12 countries were categorized as lower middle income; and 5 countries were categorized as low income.

[60]   Only Liberia is identified as low income, but would be considered "least developing" according to the U.N. classification. *See* United Nations Statistics Division—Standard Country and Area Codes Classifications (M49), http://unstats.un.org/unsd/methods/m49/m49regin.htm (last visited Mar. 28, 2011).

[61]   WJP rule of Law Index 2010, *supra* note 2 at 3.

[62]   James Podgers, *Playing Catch-Up*, 96- Dec A.B.A. J. 58.

relative to the 10 other high-income countries[63] that would likely be considered "developed," the United States ranked at or near the bottom in all of the categories, ahead of only Singapore, South Korea, and Spain.[64] The question becomes how can the United States have $214.1 billion in imports,[65] if it was not considered to be an attractive market for trade? The answer is that these indexes should not be used to judge the viability of the market, but only to provide useful information about relative markets.

Those factors selected as key economic development indicators are: 1) limited government powers; 2) absence of corruption; 3) clear, publicized, and stable laws; 4) order and security; 5) fundamental rights; 6) open government; 7) regulatory enforcement; and 8) access to civil justice.[66] "Limited government powers" include having some semblance of separation of powers, accountability among government officials, compliance with international law, and transitions of power in conformity with law.[67] The United States ranks at the bottom in the region and 9th out of 11 for high-income countries.[68] This would suggest that the United States market has the infrastructure that should accommodate imports and foreign investment, but has not been as successful in the region at encouraging trade in goods and services.

Factor 2, absence of corruption, includes the absence of bribes, improper influence, or misappropriation of funds.[69] The United States ranks relatively high in this category but at the bottom in regional and income group rankings. The United States scores the highest among the other factors at 0.83 in factor 4, order and security, which means that crime and civil conflict are effectively limited, and persons generally do not resort to physical violence to resolve grievances.[70] However, the United States is still near the

---

[63]   High income countries were Australia, Austria, Canada, France, Japan, the Netherlands, Singapore, South Korea, Spain, and Sweden. WJP rule of Law Index 2010, *supra* note 2 at 14.

[64]   James Podgers, *supra* note 63 at 58; WJP Rule of Law Index 2010, *supra* note 2 at 94.

[65]   According to U.S. International Trade in Goods and Services as of April 2011, Press Release, U.S. Census Bureau, U.S. Int'l Trade in Goods and Servs. (June 9, 2011), *available at* http://www.census.gov/foreign-trade/Press-Release/current_press_release/ft900.pdf. Exports came in much less at $167.7 billion, which results in a deficit of $46.3 billion.

[66]   This does not mean that factors 5 and 9 are not important, but will not be evaluated in determining success at stimulating investment and exports.

[67]   WJP Rule of Law Index 2010, *supra* note 2 at 9.

[68]   *Id.*

[69]   *Id.*

[70]   *Id.*

bottom relative to regional and income group rankings. This suggests that the two-party political system is not perfect and does lead to instances of corruption, but it is not widespread and should not prevent foreign entities from considering the United States as a "safe" place to do business. Where abuses occur, the U.S. legal system is relatively effective at responding to curb such abuses.

Factors 6 and 7 relate to open government and regulatory enforcement and include such sub-factors as public access to administrative proceedings, laws and regulations, and official information; effective enforcement of government regulations without improper influence; respecting due process rights; and not expropriating private property without just compensation, respectively.[71] The United States ranks 3rd overall in terms of "openness" of government and high among regional and income groups. This suggests that despite instances of corruption, most persons have the ability to know and understand the regulatory process.

Finally, factor 9 relates to access to civil justice and includes public awareness of civil remedies, access to ADR, the civil courts, affordable legal counsel, and impartial civil justice, free from improper influence, without unreasonable delays and enforcement. Unfortunately, the United States scores the lowest overall in this category, and at the bottom of regional and income groups. A foreign investor considering importing to the United States may conclude that while the U.S. has an open-government system with transparency in the rules, not everyone will have equal access to redress grievances. This would suggest that a company needs to have adequate resources to retain local counsel in the event a dispute arises, and pursue ADR to resolve disputes. It may also suggest that the United States has operational codes that influence the legal process. This is the same conclusion that most U.S. companies would reach when looking at foreign markets for business.

Overall, the decision whether to invest in the United States will not likely be determined based upon its score or ranking as the adherence to the rule of law. Its ranking on any given factor should impact on how resources will be allocated to minimize risks or identify personnel who can facilitate or expedite the process.

B. Argentina

Argentina is considered an upper-middle income country, or "developing," under UN terminology, as are all countries so designated in Latin

---

[71] *Id.*

and South Americas.[72] According to the WJP survey, Argentina ranks 33rd out of 35 globally, and toward the bottom or at the bottom on any of the principles. What is more interesting is where they rank in the region and income groups. Argentina is ranked at the bottom, like the United States, regionally and in income groups on factor 1, limited government; and near the bottom within the region on factor 3, clear and stable laws, and factor 7, regulatory enforcement.[73] The United States is ranked higher regionally and among its income group in factor 4, order and security, and factor 6, open government. Argentina has a higher regional rank than in factors 5 and 6, fundamental rights, which would seem to be consistent with its nationalist agenda to give priority to domestic interests. Those areas where the United States ranks higher are consistent with U.S. domestic priorities for an open and transparent government.

Table 10.1 below summarizes the relative rankings between Argentina and the United States.

So what does all this mean? From a business and legal perspective, it means that care should be given in selecting the type of goods and services for export to Argentina. A U.S. entrepreneur would more likely be successful licensing services, know-how, or intellectual property, such as in franchising, than exporting goods, which is subject to more regulatory requirements. Licensing software or know-how would be less risky, although piracy will still be a major problem if the services result in a consumer product that could be easily pirated. Exporting services typically are not subject to registration, tariffs, or other requirements under the General Agreement on Trade in Services ("GATS"), provided the services do not involve military, intelligence, or national security clearance. The goal should be to export U.S. services that require minimal government regulation.

Second, an entrepreneur is better served to find agents or brokers who are knowledgeable about local "business practices" or operational codes, and can help them navigate the system without violating laws prohibiting bribes and kickbacks under the Foreign Corrupt Practices Act.[74] Trade

---

[72]   United Nations Statistics Division—Standard Country and Area Codes Classifications (M49), http://unstats.un.org/unsd/methods/m49/m49regin.htm (last visited Mar. 28, 2011).

[73]   WJP Rule of Law Index 2010, *supra* note 2 at 26.

[74]   P.L. No 95-213, 91 Stat. 1494 (amended 1988 and 1998), 15 U.S.C. §78m, 78dd-1, 78dd-2. FCPA was enacted in 1977 in response to post-Watergate reports of foreign bribery and corporate slush funds. Morrison & Forrester InfoPAK, "The Foreign Corrupt Practices Act and Global Anti-Corruption Law," Association of Corporate Counsel (on file with author) www.acc.com. The FCPA prohibits

Table 10.1   Summary of the relative rankings between Argentina and the United States

Rule of Law Index Factors	Score		Global Rank		Regional Rank		Income Group Rank	
	US	AR	US	AR	US	AR	US	AR
Factor 1: Limited Gov.	.71	.32	9/35	33/35	7/7	7/7	9/11	7/7
Factor 2: No Corruption	.81	.48	10/35	20/35	7/7	3/7	10/11	4/7
Factor 3: Clear & Stable laws	.68	.39	9/35	31/35	6/7	6/7	9/11	6/7
Factor 4: Order & Security	.83	.51	11/35	25/35	6/7	2/7	9/11	5/7
Factor 5: Fundamental Rights	.74	.58	11/35	21/35	7/7	3/7	10/11	5/7
Factor 6: Open Government	.75	.29	3/35	29/35	3/7	7/7	3/11	6/7
Factor 7: Regulatory Enforcement	.71	.42	8/35	28/35	5/7	5/7	8/11	5/7
Factor 8: Access to Civil Justice	.66	.55	11/35	20/35	7/7	3/7	11/11	4/7
Factor 9: Effective Criminal Justice	.78	.43	7/35	28/35	5/7	3/7	7/11	6/7

with minimal government involvement may address this issue. In this context, the rule of law should not be the focal point in determining the viability or longevity of a trade relationship. Instead, the focus should be on how to strengthen and enhance the relationship between the parties so that the mutual expectations of the parties can be realized over the course of the transaction. Disputes should be resolved exclusively through ADR. Access to the court system should the last resort.

Third, exporting certain types of consumer goods and intellectual property, such as software or business method patents may have higher risks. For example, Argentina does not recognize software patents,[75] and so any theft or misappropriation will not be actionable. It may be better to export

---

"corruptly paying or offering to pay anything of value to a foreign official directly or indirectly to secure improper advantage; influence a foreign official in his official capacity; induce him to violate the law; or induce him to use his influence with a foreign government to affect the government's act, in order to assist in obtaining or retaining business.

[75]   Sanchez, Lupi, & Associates, *Patents in Argentina*, www.sanchezlupi.com/libreria/PATENTS.doc (last visited on Apr. 2, 2011).

intellectual property with a short shelf-life, or which cannot be easily manufactured, such as wind power or biotechnology, than other types of intellectual property.

Finally, expect that Argentina will uphold its labor and tax laws to favor local residents. This may impact on the type of agent or distributor that is used, the legal entity created, and whether income earned in Argentina will be subject to double taxation or can be extracted from the country, rather than reinvested back into the country.

IV. RECOMMENDATIONS TO INCREASE ECONOMIC DEVELOPMENT THROUGH TRANSBORDER LICENSING

Privatization of telecommunications failed to promote sustainability (?) in developing countries like Argentina because it ignored the need for buy-in from the agencies authorized to regulate and enforce the rules in these markets, or disregarded the limitations of government-imposed competition. In short, the legislated rules were not reconciled or normalized with the operational codes that were predominant and enforced at the local levels. As a result, the rule of law should be judged relative to notions of governance, focusing on a set of activities that include participation, transparency, and accountability.[76] In addition, the legal framework must empower the parties to resolve their issues, without the need for government intervention, or acknowledge its role as the forum of last resort.

A. Transborder Licensing

Opportunities in transborder licensing promise to be the new frontier for growth in the United States. There has been a 32% decline since 1982 in tangible corporate assets in favor of intangible assets.[77] Since 2000, intellectual property rights are a major source of value for U.S. companies.[78] The goods economy is being replaced with intellectual property as one of

---

[76] Chesterman, *supra* note 2 at 347.

[77] KAMIL IDRIS, INTELLECTUAL PROPERTY: A POWER TOOL FOR ECONOMIC GROWTH, 54 (Geneva, Switzerland: WIPO), *available at* http://www.wipo.int/about-wipo/en/dgo/wipo_pub_888/index_wipo_pub_888.html (last visited May 10, 2011).

[78] *Id.*

the major currencies. [79] Today, however, the paradigm has changed, and knowledge has become the new wealth."

Opportunities for exports to developing economies like Cuba, have the greatest potential if U.S. government policy encourages not only the privatization of hard assets, i.e. telecommunications, but also, and more importantly, the exchange of intellectual property. Through privatization, market access to Cuba has been limited to other Latin American countries, Mexico, and Canada. While Cuban markets have been essentially closed to U.S. companies due to the U.S.-imposed embargo for nearly five decades, that trend seems to be slowly changing.

In 2009, President Obama announced a series of changes in U.S. policy toward Cuba, which eased access to telecommunications equipment. [80] This policy shift began under President Bush, in response to a willingness by the Cuban government to increase access to cell phones, computers, and mobile communications devices, all of which are permitted but still require registration with the government.[81]

Transborder licensing between Cuba and the United States still has restrictions. For example, Section 515.206 of the C.F.R. governing exempt transactions prohibits a U.S. recording company from contracting with a Cuban musician to create and record compositions in Cuba and advance royalties to the Cuban.[82] The U.S. company could purchase preexisting materials created by the Cuban musician. If the U.S. government wants to build social trust, it should encourage such collaborations and allow parties from both countries to share in the commercial exploitation of that intellectual property.

The prescription for sustainable economic growth in developing countries should include 1) fostering more collaboration among NGOs and academic institutions in different countries; 2) overcoming the disparity in laws to achieve the intent and will of the parties by encouraging greater use of ADR to resolve disputes; and 3) building social trust through collaboration in the arts, sciences and technology transfer. In short, a strategy to nurture collaboration and cooperation among private parties of different countries must be at the center of privatization.

Conflicts of laws and the absence of a central governing body in international relations require an expanded perspective of the rule of law.

---

[79] *Id.*
[80] Stephanie Condon, *Obama Eases US-Cuba Telecom Restrictions*, CNET NEWS, Apr. 13, 2009, http://news.cnet.com/8301-13578_3-10218521-38.html.
[81] *Id.*
[82] 31 C.F.R. §515.206.

Account must be given to the nuances that distinguish different business practices. For example, business terms such as "agents" and "distributors" or "joint ventures" and "limited liability companies" have different legal interpretations in international business leading to conflicts or lack of clarity as to how a court without subject matter expertise would interpret it.

Where there is disparity in IP protection for patents or trademarks in a country, an entrepreneur has to be aware of and account for the risks associated with R&D, and to make sure there are enforceable non-disclosure, non-competition, and confidentiality agreements, or keep the IP a trade secret and consider doing manufacturing in the U.S. while assembling it elsewhere. In these cases, the law will not define success, as much as the business relationship and confidence the parties have in each other's ability to perform under the terms of the agreement.

B. Building Social Trust

The horizontal business relationship between the parties should become a key driver of sustainable economic development in international business transactions.[83] This is not to minimize the critical roles of the government as a stakeholder, regulator and/or facilitator in stimulating economic development. Instead, the point is simply that entrepreneurs should seek to stimulate and solidify the horizontal relationship between the parties, as a predicate to dealings with the vertical relationship with the government.

Building social trust begins through established relationships formed at U.S. educational institutions of higher learning; the diaspora communities; and collaborations in the arts and sciences. Academic institutions attract persons from all over the world in pursuit of a common goal: a U.S. education. The natural relationships built through study, in dorms, libraries, and coffee houses among students foster collegiality and trust, a key ingredient to identifying prospective business partners and investors. A diverse student population graduates to live and work in the United States, or return to their home country, taking those connections with them. There needs to be a way to leverage those relationships.

Diaspora communities, comprised of transplants or expatriates, also have natural connections to countries that may provide the new opportunities for exports. "Diaspora" is "that part of a people, dispersed in one or more countries other than its homeland, that maintain a feeling

---

[83] Chesterman, *supra* note 2 at 347.

of transnational community among a people and homeland."[84] Diaspora networks are important because they provide access to local information, human resources, technology, funding sources, informal contracts, and reputational enhancement.[85] In short, members of these communities are more likely to know the operational codes of more than one country. As President Obama has said about fostering better relations with Cuba, "Cuban American connections to family in Cuba are not only a basic right in humanitarian terms, but also our best tool for helping to foster the beginnings of grassroots democracy on the island."[86]

Finally, collaborations in the arts and sciences have traditionally allowed persons to overcome political and cultural differences for a common purpose or good. Collaborations provide opportunities for people to learn from each other, share and build bonds of friendship that enhance diplomacy. Innovations in technology and telecommunications have contributed to the huge increase in the volume of cross-border information exchanged between countries.[87] The potential to reduce transaction costs and stimulate consumer demand for products and services justifies more private collaborations.

Building social trust is a process that takes time, communication, and some common points for interaction. This is particularly important where there exist cultural and language challenges, as well as differences in the legal system and the administration of the rule of law. As such, starting with natural linkages with family members and between persons at academic institutions or among diaspora communities allows business partners to leverage existing networks to better understand the operational codes of a transaction, with some assurance of predictability and reliability. This builds credibility, which enhances the chance that these relationships will have longevity. Future areas of growth, such as transborder licensing, provide the best opportunity in new economies like Cuba, because the government's role (and therefore, political influence) is minimized.

---

[84]   Kingsley Aikins & Nicola White, GLOBAL DIASPORA STRATEGIES TOOLKIT, (Dublin, Ireland: Diaspora Matters 2011) p. 8.

[85]   Daniel Isenberg & William Kerr, "Take Advantage of Your Diaspora Network" GLOBAL DIASPORA STRATEGIES TOOLKIT, (Dublin, Ireland: Diaspora Matters 2011) pp. 5–7.

[86]   Stephanie Condon, *supra* note 81.

[87]   MANUEL CEREIJO, REPUBLIC OF CUBA TELECOMMUNICATIONS INFRASTRUCTURE ASSESSMENT, v (2009). University of Miami.

V.　CONCLUSION

The rule of law is an absolute prerequisite to U.S. economic development abroad. However, the rule of law will not be effective alone to stimulate entrepreneurship, without a keen recognition that existing infrastructure is inadequate to do more than create a framework for access to new markets. Technology can be used to streamline the process without interfering with the jurisdictional boundaries of local agencies, so the cost and burden on companies is more manageable. The strategy and goal to facilitate job creation and exchange of technology and innovation in countries like Cuba should be to create a regulatory environment that acknowledges the need for nationalism, but provides incentives for foreign investment in partnership with local entities. New growth areas are in franchising and licensing. Rules do not create sustainable growth; people do.

11. The making of the Durationator®: an unexpected journey into entrepreneurship

Elizabeth Townsend Gard*

I. AN UNEXPECTED ENTREPRENEUR

> The future, always so clear to me, has become like a black highway at night. We were in uncharted territory now ... making up history as we went along.[1]
>
> Sarah Connor in *Terminator 2*

The uneasy feeling of being an "entrepreneur" does not seem to subside with time. Together with my professor-spouse, we have started a spin-out LL.C. with technology from our university that we developed, and we are working on creating a business based on our research in law, literature, and history. The journey seems as impossible to achieve today as it did when we began—we are always in uncharted territory. And yet, we are slowly finding our way.

Four years ago, I was a newish professor, working on fairly obscure

* This chapter was presented as part of Tulane Law School's Faculty Brown Bag Series, July 27, 2011. Thank you to Bri Whetstone for her assistance in preparing this chapter, and Megan Carpenter for comments on early drafts, encouragement and support in the idea of sharing one's personal story of being a social entrepreneur. To Justin Levy, who has been part of the Durationator® nearly from the beginning, and has really lived every moment of this story. Thank you to Yvette Jones, Michael Bernstein, Laura Levy, John Christie, Christine Hoffman, Matt Miller, Glyn Lunney, Evan Dicharry, Ben Varadi, Jessica Edmundson, Zac Christiansen, Idea Village, Tom Dickerson, Bob Hinckley, Jule Sigall, Kenneth Crews, Peter Hirtle, Keith Werhan, Pam Samuelson, my dean(s) at Tulane Law School, Larry Ponoroff, Stephen Griffin, and David Meyer, and the countless others who have helped throughout the last years. And finally, thanks to Ron Gard, who is willing to jump in, play and help imagine our crazy adventure, to RJT, for all of our discussions on law, business, and licensing, and K. who is more of an entrepreneur than any of us.

[1] TERMINATOR 2: JUDGMENT DAY (Warner Bros. Pictures 1991).

work: one project on cultural history of women in the Great War,[2] and, connected to this, another on the copyright status of unpublished works under Section 303(a) of the 1976 Copyright Act.[3] No one seemed interested in my obsessions. It was a quiet, shy life. I knew exactly what lay ahead—teaching and writing for tenure. My path was certain and life was fairly straightforward. I liked it that way. There had been enough uncertainty in the job market. I loved the discourse and world of academia. I had no interest in clients, business, or taking chances. But even before I arrived in New Orleans to start my first tenure-track appointment, to my life and path would be added customers, business, and taking chances. In short, this chapter is the tale of the transformation of a fairly bookish tenure-track law professor who suddenly found herself being asked for the "pitch," a "business plan," and needing to decide what was the best corporate form for a university-spin out company. At any one time I felt and still feel like Eliza Doolittle, Cinderella, Frankenstein's monster, and/ or a fish out of water gasping for air.

This chapter tells the real world struggle of identifying just where the Durationator® fit within a multivalent world. We had a lot of challenges to work through before we even got to the actual start-up. What we desperately needed was a "Business for Academics" manual to help us translate discourse and understand the semiotics of our choices. Starting a business was such a different world from the law professor path. It felt much like traveling to a foreign country not knowing the language and having no translation dictionary available—a lot of pantomiming.

Professors, particularly from the humanities side of the world, have not been seen as useful entities, but rather are seen as gentle, out-of-touch souls that (maybe) contribute to understanding the world(s) in which we live(d). Ours has traditionally been seen as an economy of knowledge with a hierarchy of experience and publishing.[4] Law professors are seen as more useful, raising the new generation of judges, politicians, lawyers, and good citizens, and contributing to causes, needy clients, and the debates of the day. Law professors rarely file for patents, however. But the university

---

[2] Elizabeth Townsend Gard, "Reconstructing Vera Brittain's War Generation: A Comparative Biography" (Dissertation, 1997).

[3] *See* Elizabeth Townsend Gard, *Unpublished Work and the Public Domain: The Opening of a New Frontier*, 54 J. Copyright Soc'y U.S.A. 439, (Winter 2007) and Elizabeth Townsend Gard, *The Birth of the Unpublished Public Domain and the International Implications*, 24 Cardozo Arts & Ent. L.J. 687, (2006).

[4] *See generally* Corynne McSherry, Who Owns Academic Work?: Battling for Control of Intellectual Property, (Cambridge, Massachusetts, Harvard University Press, 2001).

has evolved in a post Bayh-Doyle Act world, even those from history, English, and law can find themselves filing a patent application.[5]

The journey began with an idea, of course, that turned into patent and trademark applications. It turns out that the patent portion of the journey was relatively easy, as was the trademark; but the actual figuring out what to do with our little invention was not so easy. The struggle was practical, but also had, at least for me, a huge psychological struggle with identity formulation. I was a professor who believed in access to knowledge and democratizing education. I would come to the heart-wrenching decision of rejecting (at least for the moment) the idea of a non-profit, to form a start-up, for-profit company using research and technology created from the work my spouse and I did as professors.

Part II is a modified version of the executive summary—what our business will do, what market need it fulfills, how we compare to the competition, and what our basic milestones will be to get to "success." Part III describes the process of how I got to the executive summary—a long, hard path, filled with learning new discourses and understanding the larger landscape of many copyright worlds. Part IV concludes with what I have learned so far in being a social entrepreneur, and what role law plays in the decisions and struggles.

II.   THE OFFICIAL VERSION

Four years ago, we identified an area of market failure: people cannot determine the copyright status of works under the current system because it takes too much time, knowledge, and expertise. Ironically, this has occurred at a time when more and more companies, industries, individuals, and academics are craving knowledge regarding the copyright status of works, particularly in relationship to posting works on the Internet. The proposed Google Book Settlement, the Europeana project, Amazon, Creative Commons, Open Knowledge Foundation, University of Michigan, Hathi Trust, and the Internet Archive are examples of high-profile entities in search of answers as to the status of copyrighted works. Some want to make money from public domain works; others want to legally tag works for others to be able to use, and still others are a mixture of both. But the problem of copyright status reaches down to any user of

---

[5]   For more information *see* Bayh-Dole @ 30: Mapping the Future of University Patenting conference papers, *available at* http://innovation.ucdavis.edu/events/bayh-dole-30-mapping-the-future-of-university-patenting/bayh-dole-30-papers.

cultural works—a second grade teacher, a collage artist, a scholar, a film-maker. To date, there has been no easy and reliable solution to determining the copyright status of a work. The Durationator® seeks to rectify this.

Invented at the Tulane University Law School, the Durationator® is a web-based tool that provides legal information to specific inquiries regarding the copyright status of cultural works. The Durationator®'s primary purpose is to make determining copyright status easy, quick, and cost effective. Through a simple, intuitive interface, a user can determine whether a particular work is protected by copyright in each country of the world, or if it has fallen into the public domain—jurisdiction by jurisdiction. As an example, if an e-book distributor wants to know where in the world a book may be sold online without copyright limitations, the Durationator® will promptly afford an easy-to-understand answer. If a library seeks to digitize a large collection for preservation as well as provide worldwide online access, the Durationator® can help ensure that doing so will not risk liability for copyright infringement. These two examples address whether a work has entered the public domain and is thus unfettered by copyright laws. However, the Durationator® can serve to reinforce copyright protection. If a film studio fears an older work in their library is being infringed and desires to claim the copyright is still valid (the first element required in bringing an infringement suit), the studio's lawyers could purchase a Durationator® Legal Report which would outline jurisdiction by jurisdiction around the world the copyright status of that work.

The Durationator® is a tool made for all users—content owners, creators, librarians, digitizers, individuals users. The target market for the Durationator® is anyone in the world who seeks to know the copyright status of a work. We see this as a fairly broad market, with sub-sections. But it turns out that whether you are Google or a second-grade school-teacher, the problem is the same. To date, except for a select group of works, it is too difficult to quickly and without substantial cost determine the copyright status of a work. We also see the markets for both the casual user as well as the heavy/serial user as having the same needs: low-cost, efficient, reliable information with low-educational requirements (i.e. you shouldn't need a law degree to figure out the copyright status of a painting). That said, we have a number of plans to reach key areas of the subgroups within the market.

We have come to see the project as fulfilling a social need where market failure has occurred. In the end, Limited Times, Inc. will develop three tools: Durationator® Basic, Durationator® for Digitizers (for digitizers and librarians), and Durationator® for Lawyers. Our current market strategy is to include key industry, academic, and non-profit users at the beta stage from experiment to product, partnering and working with them through collaborative research agreements and Durationator® Summits. If they are early adopters, we believe the smaller users will follow.

The product itself—whether as a Basic, Digg, or Lawyer version—has quantifiable benefits, as with each consumer basic the direct benefit is access to complex legal information in an accessible, understandable form at a low-cost, with the assurance that the information being provided has been vetted by the key experts in the country, and is comprehensive in scope and depth. Nothing like it exists today.

What the customer values: Our research has shown that customers are desirous of a fast, reliable, and cost-effective means of determining copyright status as an alternative to the services currently available. This is true whether the customer is a serial user, like University of Michigan or Google; public interest group, like Electronic Frontier Foundation (EFF) and Stanford Law School's Fair Use Project; or an individual artist, small publisher, or scholar.

Offering: A single determination will take a user a matter of minutes as compared to the hours or even days that a lawyer may take to manually answer the same query, for a fraction of the cost. Moreover, few lawyers would have the resources needed to answer the query globally, and therefore the service will aid lawyers in assisting their clients.

Benefits: By using the tool, users can reduce the risk of liability by making strategic decisions jurisdiction by jurisdiction, can become aware of the abundance of public domain works available for use, and can have an accurate account of the worldwide rights in their own works. Users will also be provided with information regarding options to pursue if a work is indeed protected by copyright, including library exceptions, fair use, classroom exceptions, religious use exceptions, and limiting jurisdictional use of the work.

Alternatives: Two alternatives exist. None are as comprehensive as the Durationator®.

The main alternative to Durationator® is for users to hire an attorney. This method is slow, costly, and usually unreliable as most attorneys lack the specialization necessary to make a valid appraisal. As few lawyers specialize in this particular line of work, many of those who would traditionally be considered competition would be better suited to subscribe to the Durationator® software to facilitate their work as a time-saving tool, making what historically has taken many hours to research, available in a matter of minutes and avoiding unnecessary errors by using a legal tool fully vetted and legal citations triple verified.[6]

A second set of alternatives can be found online. There are currently a handful of simple copyright calculator tools and/or tables including the ALA slider,[7] Peter Hirtle's copyright table, the OKFN public domain calculators project, and Europeana's copyright tool, to name a few. Each of these suffer from either simplicity (simplifying the law will get you to the wrong answer), complexity (one must understand subtle legal terms, as in the case of Peter Hirtle's fantastic table), or are merely wrong in their interpretation of the law (the ALA slider is a good example). None of these tools are global in scope, which is necessary in an Internet age.

Proof: The Durationator® team has developed four strategies to insure the law is correct. First, each path is initially researched, and then reviewed by two separate law students. A final revision of the work occurs independently by the Tulane Journal of Technology and Intellectual Property. Second, each path, once coded, is reviewed again for errors. Third, the path is then shown and tested locally by experts of that country and/or field. Fourth, we have begun to forge strategic partnerships with academic institutions that will help beta test the software under real-world conditions. Finally, we plan to conduct Durationator® Summits with experts from academia, industry, and libraries to discuss key questions as well as vet the software.

Beginning in 2011, the Durationator® is transitioning from experiment to product. To date, we have been funded entirely by Tulane University through grants and legal work totaling almost $180,000 and through the generous donation of unlimited student research hours from Tulane Law School (about 6000 student hours to date). All of the research, coding, and design has been done by Dr. Elizabeth Townsend Gard, Associate Professor at Tulane Law School and her Durationator® Team of students, post-grads, and experts. Tulane filed the PCT in September 2007, and the Trademark Intent-to-Use for "DURATIONATOR" in February 2008, which subsequently became a registered mark on March 30, 2010.

---

[6] Copyright search services such as Thomson's CompuMark and Bloomberg as well as the U.S. Copyright Office may be used to aid in determining the *data* necessary to determine the copyright status of a work, including registration and renewal records. However, these services only provide copyright records and no legal context in which to analyze them.

[7] AMERICAN LIBRARY ASSOCIATION, PUBLIC DOMAIN SLIDER, http://library copyright.net/digitalslider/ (last visited July 19, 2011).

The website was launched in February 2009. The closed beta version will be available in September 2012.

III. BEHIND THE SCENES OF THE OFFICIAL STORY, OR THE UNEXPECTED JOURNEY

It took me about a year to succinctly explain our project in an executive summary-type form as above. The struggle was not writer's block, but the struggle of learning a new discourse, and deciding where the Durationator® fit within many models. The intellectual property-related legal questions turned out to be fairly straightforward, and even though the research was arduous and at times unpredictable, nothing prepared me for the struggle of trying to fit the Durationator® within a larger world outside of my home law school.[8]

A. An Idea Long in the Making

As a graduate student, I had struggled greatly with trying to determine which works I could use unfettered, and which works I would need to gain permission to use more extensively than fair use would allow. It turns out that many of the works I was using were actually in the public domain, but during the writing of my dissertation were restored to copyright. I went to law school to learn the answers that seemed impenetrable and unanswerable. But my dream became much larger than merely which Vera Brittain works I could use—otherwise why would I have gone to law school! I wanted to create a place where scholars, artists, and other non-commercial users could gain reliable legal information, and even support. My spouse, Ron Gard, began to think about the structure—what would such a place look like and what kind of services would be offered? This began when he was at law school in the early 2000s. After graduation, my research while on the academic job market focused on the copyright status of unpublished works, a new addition under federal copyright. Little did I realize that I was starting to formulate building blocks of what would become the Durationator®—a software program that would make accessible complex legal information to the average user, or rather my old graduate-school self. It would not take long before the creation of software itself

---

[8] Michael Risch, *IP and Entrepreneurship in an Evolving Economy: A Case Study*, in ENTREPRENEURSHIP AND INNOVATION IN EVOLVING ECONOMIES (*infra*, Chapter 8).

and the remaining research necessary was fully underway at my new home institution, Tulane University Law School.

B. Arriving at Tulane University Law School

Our family moved from Seattle to New Orleans in the summer of 2007. After a post-doctorate fellowship and lecture position at the London School of Economics, where I started to compare U.S and U.K. copyright law, and then a Visiting Assistant Professor position at Seattle University School of Law, I had accepted a tenure-track position at Tulane University Law School. That summer, unexpectedly, the work on the Durationator® began. (The name would come that summer, too). Four key events occurred during that summer: two unsolicited e-mails, a trip to the New Orleans Public Library, 900 student research hours that began July 1, and the establishing of a very supportive relationship with my law school as well as the larger university administration.

1. Two e-mails
Two unsolicited e-mails occurred during the summer of 2007. Someone e-mailed me to ask if they could set a Vera Brittain poem to music—that is, was an early 20th century poem by a British author in the public domain in the U.S.? This seemed a reasonable question. After all, I had done my doctoral work on Vera Brittain, and I had just written two pieces on unpublished works and copyright duration. I soon realized that the problem was very complicated, and required a good deal of research and analysis, thanks to the *Twin Books* line of cases, republication of some of the poems in question in the 1930s and a reissue of the original 1918 edition in 1995 by the British Imperial War Museum.[9] But I also thought—I don't really want to have to remember all of these complex duration rules, case law and variables every time someone asks me a question. Wouldn't it be nice to have a software program where one could input specific information about a work and get a detailed working through of the law—a way to put all of my research over the last few years into a usable form? The research behind the Durationator® turned out to be quite complex, with many twists and turns as we sought to dislodge the many impediments to our quest.[10] The point of the software was to make this complex research accessible.

---

[9] *See* Elizabeth Townsend Gard, *Copyright Law v. Trade Policy: Understanding the Golan Battle within the Tenth Circuit*, 34 COLUM. J.L. & ARTS 131 (Winter 2011).
[10] Elizabeth Townsend Gard, *The (Im)Possibilities of a Usable Past: The Research behind the Durationator®*, in progress.

The second e-mail came from Matt Miller, a rising 2L at the time, who was in search of a summer research assistant position.[11] I told him of my idea—he had been a software engineer before law school. He accepted the challenge, in his quiet, confident style. He knew it could be done, and so together we set about to create a flowchart as a precursor to creating the software. Two years later, the flowchart and software had grown exponentially. Now four years later, we are on the brink of completing and coding every country in the world. We found ourselves quickly expanding to the countries of the world—as a necessary step in determining U.S. copyright law, and we also found that the U.S. law itself was far more complex than we first imagined.

2. Making accessible not only the law, but the legal means to get to an answer

During the summer 2007, I spent a good deal of my time in the basement of the New Orleans Public Library, trying to find proof of a usable past. I felt like an archeologist, like Indiana Jones, on a quest for the existence of the public domain. The reference librarian on duty would write me an improvised "pass" on a piece of scrap paper, and I would descend behind-the-scenes, where every thirty-minutes the lights turn off, marking the time I have been looking through the Catalog of Copyright Entries and the Copyright Office's official records of registrations and renewals. At the time, in 2007, these out-of-the-way, dusty records were often the only way to determine which works, written long ago, are now in the public domain or still under copyright.[12] Throughout the project, we constantly confronted new and varied problems, all related to the Catalog of

---

[11]   Since graduation, J. Matthew Miller has been an Associate at Carver, Darden in New Orleans. For more on Matt, *see* Carver Darden: J. Matthew Miller, http://www.carverdarden.com/attorneys-detail.asp?ID=35 (last visited July 19, 2011).

[12]   As our project progressed, more of the CCE records were digitized by others, but by 2010, a full version of the records was still not available online. Moreover, the records are still for the most part digitized as individual records and not yet as a searchable database. However, the records for Class A books are available online from a number of sources; *see e.g.* The Stanford Renewal Database, http://collections.stanford.edu/copyrightrenewals/bin/page?forward=home (last visited March 19, 2009). Google, with the help of Project Gutenberg, made these records available as an XML file, which we have incorporated into our *Durationator* copyright term software tool. We also found copies of the registration records for motion pictures—available at the Internet Archive. Everything else—art, musical compositions, movie renewals, commercial prints, maps, photographs, lectures, dramas, sermons, and periodicals—all of these records were not available online—only through a search of the original records.

Copyright Entries. These were the records that I was searching through in the basement of the New Orleans Public Library. These records held the key to what works were in the public domain. The CCE records were emblematic of the problem: the records were inaccessible, and so too was the law.[13]

3. 900 student hours

When I arrived at Tulane in the summer of 2007, I was also presented with 900 student research hours annually. At the time, I wondered how I would ever use those hours up—and so part of the Durationator® was designing tasks that students could accomplish that would move the project forward. After a bit of trial and error, I had students work on individual countries, while a smaller team worked with me on U.S. law. We would be focused on understanding copyright law that affected the duration for over four years. Each summer would bring intensive work, employing about a dozen students for ten weeks. It was thrilling, exciting, and sometimes overwhelming. We quickly used many more than 900 hours a year, and the law school generously found many more hours for the next few years. I also developed an efficient hierarchy, where students moved up a chain of command, with rising 2Ls being supervised by 3Ls who had worked on the project the summer before. I also used Skype to connect to each of the students. I could check in on what they were doing, or they could ask questions as they did their work.

Team Durationator® has included dozens of students, with about half a dozen taking distinct leadership roles.[14] The students' level of dedication was unmatched by anything I had seen before. They were devoted, smart, creative, careful, and each worked very, very hard both on their own and collaboratively. Students would build not only the code, but also the front end design, the initial logo, and the two-minute introductory video. As we became more interested in turning the software into a usable public form, students helped with the discussions and research on the business

---

[13]　The Internet Archive is said to be digitizing the Library of Congress' version, which includes penciled in changes. To date, however, no searchable database has been created, although a source at Google mentioned they are working on the problem. For a list of the records that have been digitized so far, *see* John Mark Ockerbloom, THE ONLINE BOOK PAGE, http://onlinebooks.library.upenn.edu/cce/ (last visited July 17, 2011).

[14]　In particular, Matt Miller is the co-inventor on the patent. Ben Varadi did the initial design work. Justin Levy served as our first Chief Legal Engineer, and is now our Senior Chief Legal Engineer. Evan Dicharry, Zac Christiansen (our new Chief Legal Engineer), Bri Whetstone (Head of Research and Social Media), and Jessica Edmundson have all played large leadership roles as well.

plan, the social media campaign, and ultimately, pricing. Three stayed on after graduation as IP fellows.[15] We all felt like we were making a difference—potentially unlocking a social good—finding the answer to such a simple question: when are works in the public domain (jurisdiction by jurisdiction)?

C. A Very Supportive University Environment

As that first summer drew to a close, an announcement for a Tulane University Research Enhancement Grant arrived by e-mail. Faculty could apply for up to $125,000 for assistance with research projects. I went to my dean at the time, Larry Ponoroff, with the idea that I needed about $5,000 for front-end website development.[16] He replied, "Dream bigger." I submitted, with his support, a much more comprehensive application, and to my surprise, I was awarded $80,000 in research money during my first semester at Tulane, and a few years later, a $25,000 IDEA grant from the Technology Transfer Office, and all of the patent, trademark and domain costs totaling so far around $60,000. To date, we have never had to take money from outside the university to complete our project, and I think we will launch in the same manner. This initial support would dramatically help form our identity, as we worked without worry of funding staying true to the project until the Beta version was completed.

The financial support was only out-matched by the emotional and intellectual support. From the beginning, before the grants and before we even had much of anything, we found support both with the Tulane administration and technology transfer office, as well as with my faculty. I always felt that my school was supporting my research, and my research happened to lead to an invention and even a start-up company. Not only did my Dean(s) supported my work with unlimited student research hours, but I felt supported and encouraged from the University administration throughout the process. Dr. Laura Levy, Provost Michael Bernstein, and especially Yvette Jones have all been incredibly kind, supportive, and helpful, both intellectually on what direction to take the project, as well as financially supportive of university funds for the project.

The Tulane Law School faculty has been especially supportive—I've

---

[15]   One, in particular, Justin Levy, came on early as our Chief Legal Engineer, and has remained on the project, now working at the Tech Transfer office at the university. He has been remarkable, and I appreciate his dedication and support with the project tremendously.

[16]   Our subsequent deans have also been very supportive, Interim Dean Steve Griffin and our new Dean David Meyer.

presented elements of the work, both the intellectual as well as practical sides, and sought out nearly everyone on the faculty for advice of one kind or another. Everyone has been very generous with their time and support of their junior colleague. I could not imagine doing this project without such collegial support—from advice on corporate formation to comparative constitutional law questions.[17] But of all the people, it was John Christie, now head of the Tech Transfer office at Tulane, who has been consistently supportive, kind, thoughtful, and patient.[18] From the first summer when I invited him to my office to discuss the idea of what would become the Durationator® through every step of the process he has let me grow, guided me with a gentle hand, and come to my rescue on a number of occasions. I know the project would not be near our beta launch without him. He is remarkable and everything a young professor could wish for when embarking on such a journey.

D. A Very Supportive Intellectual Property Scholars' Community

The intellectual journey has provided amazing connections, and as a new IP scholar, I have had to approach and have been so appreciative of the time and guidance of so many in the field—whether it was discussing key legal questions, like the rule of the shorter term, or how to fit within the open access/open source groups and the more proprietary visions of what we should become. I became part of a community, and when those I trusted did not find errors and believed in the work we are doing, my confidence began to grow that much more.[19] Besides being engaged in the

---

[17] In particular, Adeno Addis, Paul Barron, Jeanne Carriere, Alan Childress, Claire Dickerson, Onnig Dombalagian, James Duggan, Jorg Fedtke, Adam Feibleman, Robert Force, Joel Friedman, Catherine Hancock, Jancy Hoeffel, Oliver Houck, Glynn Lunney, Saru Matambanadzo, Pamela Metzger, Ron Scalice, Michael Pappas, Michael Sackey, Tania Tetlow, Amy Gajda, and Shu-Yi Oei, have been very generous and kind in their advice and suggestions at various stages, while my mentor, Keith Werhan has been tremendously supportive, every step of the way, reading papers, giving advice, and nodding supportively at important and trivial times. Part-time faculty that have also been very supportive include Sandra Queiroz, Marie Breaux, Mark Davis, David Marcello, and Robert Hinckley. But it extends not only to the faculty, but the staff as well who have been so kind and helpful at every step of the way, especially Sharon, Janice, Andrea, Cathy, Roy, Kim, Carla, Todd, Patrick, Ray, Karen, Angela, and Jerome, but there are so many more.

[18] John Christie is currently the Executive Director, Technology Transfer at Tulane University.

[19] The list of those in the IP field who have given advice and have been supportive of the underlying intellectual research is very long. But, in particular, I

actual research itself, discussing the project within the IP community has
been thrilling and incredibly intellectually exciting. I could not imagine a
better way to be introduced to this tremendous community.

IV.   THE LONG YEAR OF TRANSITION

With most academic work, one presents the findings at conferences and
publishes the results.[20] This project was different. From the first presentation at a conference, we started to face the question: how much are we
keeping proprietary? The university was pursuing trademark and patent
protection for us, which we appreciated. This time, the game was substan-
tially changing. At the same time, I needed to show my peers to see if we
were on the right track. Moreover, copyright is a world filled with many
divergent feelings and I soon realized we would have to figure out where
we fit within this world.[21] This last task would be the hardest, but as my
daughter said when she was very young, "I make my own road!" We had
to forge our own path, and this would take us a good deal of thinking to
figure out.

---

very much thank the following for the time, patience, willingness to see the latest
version, and guidance: Kenneth Crews, Graeme Dinwoodie, David Nimmer,
William Patry, Fred Von Lohmann, Diane Zimmerman, Pamela Samuelson,
Tyler Ochoa, Anthony Falzone, Peter Jaszi, Michael Carroll, James Grimmelman,
Mark Rose, Roberta Kwall, Deven Desai, Anthony Falzone, Diane Peters, Mike
Linksvayer, Anthony Reese, James Boyle, Jule Sigall, Julie Samuels, Diane Peters,
Dale Nelson, David Carson, Paul Goldstein, David Levine, David Olson, as well
as many, many others at IPSC, WIPIP, the NYLS Innovate/Activate conferences,
and the Statute of Anne conference at Berkeley. The librarian community has
also been very generous with their time, especially and most profoundly, Peter
Hirtle.

[20]   "What Should the Durationator® Be When it Grows up?" Innovate/
Activate , NYLS, September 2010; "Theorizing the Practical: the Underpinnings
of the Durationator®," SEALS, August 2010; "The Durationator® Revealed,"
Copyright @ 300, UC Berkeley, April 2010 (invited speaker); "The Making of
the Durationator™," IPSC 2009, Cardozo Law School, New York, August 2009;
"The Durationator® Experiment," WIPIP, Tulane University, October 3–4, 2008;
and "The Impossibilities of a Usable Past: Struggling with Copyright Duration in
the Basement at the New Orleans Public Library," Works-in-Progress Intellectual
Property Conference at American University, September, 2007.

[21]   We were able to show/demonstrate the Durationator® to experts at Google,
Warner Brothers, OCLC, Creative Commons, Open Knowledge Foundation,
Stanford Fair Use Project, Electronic Frontier Foundation, and other places as
well.

A. Business 101

We have spent the last year thinking about how to transition from an "experiment" to a business. I never intended to start a business, and so contemplating what to do with the Durationator® turned into an identity struggle as much as anything else. What exactly was the Durationator®, and what did we want it to become? I had these discussions with the students, with alumni, and with colleagues across the country.[22] These conversations built into long-term relationships, ones I would never have had if it had not been for having to learn Business 101.

My first experience with the business side came one afternoon at a very nice New Orleans uptown home. My students and I arrived to speak with a supportive, successful alumnus who had done very well in business. He was on a conference call in the background as he talked to us. He talked fast and had a lot to say about our potential business. He gave us advice, of which I had no idea what he was saying, and told us not to "sell" the business too early. I left his house in a whirlwind. I had just been introduced to a whole new discourse—a world with very different expectations and rules. I wanted to hide. It would take me about nine months of serious work to fully understand, if not fully embrace, the concerns and ideas he had suggested. It was an important moment—the first of many.

Over the next few months, I would have conversations with many people, as I tried to absorb the business elements of our project. I owe a tremendous debt to Tom Dickerson, husband of Tulane law faculty professor Claire Dickerson, who unintentionally became my business school tutor as he tried to explain shares, business structures, and financials.[23] Of course, my greatest struggle seemed to be the decision of whether we were going to be a for-profit or non-profit. No one wanted us to be a non-profit, except one professor at Tulane Law School and everyone outside of Tulane who wanted to use the software. To make this decision, I had to understand business from a practical side but also ontologically. How would the decision to be an LL.C., a C-corp, S-corp, or a non-profit affect the software development itself?

I began reading basic business books and, at one point, each of the

---

[22] I am particularly grateful for the repeated conversations with Jule Sigall, Pam Samuelson, Peter Jaszi, and Kenneth Crews. Their kindness and patience has been very much appreciated.

[23] Thomas Dickerson, having experience as a corporate attorney, an investment banker and chairman of a venture capital fund, is now the Managing Director of a new venture capital fund called Argent Technology Ventures, LL.C. and the Chairman of Five Star Physical Services, Inc.

students on Team Durationator® and I were engaged in doing a basic business workbook. This was actually the most helpful. I found that as I began to see examples and try to write about the Durationator® in business terms, the product and business itself started to emerge. These writing exercises led me to see the problem comparable to oil in a car—regardless of what kind of car one has, everyone needs oil. So too with copyright term information—whether it was a Google digitizing millions, a second grade teacher working on an Internet project, a graduate student, an independent filmmaker, or a multimedia conglomeration. All of these groups wanted low-cost, efficient, accessible, and fairly quick information. Sometimes they all needed legal supporting documents; other times, basic information would be sufficient.

B. Identity Struggle

We had a number of identity struggles. The product—a software tool determining the copyright status of works had no comparable product. As previously stated, there were law databases and services, like Thompson and Innography.[24] Each of these gave reports to clients on data they had regarding trademarks and patents, respectively. But nothing that exactly matched information to law—until a Tulane law faculty member during a Brown Bag presentation suggested we were "TurboTax® for copyright." Once we conceptualized the software in this manner, other elements fell into place. Some suggested that we keep a database of works whose status was known. We did not want to be responsible or appear responsible for outside data. Our mission was to understand the law. We did not want to be responsible for accurate metadata for each cultural work. The law was enough of a responsibility. We also now started to focus on the level of sophistication of our potential users.

We wanted to find a way to make it possible for the software to be widely available, and yet financially sustainable. To do this, we needed to figure out if we were going to try to charge money for the Durationator®—and how much—and if we were charging money to be self-sustaining or profitable, or if we were trying to find grants and other means of support. While we talked to a great deal of people—probably forty experts in the field

---

[24] Innography is a privately held company that focuses on patents, *see* Innography.com, Protecting Intellectual Property, Patents, Patent Infringement, Patent Software, http://www.innography.com/ (last visited July 16, 2011). Thompson Compumark is the largest supplier of trademark reports, *see* Thompson Compumark, Global Trademark Services, http://compumark.thomson.com/emea/ thomson_compumark/lang/en/ (last visited July 23, 2011).

who in one way or another were in need of the Durationator®, no one was willing to suggest what we should charge people for its use. We saw the need for our tool from many places—commercial digitizers, lawyers, the content industries, librarians, the average hobbiest, scholars, teachers— but what framework should be used to get it to market? A librarian at University of Michigan was the first to understand: "you could really make some money with this." Others had to be convinced there was something there to monetize. Still more believed it should be open sourced. Others still didn't think it could actually work. It was a mess.

As we started to talk to people who might be interested in the Durationator® — people whose work or business rely on the copyright status of works, they would continue to suggest that we open source the software, believing that somehow this was going to make it better, without understanding our closed-system process of cite-checking and researching. One day we may decide that open source would greatly benefit the project, but these conversations really felt like something else. But at the time, I was still not ready to make that leap. As I would talk with people, and "pitch" our experiment to them, they would seem interested and impressed. Some would say, "Would you mind just sending us a copy of the 'code'?" which seemed very odd. In other conversations, their first impression of "wow" would turn to "whoa"—it would suddenly sink in that we would know the actual law, and for many—librarians, non-profits, corporations—the murky unknown seemed better.

The greatest struggle I started to feel was the interest of nearly everyone we talked to either to set the code free, or give out the product for free. This would have been fine if the same people suggesting this were providing or offering funding to support the continued work, but they were not. These were really weird conversations, particularly because our system was so precise and closed. The idea of releasing unfinished research into the world seemed terrifying, to say the least. We knew that if *we* tweaked with the code in small ways, the results were wrong. We couldn't imagine this on a worldwide scale. We also knew that only a handful of experts truly understood the depth of where the research had taken us, and even when we played with others working on copyright projects, it soon became apparent that while we could help them with their questions, ours were too hard to answer.

As I talked to more and more people, it became evident that control and self-sustainability were the two key elements I found important to the project. I wanted the tool to be available for the world to use, but on our terms. Access to the software was very important: I wanted my old, graduate-student self and my theatre/artist/filmmaker friends to be able to afford to use the software tool. But I also knew that the software needed to be financially sustainable, and I surely didn't want to give the software away for free only to find we could not finish or update it, and moreover, *wrong* versions could start to pop up. We had already seen other efforts out there that led to really, really wrong answers. We were not quite at a vision of what the business would look like. It would take a few more months of thinking before the formulation of what that would actually start to look like came into place. All of this soul searching was incredibly hard.

C. Idea Village and the UC Berkeley Business Students

In 2009, we were introduced to Tim Williamson and Allen Bell, co-founders of Idea Village.[25] Christine Hoffman, Executive Director of Corporate, Foundation & Research Relations at Tulane from the beginning really saw our project as a potential start-up. One day, I went to the main administration building to have a conversation with John Christie, Christine Hoffman, Yvette Jones, and Allen Bell. Yvette Jones, Chief Operating Officer and Senior Vice President for External Affairs at Tulane, was also and still is the Chairman of the Board for Idea Village,[26] a local non-profit that helps entrepreneurs. They all had such confidence in the potential of our little experiment. It was amazing. A year later, we applied for the Idea Village Entrepreneur Class of 2010–11. With 195 applicants, we were accepted into a class of fifteen.[27] For the next six months, we concentrated on the business elements of the project—what would a business look like, writing financials, writing a business plan. We worked with a team of experts who provided us with over $80,000 worth of free business advice. Once again, I found the experience amazing and very stressful, as I learned to work within new discourses and expectations.

The Idea Village IVEC had many components. Housed downtown in the IP building, we met with our Executives-in-Residence nearly weekly, for two-hour sessions. The sessions were tailored to meet the specific needs of the business. For us, each session focused on a particular area of the business plan, or business planning. There were also seminars and

---

[25]   For more on Idea Village, and in particular Allen and Tim, *see* The Idea Village, http://ideavillage.org/Staff.php (last visited Aug. 27, 2011).

[26]   List of Idea Village Board of Directors, http://www.ideavillage.org/idea village/board.php (last visited Aug. 27, 2011).

[27]   For a full list of the IVEC class, *see* The Idea Village, http://www.idea village.org/IVECClass11.php (last visited Aug. 27, 2011); and for an overview of the program, *see* Hello from Idea Village, http://ideavillage.org/newsletter/November%202010%20Newlsetter.html (last visited Aug. 27, 2011).

classes available, which either I or my former/current students attended. Many resources were made available as well. We were actually even given equipment from HP as part of the program.

I found this process a struggle—to transition from our experiment and the language we used to a business environment. I wanted Idea Village to understand the world in which the Durationator® was made. They were patient. But for them, my struggles with discourse seemed peculiar. All of the other IVEC class entrepreneurs wanted to create *businesses,* but I still couldn't take the leap. How were we going to define the product? The Idea Village saw huge potential for our software, and they were very encouraging on how to develop it into a business. Nevertheless, I still felt we hadn't quite found our way yet. It would only be after we completed our six months with Idea Village that we would finally become an LL.C. and obtain an option from the university. Baby steps. They had wanted to do this literally on the first day we met. In many ways, we were a year too early for the program. We couldn't take advantage of all of the resources because I was still in the midst of an identity struggle. And yet, it was the environment of Idea Village that helped sort out what we might become, and helped us to start thinking of pitches, business plans, etc. We were kindergartners playing with fourth graders. My graduation was a lightening round series of "pitches" to real bankers. The experience was hard, fun, exhausting and, in the end, brought greater clarity to the project.[28]

So, as I struggled with our corporate identity, we also suddenly had the opportunity to be part of Idea Corp, which paired our project with a business-school team for a competition during New Orleans Entrepreneur week.[29] We were assigned to a team of nine students from University of California, Hass School of Business.[30] In February 2011, we flew out to Berkeley to present our project. We meet for an intensive afternoon, and then had dinner. Six weeks later, they came for a one-week intensive session. All day and night the students worked on putting together

[28] Catherine Lyons, *New Orleans Entrepreneur Week highlight events,* NOLA. COM, Mar. 21, 2011, http://www.nola.com/nolavie/index.ssf/2011/03/new_orleans_entrepreneur_week.html.

[29] *See* New Orleans Entrepreneur Week 2011, Idea Corp, Idea Village, http://noew.org/entrepreneurs/ideacorps_2011_entrepreneurs/ (last visited Aug. 27, 2011).

[30] *See* http://noew.org/info/ideacorps_teams/univertsity_of_california_berkeley_haas_school_of_business/. The Berkeley Participants were Masha Lisak, Sunil Sharma, Jamie Aaronson, Rama Kolappan, Roxan Saint-Hilaire, Iris Shim, Joe Wadcan and Sue Young.

a plan. They were being judged on where we started at the beginning of the week, and how much they contributed by the end of the week. They did an amazing job. They evaluated the potential markets, settling on the lawyer market as their focus, doing surveys, creating a price-point, and financials. We started to see our potential—what we would charge the lawyer market, and how their use would legitimize other markets. We were on our way. We had two other markets to analyze—the average users and the heavy digitizing/library crowd. But we got a lot further than anything before this. They began to put concrete examples and numbers to our business plan. They showed us one vision of how to grow into a business. It was exhilarating. At the end of the week, at 8 am, the business school students presented their work to a packed audience at IDEApitch. I stood off stage as I listened to the students talk about our potential, our hurdles, and our financials. At the conclusion of their presentation, my part was to discuss what they had accomplished for our company. They had been outsiders who had invested intellectual energy in coming up with a game plan to achieve one of the potential markets. But it was also much more. Someone else—outside of my team—had been able to understand and envision what the Durationator® would look like in concrete terms. I was no longer afraid, and I had once again had this experience in an extremely supportive environment.[31]

D. Decisions

At the end of the spring 2011, the Idea Village program had ended. I was back on my own. We still had not formed the company (or decided on whether to actually be a company), and the option with the university remained unfinished and haunting me on my computer. Then, a couple of interesting moments occurred that made the formation of the company finally a much easier jump.

At Tulane Law School, we had a second "Future of Copyright" speaker series that included Kenneth Crews, David Carson, Jule Sigall, Nina Paley, Siva Vaidhyanathan, and Jane Ginsburg.[32] As a class, we also started to

---

[31] Included in the audience had been Yvette Jones, who gave me a big hug and told me how proud she was of our progress. A photographer took our picture. It all felt very exciting. We were moving along, even at our snail's pace, and those that believed in us were right there wishing us well.

[32] The first had been part of the original Research Enhancement Grant from the University in 2007. We brought six speakers in the spring of 2009, in part, to introduce them to the Durationator®. This included Pam Samuelson, Jamie Boyle, Graeme Dinwoodie, Diane Zimmerman, Peter Jaszi, and Mark Rose.

focus on the Copyright Office's inquiry on Pre-1972 Sound Recordings. When the new 1976 Copyright Act came into existence, sound recordings were explicitly excluded from federal protection, relying instead on state law. Now, the question was arising whether fifty different laws, rather than one federal law was still the best path. Nina Paley, an independent film-maker told us the tale of her copyright woes on trying to secure permission to use eleven songs from the 1930s for her film, "Sita Sings the Blues."[33] We also had Kenneth Crews talking to us about the librarians' concerns regarding pre-1972 Sound Recordings and, in particular, the limitations on library use and preservation with Section 108.[34] Finally, we had David Carson, General Counsel for the Copyright Office, coming to speak.[35] The Inquiry was addressed to him, and so, it seemed natural in preparation for his arrival to research and prepare a reply to the comments from the call put out by the Copyright Office.

The experience was amazing—thirty-two students and one fellow, along with me researched and wrote a collaborative document regarding whether pre-1972 Sound Recordings should be federalized.[36] We looked at the comments and tried to understand the concerns of all sides. We then drafted what we thought would be a workable solution in the form of a proposed addition to the Copyright Act. Strangely, in the process, I started to find our place in the world. When I participated in the Roundtable discussion at the Copyright Office in June 2011, my latest ideas were confirmed.[37] I went to represent the law—with no stake in how anything actually turned out. I spoke only as a researcher, not as a client advocate. I saw the Durationator® in the same manner. It was not merely a product, but a state of being.

What I came away from the experience with was that we did not really

---

[33] *See* Nina Paley, *Sita Sings the Blues* FAQ, http://www.sitasingstheblues.com/faq.html.

[34] Kenneth Crews is a prominent law professor and librarian, currently at the Director of Copyright Advisor Office, Columbia University, who specializes in issues related to academics and librarians. *See* http://copyright.columbia.edu/copyright/about/director-and-staff/

[35] David Carson, General Counsel, U.S. Copyright Office. See a current organization structure of the U.S. Copyright Office at http://www.copyright.gov/docs/C-711_06-11.pdf.

[36] *See* Elizabeth Townsend Gard and the 2011 Copyright Class, Tulane University Law School, *Reply Comment Pre-1972 Sound Recordings*, http://www.copyright.gov/docs/sound/comments/reply/041311elizabeth-townsend-gard.pdf

[37] U.S. Copyright Office, Public Transcript of the June 2–3 Public Hearing, available at http://www.copyright.gov/docs/sound/ (last visited July 16, 2011).

see ourselves "siding" with any one group. We wanted to understand the
law, and the complexities of the policies involved, and then we wanted
to stay true to the "traditional contours of copyright law," for lack of a
better phrase. We wanted to code the law and support the spirit of the
law. We wanted to be trusted by the Recording Industry of America
(RIAA) and EFF, the librarians and the content owners, Google and
Internet Archive, and of course, we wanted our peers—IP scholars—to
be proud that scholars had a place in the world to contribute and even
potentially make a significant difference in problems that had not previously been solved. I wanted my research, the experiment, and ultimately
the company, to follow in the tradition of Peter Jaszi, Pam Samuelson,
and others—whose work has made significant impact in the structure and
direction of copyright law.[38]

Some still suggested that we be a non-profit, and that we try to create a
support group of libraries, industry, and academics. Others still thought
we should be an aggressive start-up company, targeting first the lawyers,
and later content owners directly. And so I made a number of decisions.
We would build and complete the software at the law school, using no
outside developers. This had begun as a law school project; the beta
version would be completed as a law school project. We would continue
to work as we had—assigning tasks to students who figured out a way to
make it work, and we would continue the extensive research the way we
had developed as well.

We were back to basics. We would build the website and user-interface,
the back-end code, and complete the research. We would make the tool
available online by September 2012, and we would begin building our two
more specialty products (for digitizers and for lawyers) from the initial
revenue. We would keep it simple—but effective. We would finish the software in a more modest way. We wanted the tool to be unencumbered by
interests—whether interests that wanted the tool to make a profit, interests
that wanted the tool to be open sourced, or interests that wanted to influence the outcome of the law. We were making our own road, and while the
journey still seemed uncertain, at least we were doing it in a way that made
the most sense for the integrity of the project.

---

[38]   For an example, *see* PATRICIA AUFDERHEIDE AND PETER JASZI, RECLAIMING
FAIR USE: HOW TO PUT BALANCE BACK IN COPYRIGHT, (Chicago, University of
Chicago Press, 2011). For examples of Pamela Samuelson's work, *see* Pam's work
regarding the proposed Google Book Settlement, http://people.ischool.berkeley.
edu/~pam/GBS.html.

V. THE ROAD AHEAD: LIMITED TIMES, INC.

We completed the negotiations with the university on the revenue-sharing agreement for the patent, and now also have an option for the licensing agreement for the start-up. We have created an LL.C.[39] We would continue to bootstrap, but in doing so, we would make it the way we want. We want to build the company with our own philosophy and interests. We want a financially sustainable company. We want to be and *be seen as* neutral, playing with everyone. We do not want to speak for anyone, but merely represent what we found in the law itself. We want to continue to do research and explore topics related to access and transparency regarding copyright law.

The experience has been life changing. First off, as a family, we now watch a lot of *Shark Tank* in our house.[40] Our product: TurboTax® for copyright. My eight-year old daughter wants to know what percentage of the company she can expect if she contributes art to the new website—she seems to have a better innate business sense than either of her parents. In the end, we realized we had to stay true to the project and forge ahead— the road is still unknown and daunting. I've come to realize that feeling of uncertainty is OK, and to merely focus on staying true to the project and the vision of the research. We are 21st century professors living in an entrepreneurial world. This is our unexpected story—so far.

---

[39] Limited Times,LL.C. was named after the U.S. Constitutional clause, I.8.8, from which the Copyright Act, and more specific duration begins: Congress is given the power to "To promote the Progress of Science and useful Arts, by securing for *limited Times* to Authors and Inventors the exclusive Right to their respective Writings and Discoveries." (italics added).

[40] *See* SHARK TANK (ABC television broadcast). Five wealthy entrepreneurs are presented with fledgling business opportunities, and then the "sharks" negotiate with the young entrepreneurs, criticize the products, or make fun of the businesses.

Index